THE PRAEGER HANDBOOK OF

RELIGION AND EDUCATION
IN THE UNITED STATES

The Praeger Handbook of
RELIGION AND EDUCATION IN THE UNITED STATES

VOLUME 2: M–Z

Edited by
James C. Carper and Thomas C. Hunt

Westport, Connecticut
London

Library of Congress Cataloging-in-Publication Data

The Praeger handbook of religion and education in the United States / edited by James C. Carper and
    Thomas C. Hunt.
        v. cm.
    Includes bibliographical references and index.
    ISBN 978–0–275–99227–9 ((set) : alk. paper) – ISBN 978–0–275–99228–6 ((vol 1) : alk. paper) –
    ISBN 978–0–275–99229–3 ((vol 2) : alk. paper)
1. Church and education–United States–Handbooks, manuals, etc. 2. Religion in the public schools–United States–
Handbooks, manuals, etc. 3. Church and state–United States–Handbooks, manuals, etc. I. Carper, James C. II.
Hunt, Thomas C., 1930– III. Praeger (Westport, Conn.)
LC111.P78 2009
0379.2'80973—dc22   2008041156

British Library Cataloguing in Publication Data is available.

Library of Congress Catalog Card Number: 2008041156
ISBN: Set: 978–0–275–99227–9
    Vol. 1: 978–0–275–99228–6
    Vol. 2: 978–0–275–99229–3

First published in 2009

Praeger Publishers, 88 Post Road West, Westport, CT 06881
An imprint of Greenwood Publishing Group, Inc.
www.praeger.com

Printed in the United States of America

The paper used in this book complies with the
Permanent Paper Standard issued by the National
Information Standards Organization (Z39.48-1984).

10 9 8 7 6 5 4 3 2 1

James C. Carper dedicates this work to the most important teachers in his life: His parents, Chris and Mary Jane Carper and Russ and Marj Wenger; sister and brother, Cherie and John; wife, Kathy; and children, Becky and Marci.

Thomas C. Hunt affectionately dedicates this work to his daughters, Staci and Eryn; and to Staci's husband, Derek, and their three sons, Nate, Zach, and AJ.

Contents

List of Entries

M

Madison, James

James Madison (1751–1836), fourth president of the United States of America, was a leading figure in the debates and political battles regarding the rights of conscience and church-state relationships in Virginia and the new nation. He was an influential actor in the Virginia struggles to redefine church-state relations in the decade following independence, the Constitutional Convention of 1787, and the first federal Congress, which framed the U.S. Constitution's First Amendment.

Madison was born in central Virginia and baptized in the Anglican Church. He received much of his early education from Presbyterian clergymen. He continued his education at the evangelical Calvinist College of New Jersey (Princeton), where he was tutored by the college president and Presbyterian divine, John Witherspoon. Madison was one of America's most theologically informed statesmen and, for a season, apparently contemplated a career in the ministry.

Madison was moved to the cause of religious liberty after observing the persecution of dissenting clergymen in his native Virginia. He was elected in 1776 to the Virginia Convention that adopted a new state constitution and declaration of rights. He soon emerged an influential figure in the Commonwealth's bitter church-state skirmishes, beginning with the adoption of the Virginia Declaration of Rights (1776) and culminating in the passage of the Virginia Statute for Establishing Religious Freedom (1786). In the first important public act of a long and distinguished political career, Madison objected to George Mason's draft article in the Declaration of Rights, providing for religious toleration. He proposed replacing Mason's statement, "all Men shou'd enjoy the fullest Toleration in the Exercise of Religion, according to the Dictates of Conscience," with the phrase, "all men are equally entitled to the full and free exercise of [religion] accord[in]g to the dictates of Conscience." Madison thought the word "toleration" dangerously implied that religious exercise was a mere privilege that could be granted or revoked at the pleasure of the civil state and was not assumed to be a natural, indefeasible right. The Declaration's sixteenth article, as adopted, reflected Madison's amendment, affirming that all citizens enjoyed equality in religious exercise.

Nearly a decade later, Madison led the opposition in the Virginia legislature to a 1784 proposal for a property tax "for the support of Christian teachers." This bill violated the equality among religious groups that Madison thought was essential to religious liberty. He successfully orchestrated the proposal's defeat by delaying legislative action on the bill and by mobilizing popular opposition to it. As part of a campaign to turn public opinion against the measure, Madison authored and circulated for public signature a "Memorial and Remonstrance against Religious Assessments" (1785), which outlined 15 reasons for rejecting the tax bill. The "Memorial and Remonstrance" is widely regarded as Madison's most philosophical defense of religious liberty.

Madison began by quoting familiar language from Article 16 of the Virginia Declaration of Rights: "Religion or the duty which we owe to our Creator and the manner of discharging it, can be directed only by reason and conviction, not by force or violence." Religion, he argued, is outside the cognizance of civil government. All citizens are entitled to the full, equal, and natural right to exercise religion according to the dictates of conscience. "[T]he same authority which can establish Christianity, in exclusion of all other Religions," Madison warned, "may establish with the same ease any particular sect of Christians, in exclusion of all other Sects." An exclusive ecclesiastical establishment "violates that equality which ought to be the basis of every law." Furthermore, it is "an arrogant pretension" to believe "that the Civil Magistrate is a competent Judge of Religious Truths; or that he may employ Religion as an engine of Civil policy." The lesson of history, he said, is "that ecclesiastical establishments, instead of maintaining the purity and efficacy of Religion, have had a contrary operation." Madison reported that established churches produce "pride and indolence in the Clergy, ignorance and servility in the laity, in both, superstition, bigotry and persecution." A religious establishment in Virginia would be a regrettable "departure from that generous policy, which, offering an Asylum to the persecuted and oppressed of every Nation and Religion, promised a lustre to our country, and an accession to the number of its citizens." Madison also rejected the notion that religion could not survive without the sustaining aid of civil government or that civil government could not preserve social order and stability without the support of an established church. He believed, to the contrary, that true religion flourished in the public marketplace of ideas unrestrained by an exclusive arrangement with the civil authority. He thought it was a contradiction to argue that discontinuing state support for Christianity would precipitate its demise, because "this Religion both existed and flourished, not only without the support of human laws, but in spite of every opposition from them.... [A] Religion not invented by human policy, must have pre-existed and been supported, before it was established by human policy." If Christianity depended on the support of civil government, then the "pious confidence" of the faithful "in its innate excellence and the patronage of its Author" would be undermined. He concluded that the best and purest religion relied on the voluntary support of those who profess it, without entanglements of any sort with civil government, including those arising from financial support, regulation, or compulsion.

After only brief consideration in the fall of 1785, the assessment bill died quietly in committee. Madison used the momentum generated by its demise to push for final passage of Jefferson's "Bill for Establishing Religious Freedom," which became law in January 1786.

Madison was a key figure in the Convention that drafted the U.S. Constitution of 1787 and in the ratification debates that followed. Although he initially opposed adding amendments to the proposed Constitution, he belatedly and reluctantly acceded to demands for amendments in order to secure the Constitution's ratification. After taking a seat in the first federal Congress, he became a leading advocate for amendments, including language explicitly protecting religious freedom from infringement by the new national government. His first religion proposal stated that the "civil rights of none shall be abridged on account of religious belief or worship, nor shall any national religion be established, nor shall the full and equal rights of conscience be in any manner, or on any pretext infringed." This text was eventually shaped into what later became the First Amendment. Given the many congressmen who contributed to the debates on the measure, it would be inaccurate to credit Madison alone for the First Amendment. Madison's proposal that "No state shall violate the equal rights of conscience," which would have undermined the federalism character of the Bill of Rights, failed to gain passage.

As president, Madison vetoed a bill "incorporating the protestant Episcopal Church in the Town of Alexandria in the District of Columbia" and a bill setting apart federal land in the Mississippi territory for a Baptist church because they violated the First Amendment prohibition on making "law respecting a religious establishment." He also issued four religious proclamations during his presidency recommending days for public humiliation, fasting, prayer, and thanksgiving to Almighty God.

In his retirement years, Madison opined that legislative chaplains paid from public funds and executive proclamations of days for public thanksgiving and prayer violated the ban on a religious establishment. This position contrasts with his actions as an elected official when, as a Virginia legislator in 1785, he introduced a "Bill for Appointing Days of Public Fasting and Thanksgiving" and, as president, he recommended days for religious observance.

Madison believed that religion, which is a matter of conviction and conscience, should be placed beyond the reach of civil authorities. Civil government should neither privilege nor penalize citizens, institutions, or conduct on account of religion; rather, it should take no cognizance of religion in the exercise of its authority. All citizens, he thought, are "equally entitled" to the free exercise of their religion, and civil government must treat all religious sects equally. Therefore, he opposed any arrangement that gave legal preference to one religion over others. He also thought the best security for religious liberty is a multiplicity of contending religious groups that would check one sect or group of sects from gaining official favor. *See also:* First Amendment Religion Clauses and the Supreme Court; Jefferson, Thomas; Separation of Church and State/Wall of Separation between Church and State.

Further Reading: Robert S. Alley, ed., *James Madison on Religious Liberty* (Buffalo, NY: Prometheus Books, 1985); Eva T.H. Brann, "Madison's 'Memorial and Remonstrance': A Model of American Eloquence," in *Rhetoric and American Statesmanship,* ed. Glen E. Thurow and Jeffrey D. Wallin (Durham, NC: Carolina Academic Press, 1984); Daniel L. Dreisbach, "Church-State Debate in the Virginia Legislature: From the Declaration of Rights to the Statute for Establishing Religious Freedom," in *Religion and Political Culture in Jefferson's Virginia,* ed. Garrett Ward Sheldon and Daniel L. Dreisbach (Lanham, MD: Rowman and Littlefield, 2000); Vincent Phillip Munoz, "James Madison's Principle of Religious Liberty," *American Political Science Review* 97 (February 2003): 17–32; Garrett Ward Sheldon, *The Political Philosophy of James Madison* (Baltimore: Johns Hopkins University Press, 2001).

Daniel L. Dreisbach

Mann, Horace

Horace Mann (1795–1859) was born in southeastern Massachusetts and, after practicing law in the Boston area and serving in the state Senate, became a leader in social reform. With the establishment of the state Board of Education in 1837, Mann was appointed its secretary, a position that he occupied until 1848, when he replaced John Quincy Adams in Congress.

As the first state education official and through his widely read *Annual Reports,* Mann made himself the most influential spokesman for the emerging program of the "common" public school. His religious views both facilitated the acceptance of that program and influenced the role that religion came to play in American public schools compared with those in other Western nations.

Mann's own religious views are thus of more significance than is ordinarily the case with a public official. A biography prepared by his second wife after his death includes a long extract from a letter Mann wrote to a friend, recounting his formative experiences growing up in the town of Franklin. The strongly orthodox teaching of Nathanael Emmons, his childhood pastor, produced a reaction, first of anxiety and then of rejection, according to this account:

> More than by toil, or by the privation of any natural taste, was the inward Joy of my youth blighted by theological inculcations. . . . He was an extra or hyper-Calvinist,—a man of pure intellect, whose logic was never softened in its severity by the infusion of any kindliness of sentiment. He expounded all the doctrines of total depravity, election, and reprobation, and not only the eternity, but the extremity, of hell-torments, unflinchingly and in their most terrible significance; while he rarely if ever descanted upon the joys of heaven, and never, to my recollection, upon the essential and necessary happiness of a virtuous life. . . . The consequences upon my mind and happiness were disastrous in the extreme. . . . I remained in this condition of mind until I was twelve years of age. I remember the day, the hour, the place, the circumstances. . . when, in an agony of despair, I broke the spell that had bound me. From that day, I began to construct the theory of Christian ethics and doctrine. . . which, with such modifications as advancing age and a wider vision must impart, I still retain, and out of which my life has flowed. (Howe, 1970, pp. 172–173)

Leaving no doubt about his private opposition to the dominant, though waning, religious current of his day and to its inclusion in schools, he wrote bitterly in another letter, "what an unspeakable calamity a Calvinistic education is" (Glenn, 1988, p. 143). Mann and other elite reformers of the 1830s and 1840s assumed, inaccurately as it turned out, that the Unitarianism that most of them shared would replace traditional Christianity— as, indeed, Jefferson had predicted a generation before.

Mann's extreme aversion against Protestant orthodoxy did not lead him, as the state official responsible for promoting the common public schools, to seek to ban religion from the classroom; to the contrary, in a compendium of Massachusetts education law and policy, Mann observed that "the policy of the State promotes not only secular but religious instruction." In his *Eleventh Report* as Secretary (1848), he boasted that

> I suppose there is not, at the present time, a single town in the Commonwealth in whose schools [the Bible] is not read. . . . By introducing the Bible, they introduce what all its believers hold to be the rule of faith and practice; and although, by excluding theological

systems of human origin, they may exclude a peculiarity which one denomination believes to be true, they do but exclude what other denominations hold to be erroneous....If it be the tendency of all parties and seers, to fasten the mind upon what is peculiar to each, and to withdraw it from what is common to all, these provisions of the law counter-work that tendency. They turn the mind towards that which produces harmony, while they withdraw it from sources of discord. (Glenn, 1988, p. 166)

Far from desiring to exclude religious instruction from the common school, as his accusers had it, Mann insisted, "I could not avoid regarding the man who should oppose the religious education of the young, as an insane man." Mann pointed out that he and the board had continually promoted the use of the Bible in the common school, and "if this Bible is in the schools, how can it be said that Christianity is excluded from the schools?" The Bible was allowed to "speak for itself," and what could be more fair or reverent? But this admirable and "Christian" system was under attack, and now not only from Protestant orthodoxy but from the claim of the Catholic clergy to provide education for the children of Irish immigrants. Nothing, he insisted, could be more unfortunate (Glenn, 1988, pp. 168–169).

Mann saw the common school itself as having an essentially religious mission, one of "elevating" and "purifying" humanity. Contradicting the "gloomy" doctrines about human sinfulness and the need for a Redeemer prevalent among Protestants and Catholics alike, the school would reveal to the rising generation of young Americans a new gospel of essential human goodness and the pure morality that guaranteed happiness in this world and beyond.

Mann argued that he was actively engaged in promoting religion and that his opponents could only be motivated by fanaticism and hostility to the true interests of humanity.

Mann persuaded himself that "the Religion of heaven" was different from, higher than, and in conflict with "the creeds of men." The common school would cultivate the moral nature and, at the same time, develop the highest form of religious sentiment and piety of which children were capable. It was in the service of this mission, and not simply to avoid controversy, that the school must exclude the doctrinal tenets of orthodoxy. It was not that the exclusion of these traditional teachings from the school was an unfortunate consequence of the religious divisions in the community but rather that their inclusion, under any circumstances, would be fatal to the teaching of true religion and morality.

The "peculiarities" that should be excluded, of course, included the belief that the death and resurrection of Jesus Christ were of decisive and irreplaceable importance, a doctrine that, according to Mann, could not be taught in the schools. He appears sincerely not to have recognized the extent to which his own belief in human goodness and the centrality of morality to religion constituted an alternative faith—essentially that preached Sunday by Sunday in Unitarian churches—which could not fail to conflict with traditional Christian beliefs, whether of Protestants or of Roman Catholics.

Unlike the state-sponsored schools of Prussia, which he devoted his honeymoon to visiting and wrote about in his seventh *Annual Report,* and unlike those at the time and since in England, Ireland, and Canada, the schools that Mann promoted were not denominationally specific. The United States did not generally develop separate Protestant and Catholic public schools, with a few exceptions based on local compromises. The thrust of Mann's efforts was toward Christianity so devoid of doctrine that, in fact, it corresponded very well with his own Unitarianism.

As a Unitarian of his time, Mann considered himself a Christian who would preserve all that was pure, noble, and true of the teaching of Jesus Christ, without the accretions of legend and speculative doctrine that, in his view, had been added by superstition and the calculation of a priestly caste. He was quite sincere in considering his views "nonsectarian." Teaching that sought to form a sincere piety directed toward the Creator, a morality based upon the example and ideals of Jesus and conducive to civic peace and social righteousness —how could that "favor the tenets of particular sects?" (Glenn, 1988, p. 131).

He was not alone. Of the 11 original members of the Massachusetts Board of Education, eight were Unitarians, including the governor and the other moving spirits in the creation and selection of the board. Charles Brooks, the advocate of state action to create normal (teacher-training) schools, was a Unitarian minister, as were Cyrus Peirce, appointed by the board as principal of the first such school, and his successor Samuel J. May. The principal of the normal school at Bridgewater was a Unitarian layman, and the "special visitors" assigned by the board to oversee these institutions in 1839 were two Unitarian clergymen and two Unitarian laymen.

The conflict between religious liberalism and orthodoxy was the leading drama in Massachusetts for more than a generation, until abolition and immigration came to replace it in the public consciousness. The conflicts over the religious mission of the common school were not, as Mann presented them, a struggle between an outmoded and moribund (but still malignant) orthodoxy on the one hand and the forces of progress and love of humanity on the other but rather a conflict between two dynamic movements, each determined to shape the mind of the growing nation. *See also:* The Bible in the Public Schools; Common School; Prayer in the Public Schools.

Further Reading: Lawrence A. Cremin, ed., *The Republic and the School: Horace Mann on the Education of Free Men* (New York: Teachers College Press, 1957); Raymond B. Culver, *Horace Mann and Religion in the Massachusetts Public Schools* (New Haven, CT: Yale University Press, 1929); Charles L. Glenn, Jr., *The Myth of the Common School* (Amherst: University of Massachusetts Press, 1988); Daniel Walker Howe, *The Unitarian Connection: Harvard Moral Philosophy, 1805–1861* (Cambridge, MA: Harvard University Press, 1970); Neil G. McCluskey, *Public Schools and Moral Education: The Influence of Horace Mann, William Torrey Harris, and John Dewey* (New York: Columbia University Press, 1958); Jonathan Messerli, *Horace Mann: A Biography* (New York: Alfred A. Knopf, 1972).

Charles L. Glenn, Jr.

McCollum v. Board of Education

The practice of permitting educational officials in public schools to release children during the class day so that they could receive religious instruction in their public schools reached the U.S. Supreme Court in a dispute from Champaign, Illinois, *People of State of Illinois ex rel. McCollum v. Board of Education of School District No. 71, Champaign County* (1948). At issue in *McCollum* was a local school board's practice of permitting members of the Jewish, Roman Catholic, and Protestant faiths, who formed a voluntary association and obtained its approval for a cooperative plan, to offer religion classes to children whose parents agreed to have them take part in the program. Students had to be released from their public schools while their religion instructors notified their regular teachers if they were absent. The classes were taught in regular classrooms, in three separate groups, by Protestant teachers, Catholic priests, and a Jewish rabbi. Students who did not attend religious instruction had to go to some other place in their schools to pursue their secular studies. After a trial court, affirmed by the Supreme Court of Illinois, refused to order school officials to discontinue the practice, opponents sought further review.

Writing for the U.S. Supreme Court in its relatively brief eight to one judgment in *McCollum,* Justice Hugo Black identified the issue as "the power of the state to utilize its tax-supported public school system in aid of religious instruction." To this end, he reversed in favor of the opponents of the plan, on the basis that it violated the Establishment Clause's mandate of complete separation of church and state, language that is not in the text of the First Amendment. Interestingly, it was Black himself who introduced the Jeffersonian metaphor calling for a "high wall of separation of Church and State" in his majority opinion in *Everson v. Board of Education* (1947) wherein the Court upheld a statute from New Jersey that allowed parents to be reimbursed for the cost of transportation associated with sending their children to their religiously affiliated nonpublic schools.

At the heart of his analysis, Black focused on the need to separate church and state by declaring that "No tax in any amount, large or small, can be levied to support any religious activities or institutions, whatever they may be called, or whatever form they may adopt to teach or practice religion." In conclusion, he maintained that the program ran afoul of the First Amendment for two reasons. First, Black was of the opinion that it was impermissible that tax-supported public school buildings were being used to disseminate religious doctrine. Second, he pointed out that public school officials provided religious groups with an invaluable, albeit impermissible, aid in helping them by providing students for their classes via the state's compulsory education system.

Justice Felix Frankfurter, joined by Justices Robert Jackson, Wiley Rutledge, and Harold Burton, filed a separate concurrence in which they expanded Black's views on the need for the separation of church and state. Although he had some reservations about the Court's asserting jurisdiction in the dispute, Justice Jackson also filed a concurring opinion.

In his dissent, Justice Stanley Reed acknowledged that he agreed with the constitutional dictate that Congress (and the states) was forbidden from establishing a religion; this is not what took place in the dispute at bar. Yet, if anything, he determined that the released-time program was provided in furtherance of protecting freedom of religion and did not violate the First Amendment. *See also:* Released Time for Religious Instruction; *Zorach v. Clauson.*

Further Reading: *Everson v. Board of Education,* 330 U.S. 1 (1947); *People of State of Illinois ex rel. McCollum v. Board of Education of School District No. 71, Champaign County,* 333 U.S. 203 (1948).

Charles J. Russo

McGuffey Readers

The famous *McGuffey Readers,* named after William Holmes McGuffey, although he wrote but several of the first edition, were next to the Bible in importance of books used in the nineteenth and early twentieth century American schools. Their estimated sales reached 122 million by 1920.

Usually grouped together, the various editions reflect a different moral base. McGuffey himself, a Presbyterian minister, preached a message of Calvinistic morality. Subsequent editions, however, reflect a more secularized version of morality. Nonetheless, the *Readers* are connected with teaching moral and ethical standards, and have been nostalgically remembered by many. McGuffey himself emphasized the moral virtues of industry, honesty, and temperance. The various editions were the textbooks of the American middle class, especially on the frontier. The *Readers* promised a reward, heavenly and earthly at first, later focusing on the earthly, for those who practiced the virtues. Gambling, drinking, and other forms of self-indulgence were to be avoided.

The *Readers* were bastions of Protestant Christianity in the American common school. Their mix of patriotism and religion was clear: George Washington, for instance, was compared to Moses. They advanced the values of Protestant morality and thus were favored partners of the Protestant faith. They combined the teaching of love of God and country, duty to parents, and respect for property with the certainty of progress and the superiority of the United States. They served, for many Americans of their time, as the largest storehouse of ethical teaching outside of the Bible.

As mentioned above, the *Readers* preached middle-class values. God, they proclaimed, blessed the industrious. Those so blessed, however, had a moral obligation to do good with their wealth. Their teaching fit neatly within the culture of the second half of the nineteenth century, which featured Protestant morality, patriotism, and social order.

The impact of the *McGuffey Readers* has been described by some as monumental. The emphasis on moral conduct, that virtue is rewarded and vice is punished, reached a huge audience. Their lessons reached a number of generations, and the books influenced the nation's schoolchildren not only in morality and religion but also in their taste for literature and social development. They were, indeed, more influential in forming the American character than any other book outside of the Bible. *See also:* Civil Religion and Education; Common School.

Further Reading: Lewis Atherton, *Main Street on the Middle Border* (Bloomington: Indiana University Press, 1954); Harvey C. Minnich, *William Holmes McGuffey and His Readers* (New York: American Book Company, 1936); Richard D. Mosier, *Making the American Mind: Social and Moral Ideas in the McGuffey Readers* (New York: King's Crown Press, 1947); Henry H. Vail, *A History of the McGuffey Readers* (Cleveland, OH: The Burruss Brothers Co., 1911); John H. Westerhoff, *McGuffey and His Readers* (Nashville, TN: Abingdon, 1978).

Thomas C. Hunt

Meek v. Pittenger

Meek v. Pittenger (1975) involved a challenge to a far-reaching statute from Pennsylvania that provided aid to students who attended primarily religiously affiliated nonpublic schools. One part of the law allowed the loans of instructional materials, including textbooks and other printed materials, to religiously affiliated nonpublic schools; instructional materials included periodicals, maps, charts, recordings, and films. Another part of the statute permitted educators from public schools to provide auxiliary services on-site to students who attended these schools; among these services were speech and hearing therapy, counseling, psychological services, and testing.

A federal trial court upheld the constitutionality of the loans of textbooks, instructional materials, and the auxiliary services programs. At the same time, the court struck down the loan of instructional equipment on the ground that the materials could be used for religious purposes. The U.S. Supreme Court agreed to hear an appeal.

On further review in *Meek,* Justice Potter Stewart, writing for the Supreme Court, followed the precedent that it set in *Board of Education v. Allen* (1968) in affirming the constitutionality of the textbook loans. Relying on the test that the Court created in *Lemon v. Kurtzman* (1971), he invalidated the provisions dealing with periodicals and other instructional aids and material in declaring that the statute had the primary effect of advancing religion in light of the predominantly religious character of the participating schools. Stewart was not satisfied that there were sufficient safeguards in place to prevent against impermissible governmental aid to religious schools insofar as the only statutory requirement imposed on the schools to qualify for the loans was that they provide for the subjects and activities called for by the commonwealth's board of education. To this end, he was of the opinion that since the religious schools were the primary beneficiaries, the significant amount of aid that they received to their educational functions necessarily, and unconstitutionally, provided assistance to their sectarian enterprises as a whole.

In another aspect of his holding in *Meek,* Stewart invalidated that part of the law that permitted educators from public schools to provide auxiliary services on-site in the religiously affiliated nonpublic schools. He also prohibited the delivery of a variety of instructional programs, guidance counseling and testing, and services for children who were educationally disadvantaged. Stewart feared that in ensuring that the instructional aid that the students received, no matter how educationally disadvantaged they were, would have required such a degree of supervision to make sure that it did not include religious ideology that it violated the requirement that it not lead to excessive entanglement between church and state in violation of the *Lemon* test.

Justice William Brennan's partial concurrence and partial dissent, joined by Justices William Douglas and Thurgood Marshall, would also have struck down the textbook loans as constitutionally impermissible. Justice William Rehnquist, joined by Justice Byron White, concurred separately in explaining why he voted to uphold the textbook loan provision.

Interestingly, in a plurality opinion in *Mitchell v. Helms* (2000), a dispute from Louisiana, the Supreme Court upheld the constitutionality of a federal law that permits the loans of instructional materials including library books, computers, television sets, tape recorders, and maps to religiously affiliated nonpublic schools (among others). While the plurality explicitly reversed those parts of *Meek* that were inconsistent with its judgment in this regard, insofar as less than the required five justice majority signed on to the same opinion, the status of such loans remains uncertain. *See also: Board of Education v. Allen; Cochran v. Louisiana State Board of Education; Mitchell v. Helms; Wolman v. Walter.*

Further Reading: *Board of Education v. Allen,* 392 U.S. 236 (1968); *Lemon v. Kurtzman,* 403 U.S. 602 (1971); *Meek v. Pittenger,* 421 U.S. 349 (1975); *Mitchell v. Helms,* 530 U.S. 793 (2000), *rehearing denied,* 530 U.S. 1296 (2000), *on remand sub nom. Helms v. Picard,* 229 F.3d 467 (5th Cir. 2000).

Charles J. Russo

Meyer v. Nebraska

In its landmark decision in *Meyer v. Nebraska* in 1923, the U.S. Supreme Court laid the foundation for the constitutional protection of nonpublic education. The Court in *Meyer* invoked the Due Process Clause of the Fourteenth Amendment to invalidate Nebraska and Iowa statutes prohibiting the teaching of foreign languages in elementary schools and an Ohio law banning the teaching of German in elementary schools.

These statutes were similar to laws enacted by at least 16 other states in the wake of the First World War in an effort to encourage patriotism and to stimulate assimilation among ethnic citizens, particularly German Americans. During the war, nativists and other proponents of so-called "100 percent Americanism" feared that the widespread use of foreign languages in the nation's many flourishing ethnic communities would encourage subversion and impede national unity. Officials in many states promulgated various formal and informal measures to discourage the use of foreign languages in church services, schools, and even in the streets and over the telephone. After the war, proponents of more rapid assimilation focused on education with the enactment of laws designed to ensure that children would not learn foreign languages during their formative years.

Although many public educators tried to prevent the enactment of these laws, the principal legal challenges arose from Lutheran parochial schools. During the early twentieth century, German-American Lutherans maintained the nation's second largest network of parochial schools, the result of an effort to transmit German cultural traditions and to ensure that children received thorough instruction in Lutheran doctrine. At a time when many German-American Lutheran parishes still conducted services and confirmation classes in German, instruction in the German language enabled children to understand the Lutheran catechism and to follow the liturgy, hymns, and sermons in churches that had not yet made the transition to the English language.

During 1919 and 1920, teachers at several Lutheran parochial schools in Nebraska, Iowa, and Ohio were convicted of violating the laws, which they had openly defied. Robert T. Meyer, the teacher at a school operated by Zion Lutheran Church near Hampton, Nebraska, was arrested and fined $25 after a county attorney who entered his classroom found Meyer teaching a Bible story in German to a ten-year-old boy, Raymond Parpart. Knowing that the county attorney was planning to visit his classroom and that he would not arrest him if he conducted the class in English, Meyer boldly decided to risk prosecution because he believed that he had a constitutional right to teach children the religion of their parents in the language of their parents. "I had my choice," he later explained to his attorney. "I knew that, if I changed into English, he would say nothing. If I went on in German, he would arrest me. I told myself that I must not flinch. And I did not flinch. I went on in German."

The supreme courts of Nebraska, Iowa, and Ohio sustained the convictions of the teachers, and the Nebraska Supreme Court also denied a motion by what is now the Lutheran Church–Missouri Synod and the Polish American father of a student at a Roman Catholic parochial school to enjoin enforcement of a similar law that replaced the one under which Meyer had been prosecuted.

Motivated primarily by their desire to impart religious instruction in foreign languages, opponents of the laws argued in state courts that the statutes interfered with their free exercise of religion under the state constitutions. They were not able to contend that the statutes violated the First Amendment Free Exercise Clause because the U.S. Supreme

Court had not yet held that the clause applied to the states. Mindful that courts of this era were more solicitous of property rights than personal liberties, they also argued that the laws interfered with the contractual rights of the parents and the schools and the right of teachers to earn a livelihood. Moreover, they contended that the law would economically harm the schools because many parents would send their children to public school if the schools no longer could teach their ethnic language. In rejecting these arguments, the state courts held that the laws were reasonably related to the compelling need of the states to ensure that children were well grounded in the English language and American values before they learned foreign languages.

In their arguments before the U.S. Supreme Court, the opponents of the laws acknowledged that states had a legitimate need to ensure that their citizens were fluent in English, but argued that banning foreign language instruction was not rationally related to this goal. The states insisted that the laws were appropriate exercises of their inherent power to protect the public safety and welfare.

In two separate decisions on June 9, 1923, the Supreme Court held that the statutes unconstitutionally deprived parents and teachers of their liberty and property in violation of the Fourteenth Amendment Due Process Clause. Justice James C. McReynolds read both decisions aloud in a sarcastic tone that appeared to mock legislators who attempted to deprive citizens of fundamental rights.

Consistent with its tradition of invoking the Fourteenth Amendment to protect economic rights from undue state interference, the Court based its decisions partly upon the right of parents to hire foreign language teachers and their right to follow their vocation. The Court also, however, suggested that the law interfered with personal liberties, particularly the rights of students to acquire knowledge, and with the right of parents to supervise the education of their children.

Although the Court acknowledged that "the state may do much...in order to improve the quality of its citizens," it declared that "the individual has certain fundamental rights which must be respected." While the Court explained that it was not necessary to define these rights "with exactness," the Court declared,

> [w]ithout doubt that the Fourteenth Amendment denotes not merely freedom from bodily restraint but also the right of the individual to contract, to engage in any of the common occupations of life, to acquire useful knowledge, to marry, establish a home and bring up children, to worship God according to his own conscience, and generally to enjoy those privileges long recognized at common law as essential to the orderly pursuit of happiness by free men.

Two justices, Oliver Wendell Holmes, Jr. and George Sutherland, dissented from the Court's decision because they contended that the statutes were rationally calculated to facilitate the reasonable goal of a common language. Although Holmes acknowledged that he dissented "with hesitation and unwillingness," he explained that

> youth is the time when familiarity with a language is established and if there are sections in the State where a child would hear only Polish or French or German spoken at home I am not prepared to say that it is unreasonable to provide that in his early years he shall hear and speak only English at school.

While proponents of parochial education hailed *Meyer* as a victory for religious freedom, the Court did not rely upon the First Amendment Free Exercise Clause or any other specific provision of the Bill of Rights, which the Court had not yet begun to incorporate into state law. *Meyer's* emphasis on personal liberties, however, foreshadowed the Court's incremental nationalization of most of the provisions of the Bill of Rights, beginning later in the 1920s.

The *Meyer* decision had important implications for parochial education. The decision was well timed because many of the same forces that had worked to ban foreign language were engaged in a nationwide campaign to require all elementary schoolchildren to attend public school. Only seven months earlier, Oregon voters had approved a compulsory public education law. Meyer's attorney, Arthur T. Mullen, a prominent Roman Catholic layman, was well aware that the Court's nullification of the language laws would cast a dark shadow over the constitutionality of any compulsory public education law. During his oral argument before the Court, Mullen declared that the state had no power to require children to attend public schools, and he believed that this assertion won over McReynolds by making him understand that *Meyer* involved broad questions about the state's power over parental rights. Two years after *Meyer,* the Court in *Pierce v. Society of Sisters* invalidated the Oregon law on grounds that were similar to those on which it had based its decision in *Meyer. See also: Farrington v. Tokushige; Pierce v. Society of Sisters;* State Regulation of Religious Schools.

Further Reading: *Meyer v. Nebraska,* 262 U.S. 390 (1923); *Pierce v. Society of Sisters,* 268 U.S. 510 (1925); William G. Ross, *Forging New Freedoms: Nativism, Education, and the Constitution, 1917–1927* (Lincoln: University of Nebraska, 1994).

William G. Ross

Minersville School District v. Gobitis

The Gobitis children, Lillian, 12 years old, and her brother, William, aged 10, were expelled from the Minersville, Pennsylvania, public school for refusing to say the Pledge of Allegiance to the American flag. The Minersville school board policy required all pupils and teachers to pledge the flag. Since Pennsylvania had a compulsory attendance statute, the children were denied a free education after being expelled and therefore were required to attend private schools that charged tuition.

The members of the Gobitis family were Jehovah's Witnesses. They and others of their faith conscientiously believed that saluting the flag was forbidden by Scripture. Their beliefs rested on parts of the Ten Commandments that state: "Thou shalt have no other gods before me" and "Thou shall not make unto thee any graven images or any likeness of any thing that is in heaven above." Pledging allegiance to the flag was, in their understanding of Scripture, bowing down before a graven image.

In its deliberation of the *Gobitis* (1940) case, the U.S. Supreme Court opined: "We must decide whether the requirement of participation in such a ceremony, exacted from a child who refused upon sincere religious grounds, infringes without due process of law the liberty guaranteed by the Fourteenth Amendment." In an 8-1 decision handed down on June 3, the Court upheld the school district's policy. The court reasoned that since the legislature had established the flag salute, with no exemption, because of the desire for a common experience, not to uphold the legislature would mock reason and denigrate "our history." The court further stated "[t]he mere possession of religious convictions which contradict the relevant concerns of a political society does not relieve the citizen from discharge of political responsibilities." The religious conviction of an individual does not override the powers of government to maintain an "orderly, tranquil and free society." Therefore, the Court ruled that a child could be required to salute the flag in a public school.

Justice Harlan Fiske Stone was the lone dissenter. Justice Frankfurter who wrote the majority opinion for the Court wrote a personal letter to Justice Stone invoking judicial self-restraint. Justice Stone replied "I must distinguish between a vulgar intrusion of law in the domain of conscience and legislation dealing with the control of property. The Courts' responsibility is the larger in the domain of conscience."

A short three years later the decision in *Gobitis* was reversed. In 1943 in the case of *West Virginia v. Barnette,* the Supreme Court ruled that a child could not be forced to recite the Pledge of Allegiance as such action would violate the child's right of free exercise of religion guaranteed by the First Amendment. *See also:* First Amendment Religion Clauses and the Supreme Court; The Pledge of Allegiance; *West Virginia State Board of Education v. Barnette.*

Further Reading: Archibald Cox, *The Court and the Constitution* (Boston: Houghton Mifflin Company, 1987); *Elk Grove Unified School District v. Newdow,* 543 U.S. 1 (2004); *Frazier v. Alexandre,* 434 F. Supp. 2d 1350 (S.D. Fla., 2006); *Minersville School District v. Gobitis,* 310 U.S. 586 (1940); *West Virginia State Board of Education v. Barnette,* 319 U.S. 624 (1943).

M. David Alexander

Mitchell v. Helms

In *Mitchell v. Helms* (2000) a plurality of the U.S. Supreme Court expressly overruled earlier precedent to the contrary in upholding the constitutionality of Chapter 2 of Title I of the Elementary and Secondary Education Act of 1965 (reauthorized in 1981 as the Education Consolidation and Improvement Act). Chapter 2 is a far-reaching federal statute that permits states to loan instructional materials such as library books, computers, computer software, television sets, tape recorders, and maps to religiously affiliated nonpublic schools.

Helms initially involved three issues. Only the third issue reached the Supreme Court. In the parts of *Helms* not reviewed by the Court, the Fifth Circuit Court of Appeals found that after *Agostini v. Felton* (1997), wherein the Supreme Court upheld the on-site delivery of federally funded remedial programs for poor students in religious schools in New York City, a Louisiana statute allowing the on-site delivery of special education services in religious schools did not violate the Establishment Clause of the First Amendment. The appellate court also affirmed that a nonprofit corporation that received government funds and paid for transporting children to and from their religious schools was constitutional. The most contentious part of the case before the Supreme Court was the Fifth Circuit's vitiating Chapter 2.

A splintered Court, in a plurality opinion authored by Justice Clarence Thomas and joined by Chief Justice William Rehnquist, and Justices Anthony Kennedy and Antonin

Scalia, reversed the Fifth Circuit in upholding the constitutionality of Chapter 2. Although not explicitly naming it, Thomas expanded the parameters of the Child Benefit Test. In its analysis, the plurality overruled language in *Meek v. Pittenger* (1975) and *Wolman v. Walter* (1977) that prohibited loans of various types of instructional aids such as films, laboratory equipment, library books, maps, and periodicals to religiously affiliated nonpublic schools on the basis that they aided their "sectarian" activities.

Justice Thomas noted that *Agostini* modified the tripartite *Lemon v. Kurtzman* (1971) test, which asks whether governmental aid has a secular legislative purpose, has a principal or primary effect that neither advances nor inhibits religion, and does not create excessive entanglement of government and religion, by reviewing only its first two parts while examining entanglement as one criterion in evaluating the statute's effect. Insofar as the purpose part of the test was not challenged, Thomas limited his analysis to the effects of Chapter 2.

Thomas applied two principles from *Agostini* in reasoning that Chapter 2 did not have the primary effect of advancing religion. First, he noted that Chapter 2 recipients are not defined by reference to religion in pointing out that the aid was available on a nondiscriminatory basis to all schools on the basis of neutral, secular criteria that neither favor nor disfavor religion. Second, he asserted that Chapter 2 did not foster governmental indoctrination of religion since eligibility was not only determined on a neutral basis, using a broad array of criteria, without regard to whether a school was religious but also because parents made private choices in selecting where their children would be educated. This language later came into play in *Zelman v. Simmons-Harris* (2002) wherein the Supreme Court upheld the Cleveland voucher program. In that decision, the majority recognized the private choice of parents with regard to directing the education of their children. Thomas concluded that Chapter 2 did not have the effect of advancing religion, even though the aid could be described as direct, since it was secular, neutral, and nonideological and there was not evidence that any of the equipment was diverted to religious purposes.

In a lengthy concurrence, Justice Sandra Day O'Connor, joined by Justice Stephen Breyer, thought that Justice Thomas went too far in implying that he might uphold any form of aid to students in religious schools as long as it is secular and offered on a neutral basis. Justice David Souter's lengthy dissent, joined by Justices John Paul Stevens and Ruth Bader Ginsburg, argued that Thomas's opinion departed radically from the Court's precedents prohibiting substantial aid to religious schools. This deep disagreement on the interpretation of the Establishment Clause as applied to the question of government aid to religious schools emerged again two years later in the *Zelman* decision. *See also: Agostini v. Felton;* Government Aid to Religious Schools; *Meek v. Pittenger; Wolman v. Walter; Zelman v. Simmons-Harris.*

Further Reading: *Agostini v. Felton,* 521 U.S. 203 (1997); *Lemon v. Kurtzman,* 403 U.S. 602 (1971); *Meek v. Pittenger,* 421 U.S. 349 (1975); *Mitchell v. Helms,* 530 U.S. 793 (2000); *Wolman v. Walter,* 433 U.S. 229 (1977); *Zelman v. Simmons-Harris,* 536 U.S. 639 (2002).

Charles J. Russo

Moments of Silence

In 1985, in *Wallace v. Jaffree,* the U.S. Supreme Court struck down Alabama's moment-of-silence legislation, but then suggested that moment-of-silence statutes that do not manifest an overt religious purpose might be constitutional. Many states took the message to heart and passed new (in some cases revising old) moment-of-silence statutes. The Court has not seen fit to revisit the issue to put its official stamp of approval on any of these statutes, but it is now widely assumed that moment-of-silence observances are constitutional, provided the Court's unofficial suggestions are followed.

Approximately 30 states now have moment-of-silence statutes. These statutes generally were crafted on the theory that some form of prayer should be permitted, even encouraged, in the nation's public schools. More overt forms of prayer had already been held to be unconstitutional in *Engel v. Vitale* (1962) and *Abington Township School District v. Schempp* (1963).

In *Engel,* the Court struck down a 22 word, nondenominational prayer written by the New York Board of Regents for official use in the public schools of New York. Pupils could remain silent or be excused from the room while the prayer was recited. The Court's decision was one of the most controversial in its history.

Undaunted by the public vilification it received following the *Engel* decision, the Court considered the next year (1963) two more cases dealing with religion in the public schools. One involved a Pennsylvania statute requiring that at least ten Bible verses should be read daily in all classrooms; the other challenged a Maryland statute that provided for the daily reading of a chapter from the Bible and/or reciting the Lord's Prayer. Deciding the cases together in *Abington Township School District v. Schempp,* the Court disallowed both practices as violations of the Establishment Clause.

Neither *Engel* nor *Schempp* dealt specifically with moments of silence. In *Schempp,* however, Justice William Brennan, in making the point that states could not use religious means to achieve secular ends when nonreligious means would suffice, noted by way of example that a state could not be prohibited from permitting "daily recitation of the Pledge of Allegiance, or even the observance of a moment of reverent silence." While it was not possible to compose prayers to be recited in classrooms, it did appear that periods of meditation, even periods of silence specifically for prayer, might be constitutional. Lower courts were divided on the constitutionality of these statutes, and it therefore came as no surprise that the Supreme Court felt compelled, in 1985, to address the constitutionality of moments of silence in the *Jaffree* case.

Jaffree was a challenge to three separate Alabama statutes. One provided that teachers could lead "willing students" in a recital of a specified prayer that was set out in the statute. The Supreme Court upheld the lower courts' invalidation of this statute, in essence reaffirming *Engel v. Vitale.* A second statute authorized a one-minute period of silence for "meditation." The district court upheld this statute, and it was not challenged on appeal; it was the opinion of all concerned parties that a period calling for meditation alone did not invoke Establishment Clause concerns. The third statute provided for "meditation or voluntary prayer." It was this statute that was the focus of the case and that the Supreme Court, in a 6-3 vote, found to violate the Establishment Clause.

Justice John Paul Stevens, who authored the majority opinion, emphasized that the State of Alabama failed to "present evidence of *any* secular purpose" for the statute, as required under the first or "secular purpose" prong of the three-prong test articulated in *Lemon v. Kurtzman* (1971). Thus, since the statute endorsed prayer as a favored practice, it violated the Establishment Clause.

It was not Justice Stevens, however, but Justices Lewis Powell, Jr. and Sandra Day O'Connor, who in separate concurring opinions strongly intimated that a moment of silence, untainted by the religious purpose that so obviously characterized the statute in the *Jaffree* case, would be permissible. Justice Powell, after concluding that the Alabama statute failed the secular purpose prong of the *Lemon* test, commented that a better-worded statute would not necessarily violate the second and third prongs. "I note," he stated, "that the 'effect' of a straightforward moment-of-silence statute is unlikely to 'advance or inhibit religion.' Nor would such a statute 'foster an excessive entanglement with religion.'" According to O'Connor,

> the relevant issue is whether an objective observer, acquainted with the text, legislative history, and implementation of the statute, would perceive it as a state endorsement of prayer in public schools. A moment of silence law that is clearly drafted and implemented so as to permit prayer, meditation, and reflection with the prescribed period, without endorsing one alternative over the others, should pass this test.

These statements adequately outlined how a constitutional statute might be written.

A majority of states now have moment-of-silence statutes that appear to meet the Stevens-Powell-O'Connor guidelines. Some statutes mandate moments of silence, some make the practice optional, leaving the decision in the hands of local school districts, and some require that moments of silence be implemented only at the request of students. Whatever their form, critics contend that moments of silence trivialize prayer and violate church-state separation, but they are today widely practiced in many public schools. In many cases, moments of silence have been incorporated into a range of school activities, such as assemblies, graduation ceremonies, and sporting events. Moments of silence thus seem to have achieved an honored and lasting status in America's public schools. *See also: Abington School District v. Schempp* and *Murray v. Curlett; Engel v. Vitale;* Prayer in the Public Schools; *Wallace v. Jaffree.*

Further Reading: *Abington v. Schempp,* 374 U.S. 203 (1963); Robert S. Alley, *School Prayer: The Court, the Congress, and the First Amendment* (Buffalo, NY: Prometheus Books, 1994); Derek H. Davis, "*Everson* and Moments of Silence: Constitutional and Ethical Considerations," in *Everson Revisited: Religion, Education, and Law at the Crossroads,* ed. Jo Renee Formicola and Hubert Morken (Lanham, MD: Rowman &Littlefield Publishers, Inc., 1997); *Duffy v. Las Cruces Public. Schools,* 557 F.Supp. 1013 (D.N.M. 1983); *Engel v. Vitale,* 370 U.S. 421 (1962); *Gaines v. Anders,* 421 F.Supp. 337 (D. Mass. 1976); *May v. Cooperman,* 572 F.Supp. 1561 (N.D. N.J. 1983); *Wallace v. Jaffree,* 472 U.S. 38 (1985); Deena Yellin, "Guide to Understanding: Handbook Explains Special Needs of Muslim Students," *The Record* (NJ), February 11, 1999, 2 Star B.

Derek H. Davis

Moral Education

Moral education in American schools owes much to Swiss psychologist Jean Piaget's research in the 1930s on moral development in children. According to Piaget, children's moral thinking involves two distinct stages. For children younger than 10 or 11 years of age, moral judgments are based on the consequences of actions. At this early stage of moral development, rules are considered to be absolute and constant. After the age of 10 or 11, children begin to base their moral judgments on the intention of actions rather than the consequences. At this later stage, rules become more flexible and subject to change. This two stage theory of moral development strongly influenced the work of developmental psychologist Lawrence Kohlberg, who focused on a stage theory of moral thinking that extended well beyond Piaget's understanding. According to Kohlberg, the stage of formal operations marked by Piaget's second stage of development actually continues beyond the 10 or 11 year window. By interviewing children and adolescents through age 16, Kohlberg found six stages of moral development, the first three of which shared many features with Piaget's stages. In Kohlberg's first stage, children equate morally right action with whatever the primary authority says is right. The rule of thumb is to obey authority and avoid punishment. At stage two, children begin to recognize multiple sources of authority and to weigh multiple responses to moral dilemmas. Because both of these stages rely on moral judgments based primarily on self-interest and avoidance of punishment, they represent the level of preconventional moral reasoning, according to Kohlberg.

The next two stages involve moral reasoning that recognizes the conventional values and expectations of society. In stage three, children begin to identify themselves as good or bad people, and they understand that being good means having the acceptance and approval of those around them. At the fourth stage, they recognize the value in obeying laws in order to protect the larger society. Because both of these stages rely on moral judgments based primarily on considerations of the expectations of others, Kohlberg labeled this the conventional level of moral reasoning. In the last two stages, the level of postconventional moral reasoning, Kohlberg concluded that we are more concerned with adhering to universal moral principles than with the particular consequences of actions for certain groups. At this level of reasoning, the morally right action requires consideration of all interests, not just those within one's own particular society and familial associations. Because Kohlberg's final stages are best evidenced by an open and democratic conceptual framework for moral reasoning, this postconventional level requires less conformity to authority and greater emphasis on contextual considerations that may influence one's moral judgments.

In addition to the considerable work of Piaget and Kohlberg, moral education has also been influenced by the values clarification theory, which can be traced back to John Dewey, who described moral education as a process of deliberation called "valuation" in which students critically analyze the merits of a variety of behavioral responses to certain ethical dilemmas. Dewey's method of valuation was the basis for "values clarification" by Sidney Simon, Leland Howe, and Howard Kirschenbaum (1972), which introduced the theory that moral judgments are essentially relative, and therefore best made by discerning the individual thought processes required for autonomous moral decision making. Described as a pedagogical method that would purportedly clarify ethical behavior for students, the authors suggested that teachers should encourage students to make fully autonomous ethical decisions based on personal choice and analysis of particular situations that presented themselves as moral dilemmas. Values clarification in moral education programs can be viewed as any process an individual chooses that will help him or her better articulate and clarify the values that he or she believes are important. This methodology also relies heavily on the assumptions of humanistic psychology, particularly the view that valuation involves a process of self-actualization, and the potential to freely act upon one's choices. Because our value systems are believed to impact all conscious decisions and actions in our lives, it is important to understand the basis for our values and to align them with our behavior.

One of the primary stated aims of the values clarification approach is to help students use emotional awareness to reflect upon personally held beliefs and to clarify such beliefs with respect to their own personal value systems. Therefore, the benefits of engaging in any dialogue involving moral language could only be understood in terms of individual choices and tolerance for all perspectives (since none could be empirically confirmed or denied). The values clarification approach to moral education emphasized the role of teachers as facilitators of discussion. As facilitators, teachers were not to suggest their own personal values, nor suggest shared societal values as moral options for their students. Teachers were instead guided to help students clarify their own personal values by following a seven step valuing process. This sevenfold process describing the guidelines of the values clarification approach was formulated by Simon et al. (1972): choosing from alternatives, choosing freely, prizing one's choice, affirming one's choice, acting upon one's choice, considering the consequences of acting, and acting consistently over time. For example, students are encouraged to reflect on the significance of values in their own lives, and then assess and prioritize such values based on the utilitarian benefit they have attached to that significance. Thus, a value does not become valuable until it is autonomously chosen by an individual based on his or her assessment of the usefulness of the value. Viewed in this light, values are construed as having no intrinsic worth in and of themselves.

Practices used in the values clarification method most commonly include small group discussions, hypothetical scenarios posing some moral dilemma, rank order scaling exercises for prioritizing personal values, and personal journals or diaries. The values clarification model of moral education assumes that the valuing process is internal to each person; it rejects the idea that there are some universally accepted set of core values. Instead, there are three primary areas of foci, which are described as prizing one's beliefs and behaviors, choosing one's beliefs and behaviors, and acting on one's beliefs. The values clarification method teaches that behavior is not morally good or evil, but is rather well chosen or foolish actions that will vary based on considerations of time, place, and other relevant circumstances. According to this method of moral education, a choice is good, healthy, or wise if its outcome is pleasing to the individual after consideration of the sevenfold criteria, and a choice is bad, unhealthy, or unwise if it fails to meet these criteria.

The values clarification methodology uses a process approach in teaching moral education that relies on "value neutrality" and the nonjudgmental analysis of hypothetical moral dilemmas. Because tolerance for different perspectives is considered to be deeply valued in our pluralistic and individualistic society, the values clarification method appealed to those who viewed "traditional" moral education as overly dogmatic and insensitive to the expression of different moral values. It is often difficult to discern, however, the difference between values clarification programs and the advocacy of ethical relativism. Both secular and theistic moral philosophers have found ethical relativism to be problematic for several reasons. A strong objection to the values clarification theory relies on a critical consideration of the consequences of complete value neutrality. For example, by promoting the acceptance of all values as equally appropriate, the values clarification method yields the rather bizarre consequence of requiring the acceptance of practices that we would otherwise find to be morally reprehensible, like slavery, ethnic cleansing, and apartheid. Therefore, a careful analysis of value neutrality actually leads to an opposite conclusion, viz., the recognition that we ought not to be equally tolerant of all values and that some values are, in fact, more desirable than others. Unfortunately, the values clarification agenda denies this conclusion by explicitly declining to criticize or devalue any particular moral value.

Frustrated by the lack of success in the values clarification approach to moral education, and supported by a strong public agenda to reintroduce so-called traditional character education into the public schools, educators have observed a resurgence of interest in "core virtues" and character education programs that would support the same. The 1994 Gallup Poll of the Public's Attitudes toward the Public Schools, conducted by Phi Delta Kappa, indicated a strong and growing public support for character education programs, and a majority of those polled favored stand-alone courses on habit formation of values and appropriate ethical behavior in the public schools. An even more interesting finding of the 1994 Gallup Poll was that over 90 percent of the respondents approved the teaching of core moral values, and two-thirds of those surveyed also valued instruction about world religions. Given the violent and uncivil cultural milieu of our country during these decades, we should not be surprised by this growing public support for character education programs in our public schools. As concerns about crime, delinquency, drug and alcohol abuse, and juvenile gang violence have grown, so has our interest in finding character education programs that work.

The character education movement promotes the teaching of core values that can be embedded in academic programs through the formal curriculum, especially in literature, social studies, and social science classes. Most of the character education programs promote a strong emphasis on student accountability and hold students to high levels regarding academic achievement. In schools that have adopted a character education program, service learning pedagogy is also a major source for delivery of core values instruction for most middle school and high school students. Service learning provides students with an opportunity not only to incorporate values into their own character framework but also to act on those values in socially responsible and meaningful ways. Schools that actively engage students in community and civic service projects may also use those experiences as the source of discussions in the classroom regarding civic and social responsibility in a democratic society.

A variety of interdisciplinary and cocurricular activities are also employed in the promotion of character education in public schools. For example, school organizations and club activities such as drama, sports, and student government also provide a myriad of opportunities for students to make important decisions about core values. Many of these programs have strong character education components as an integral part of the students' experience and are designed to encourage students to practice values such as initiative, diligence, loyalty, tact, generosity, altruism, and courage. In schools that report positive developments for students with respect to character education, there are common expectations among students, administrators, teachers, and staff. For example, students are encouraged to be active rather than passive members of policy and rules committees that set standards for school behavior. Because the students in these schools have contributed to setting the policy standards, they tend to accept responsibility for meeting those standards (and/or dealing with the consequences of noncompliance). According to Leming (1993), this research suggests that discipline, when established by the students themselves, is a strong component of character education programs.

Although most of the values that may be considered to be universal are well rooted in world religions, there are some religious groups that object to teaching these core values without their explicit identification with a divine source. Such groups accuse schools of teaching secular humanism by their omission to identify God as the source of core values. Although the Constitution itself contains no language regarding religion, the First Amendment, approved in 1791 as part of the ten amendments known as the Bill of Rights, contains a clause that states that Congress cannot prohibit the free exercise of religion. It is interesting to note that teachers and administrators have occasionally met resistance from parent organizations that would otherwise support character education, but worry that educators are promoting a secular humanist education with their teaching of core values. Given that the Supreme Court's interpretation of the Establishment Clause of the First Amendment prevents public schools from directly teaching religious values, the charge of secular humanism levied by religious groups against public educators may seem, on the surface, to be unwarranted. Religious groups, however, are concerned to preserve both tenets of the First Amendment, and they rightly point out that while schools are careful not to "establish religion" in the classroom, they have not been vigilant in preserving the students' right to freely exercise their religious values.

This dilemma poses itself as almost intractable in the public school domain, particularly when character education curricula materials are reviewed by teachers, administrators, and school boards. For example, the idea of a core set of moral values has traditionally been strongly associated with the religious teachings of both Judaism and Christianity. Religious parents (and educators) see no good reason to diminish that association, although they also recognize the need to present multiple representations of the core values. Their complaint arises when schools insist on representing such core values as completely devoid of association with any religious tradition. This complaint is legitimized when we consider that intentionally severing the discussion of core values from religion is historically inaccurate; that is, the analysis of core values as having been created exclusively by humans misrepresents the richness and historical influence of the role of religion in articulating such values.

Although public school educators are required by law to separate church and state, they may still teach certain core values that are accepted by both secular and religious teachings. Such a compromise may be our best hope in order not to leave our public school educators in a precarious dilemma with respect to the promotion of character education curriculum. In the meantime, we need to promote dialogue about the meaning of right and wrong, of the ethical values that are good as opposed to evil, and continue to discuss what constitutes a set of core values that can be accepted by both religious and nonreligious members of our community. *See also:* The Bible in the Public Schools; Secularism.

Further Reading: Stanley M. Elam, Lowell C. Rose, and Alec M. Gallup, "The 26th Annual Phi Delta Kappa/Gallup Poll of the Public's Attitudes Toward the Public Schools," *Phi Delta Kappan* 76 (September 1994): 41–64; Lawrence Kohlberg, *Essays on Moral Development* (New York: Harper & Row, 1981); James. S. Leming, "Synthesis of Research: In Search of Effective Character Education," *Educational Leadership* 51 (November 1993): 63–71; Thomas Lickona, *Character Matters: How to Help Our Children Develop Good Judgment, Integrity, and Other Essential Virtues* (New York: Touchstone, Simon & Schuster, 2004); B. Edward McClellan, *Schools and the Shaping of Character: Moral Education in America, 1607–Present* (Bloomington, IN: ERIC Clearinghouse for Social Studies/Social Science Education and the Social Studies Development Center, Indiana University, 1992); Jean Piaget, *The Moral Judgment of the Child* (London: Kegan Paul, Trench, Trubner and Co. 1932); Sidney Simon, Leland Howe, and Howard Kirschenbaum, *Values Clarification: A Handbook of Practical Strategies for Teachers and Students* (New York: Hart, 1972).

Monalisa M. Mullins

Moral Majority

In 1976, millions of evangelical Christians voted for fellow-believer Jimmy Carter, helping him gain the presidency in a close race with Gerald Ford. George Gallup reported that as many as 50 million Americans could be described as evangelicals, and *Newsweek* magazine ran a cover story calling 1976 "The Year of the Evangelical." Disappointed by Carter's support of the Equal Rights Amendment, his refusal to condemn all abortions, and his stance that homosexuals should enjoy equal rights, many conservative Protestants began looking for ways to use their newfound political muscle to push the country in a more rightward direction.

By the end of the 1970s, Jerry Falwell (1933–2007), pastor of the fundamentalist Thomas Road Baptist Church in Lynchburg, Virginia, was beginning to use his widely aired radio and television programs to speak against gay rights, abortion, and other issues he traced to the influence of "secular humanism." In 1979, with the encouragement and assistance of political activists who referred to themselves as the New Right or "movement conservatives" and were associated with such organizations as the Heritage Foundation and the Free Congress Foundation, Falwell founded Moral Majority, declaring that it would be "pro-life, pro-family, pro-moral, and pro-American." (He sometimes added "pro-Israel," a reflection of a theological doctrine known as "dispensationalist premillennialism," which holds that full restoration of the nation of Israel, including complete possession of "Judea and Samaria," aka the West Bank, home to millions of Palestinians, is a prerequisite to the second coming of Jesus.) Its stated aims included registering evangelical Christians to vote, informing members about what was going on in Washington and in state legislatures, lobbying to defeat "left-wing social welfare bills," and pushing for legislation that would protect and advance a conservative social agenda. Prominent pastors Charles Stanley, James Kennedy, Tim LaHaye, and Greg Dixon were on the founding board; Robert Billings served as executive director. During the same period, an organization called Religious Roundtable worked to mobilize Southern Baptists, and Christian Voice played a comparable role among charismatic and Pentecostal Christians. Because of Falwell's attention-getting message and style and his ubiquitous presence on television and in the press, however, Moral Majority became the best-known representative and symbol of the movement that came to be called the "Religious Right."

As an openly political organization, Moral Majority did not have tax-exempt status, but Falwell was able to use his *Old Time Gospel Hour* broadcasts and Liberty University, which he founded and served as Chancellor, as tax-exempt vehicles to promote the organization and its agenda. For years, he had used the broadcast to raise money for Liberty University and, since the bicentennial year of 1976, he had been holding "I Love America" rallies on the steps of state capitols throughout the country. The rallies, which often drew thousands of people who had been alerted by Falwell's broadcasts and direct mail to his supporters, featured a band and chorus of squeaky-clean Liberty students who performed rousing renditions of religio-patriotic songs, followed by a stirring Falwell jeremiad and call for national repentance and, typically, warm endorsements of the event by high-ranking state officials and other well-known local figures. Paid for by tax-exempt contributions from supporters of *The Old-Time Gospel Hour,* the rallies attracted coverage by local news media and increased and legitimized Falwell's public stature. After the founding of Moral Majority, they enabled him to invite all the pastors present—often several hundred—to a complimentary luncheon where he explained the rationale and strategy of the Moral Majority, urged them to establish local chapters and to use their churches as a base for registering people to vote, and provided them with basic information on such issues as abortion, pornography, homosexuality, and the ERA. Only the modest expense of the meal had to be paid for by nonexempt Moral Majority funds. During 1979 and 1980, Falwell spent most of his time on the road, traveling upwards of 300,000 miles per year, often speaking several times a day at churches, public gatherings, luncheons, dinners, and press conferences, and meeting privately with the network of people who were helping set up Moral Majority chapters throughout the country. By the end of 1980, he claimed to have contacted 72,000 preachers to acquaint them with Moral Majority and its purposes.

As one who, in a widely distributed 1960s sermon, had warned preachers to eschew such activity, Falwell recognized that riding into the political arena in such a visible vehicle constituted a direct challenge to fundamentalist pietism, which traditionally manifested itself not only in disciplined devotional practice and strict standards of personal morality, but also in a general stance of separation from "the world." Millions of conservative Christians were not even registered to vote. He not only worked to convince the pastors to join his cause, but provided them with materials to help them explain to their flocks why fundamentalists had to change their old attitude toward politics and, having done so, get them registered to vote. In addition to convincing them they had a duty to become involved in politics, Falwell also worked hard at breaking down their separatist impulses, persuading them that, to accomplish goals beneficial not only to Christians but to the nation as a whole, they would have to be willing to collaborate with people with whom they disagreed on matters of doctrine—Catholics, Jews, perhaps even Mormons—but who shared their views on such matters as the family, abortion, and homosexuality. As a consequence of their association with "movement conservatives," Moral Majority and kindred organizations soon fleshed out their platforms to include positions not ordinarily dealt with in Sunday School, going on record to oppose the strategic arms limitation treaty (SALT II), economic sanctions against Rhodesia, abrogation of the U.S. military treaty with Taiwan, and the relinquishing of control of the Panama Canal. On the positive side, they regularly lined up in favor of increased spending for national defense.

In 1967, Falwell had established Liberty Christian Academy, which began as a K–5 elementary school, later expanded to K–12 status, and led ultimately to Lynchburg Baptist College, later renamed Liberty Bible College, then Liberty University. Though regarded by many as a white-flight school, Falwell insisted that he was acting in response to Supreme Court decisions banning school-sponsored prayer and Bible reading, as well as to other developments he felt were detrimental to a Christian worldview, including a perceived onslaught from secular humanists, whom Falwell and his colleagues tended to blame for virtually any ill they found in society. (Board member Tim LaHaye's 1980 book, *The Battle for the Mind,* played a major role in alarming conservative Christians of the putative menace.) Not surprisingly, Moral Majority advocated, as Falwell's schools practiced, school prayer, abstinence-only sex education, and the teaching of alternatives to Darwinian evolution. It also favored taxpayer-funded vouchers that could be used in private, religiously oriented schools and tax credits for tuition paid to such schools. The organization also frequently criticized textbooks used in public schools.

When Ronald Reagan won the presidential election and Republicans gained a majority in the Senate, Falwell and his Moral Majority colleagues took considerable credit for the achievement. They were therefore understandably disappointed at the failure of the Reagan administration to give strong support to the social goals central to their agenda, such as a school prayer amendment, and they had never developed sufficiently effective political technique and organization to have much real leverage. In 1986, faced with failure to achieve major legislative victories for the organization's "pro-moral, pro-family" agenda and chronic financial problems at Liberty University, Falwell announced that Moral Majority would be folded into a new entity known as the Liberty Federation. In effect, this was a face-saving way for both Falwell and Moral Majority to withdraw from an arena in which they were no longer effective. The Liberty Federation proved to be a cipher; after two articles at the time of its inauguration, the *New York Times* never mentioned it again during the entire year, a marked contrast to the enormous amount of attention Moral Majority had received during its early years. Though not formally disbanded until 1989, Moral Majority's day had clearly been over for several years, and its mantle was picked up by other organizations, most notably Christian Coalition, founded by religious broadcaster Pat Robertson and led by Ralph Reed. Still, by helping to convince thousands of fundamentalist pastors and millions of their flocks that it was their Christian duty to get involved in a realm they had long eschewed, Falwell and Moral Majority have left a lasting mark on American politics. *See also:* Christian Coalition; Humanism and the Humanist Manifestos; Secularism.

Further Reading: Sara Diamond, *Roads to Dominion* (New York: Guilford Press, 1995); William Martin, *With God on Our Side: The Rise of the Religious Right in America* (New York: Broadway Books, 1996; 2004).

William Martin

Mueller v. Allen

At issue in *Mueller v. Allen* (1983) was the constitutionality of a statute from Minnesota that granted all parents state income tax deductions for the actual costs of tuition, textbooks, and transportation associated with sending their children to elementary or secondary schools in the state. The statute granted parents deductions of $500 for children in grades K–6 and $700 for those in grades 7–12. In upholding the constitutionality of the statute, *Mueller* stands out as the only case between the Court's 1971 ruling in *Lemon v. Kurtzman* and the shift in its jurisprudence that began in 1993 with *Zobrest v. Catalina Foothills School District* that permitted aid other than transportation to parents who sent their children to religiously affiliated nonpublic schools.

The federal trial court in Minnesota rejected an initial challenge to the statute in finding that it did not violate either the Establishment or Free Exercise Clauses of the First Amendment to the U.S. Constitution. The court was satisfied that the statute was constitutional because it passed all three prongs of the *Lemon* (1971) test. The Eighth Circuit Court of Appeals affirmed for essentially the same reasons.

On further review in *Mueller,* writing for a closely divided 5-4 Court, Justice, later Chief Justice, William Rehnquist, upheld the statute's constitutionality. Rehnquist distinguished *Mueller* from the Court's earlier judgment in *Committee for Public Education v. Nyquist* (1973), wherein it struck down a statute from New York that provided income tax benefits to parents whose children attended religiously affiliated nonpublic schools. Rehnquist reached a different outcome in *Mueller* primarily because the tax benefit was available to all parents, not only those whose children were in nonpublic schools and that the deduction was one among many rather than a single, favored type of taxpayer expenditure.

At the heart of his analysis, Rehnquist applied the three-part *Lemon* test. First, he agreed that the statute had a secular legislative purpose in acknowledging the legislature's broad latitude to create classifications and distinctions in tax statutes, and that the state could have been considered to benefit from the scheme since it promoted an educated citizenry while reducing the costs of public education. Second, Rehnquist was of the opinion that the law did not have the primary or principal effect of advancing religion because the deduction was available to all parents, regardless of where their children attended school. At the same time, Rehnquist was not concerned with the fact that since Minnesota's public schools were essentially free, the expenses of parents with children in them were at most minimal and that about 96 percent of the taxpayers who benefited had children who were enrolled in religious schools. Third, he reasoned that the law did not create excessive entanglement since officials might have had to question educational expenses associated with textbooks. Instead, he harkened back to *Board of Education v. Allen* (1968), wherein the Court upheld a mandatory textbook loan in secular subjects for students regardless of whether they attended religiously affiliated nonpublic schools in New York, in concluding that the law did not violate the Establishment Clause.

Justice Thurgood Marshall's dissent rejected the majority's distinction between *Nyquist* and *Mueller*. Instead, he maintained that insofar as the statute ultimately benefited religiously affiliated nonpublic schools, it failed to pass constitutional muster. *See also:* Government Aid to Religious Schools; *Lemon v. Kurtzman* and *Earley v. DiCenso;* Tuition Tax Credits; *Zobrest v. Catalina Foothills School District.*

Further Reading: *Board of Education v. Allen,* 392 U.S. 236 (1968); *Committee for Public Education v. Nyquist,* 413 U.S. 756 (1973); *Lemon v. Kurtzman,* 403 U.S. 602 (1971); *Mueller v. Allen,* 463 U.S. 388 (1983); *Zobrest v. Catalina Foothills School District,* 509 U.S. 1 (1993).

Charles J. Russo

N

National Association of Evangelicals

The National Association of Evangelicals (NAE) traces its origins to April 7–9, 1942, when a group of 147 moderate Christian evangelicals gathered in St. Louis for the "National Conference for United Action among Evangelicals." The attendees represented over 75 denominations, and they sought to unify disparate evangelical organizations in an effort to inspire political activism and encourage cooperative ministry. The conveners believed that conservative Protestantism had lost its relevance and was unfavorably viewed by many as an anti-intellectualist and politically sedentary faction. According to Christian Smith, those present at the seminal meeting sought to "launch a religious movement they hoped would transform the character of conservative Protestantism and literally alter the course of American religious history" (Smith, 1998, p. 1).

The NAE today is composed of 45,000 churches representing approximately 60 denominations. It is engaged in a broad array of social and political issues that includes (but is not restricted to) those that have been championed by conservative Christian groups for decades. For example, while its opposition to issues such as legalized abortion, embryonic stem cell research, and same-sex marriage remains strong, in 2007 the NAE board also took stances that were considered controversial by other established Christian conservatives such as opposing torture and reaffirming a commitment to care for "the creation."

The NAE also has a long history of advocacy regarding issues related to religion and education that is exemplified in a series of statements, resolutions, and lobbying campaigns that span from 1962 to the present day. Following the highly controversial Supreme Court decision in *Engel v. Vitale* in 1962 banning school-sponsored prayer, the NAE issued a strongly worded statement condemning interpretations of the separation of church and state that support "surrender to secularism and atheism through the exclusion from our public schools of all reference to God" (National Association of Evangelicals, at www.nae.net). At that time, the NAE emphasized a definition of "separation" as a protection against government encroachment upon religious affairs and thus interpreted rulings like *Engel v. Vitale* as a violation of free exercise rather than a valid interpretation of the Establishment Clause. A 1965 resolution entitled "Religion and Education" represented similar assumptions in its assertion that it is the "duty" of the public school "to do full justice to the large place of the Judeo-Christian tradition in our American heritage" and that "an objective presentation of the contribution made by the Christian faith to the development of that heritage" should be represented throughout the curriculum. The resolution also affirms the "freedom" that "Christian teachers" have "to teach from a Christian standpoint and to witness by example and personal life the effects of Christian commitment" (National Association of Evangelicals, at www.nae.net).

Two years later, however, the NAE appeared to be resigned to the fact that the public schools were increasingly secular spaces. In a 1967 statement entitled "Christian Day Schools" the organization recognized that in "most public classrooms in America today the Bible is not taught as God's revelation, the distinctiveness of the faith cannot be inculcated and a Christian philosophy of history is not suggested" (www.nae.net). In response, the statement called for those in the NAE to learn more about the education their children are receiving in the public schools and to compare it with the educational opportunities available in Christian schools. The statement also called for support of Christian schools as a defense against the "prevailing secular philosophies of the day" (www.nae.net).

Between 1960 and 2000 the NAE was involved in many of the school prayer amendments initiated in Congress, and its position gradually shifted over the years from vigorous endorsement and lobbying (Becker Amendment, 1964) to endorsement (Wylie Amendment, 1971) to perfunctory support (Reagan Amendment, 1982) to opposition (Istook Amendment, 1995–1997). This shift represented a broader division among conservative Christian groups regarding strategies for strengthening the role of religion in public schools. In the early 1980s, the NAE frequently found itself in alignment with organizations such as the Christian Legal Society and the Southern Baptist Convention in their shared concern that increased government involvement with religion through measures such as a constitutional amendment supporting government-endorsed prayer would actually serve to jeopardize rather than enhance the free exercise of religious beliefs. An alternative strategy was one that supported providing "equal access" to school facilities, funds and services for student-led religious groups and clubs, thereby expanding the opportunities for individual religious expression through that venue. This was the general approach endorsed by the NAE as represented through its lobbying efforts in support of the equal access bill that Senator Mark Hatfield introduced in 1982. Though the NAE technically endorsed the competing Reagan Amendment, it used its considerable political clout in support of this alternative strategy. Its decision not to support the Istook Amendment in 1995 was an even more explicit representation of its shift in political focus.

Another related initiative was taking shape in the early 1990s that involved a coalition of diverse religious and secular groups who disagreed ideologically about many dimensions of the religion in the schools' controversies but were able to unite on the desire to help better clarify current law. A group of lawyers from this coalition (including representation from the NAE) came together to draft a statement outlining key components of the law and the implications they held for public schools. The Clinton administration was also keen to address issues related to religion in the schools to challenge the perception that those who opposed a constitutional amendment supporting school prayer were against religion itself. Secretary of Education Richard Riley learned about the coalition that was drafting the statement on clarifying the law and offered to utilize the resources of the Department of Education to further the initiative and to distribute the final document to teachers and administrators nationwide. This offer frustrated many of the more ideologically conservative members of the coalition who believed a move like this would politicize the effort in ways that would be detrimental to their interests. Clinton was in the midst of a reelection campaign, and they believed that his alignment with this initiative would boost his credibility and ultimately undermine their efforts to pass a constitutional amendment supporting school prayer. The NAE was one of only a small handful of conservative evangelical groups who decided to sign the final document entitled "Religion in the Public Schools: A Joint Statement of Current Law," and those who did were highly criticized by fellow conservatives for lending credibility to this effort.

Another issue related to religion in the schools that the NAE has engaged in ways that are more aligned with their conservative colleagues in other organizations is support for school choice through vouchers. The NAE believes it is constitutionally sound for governments to support the right of parents to send their children to the school of their choice by issuing vouchers for those who choose independent versus public schools. The vouchers are drawn from tax revenues and are used to offset private school tuition costs. The NAE joined the petitioners in the landmark U.S. Supreme Court case *Zelman v. Simmons-Harris* (2002) where the Court ruled in a 5-4 vote that a school voucher program in Cleveland, Ohio, did not violate the no establishment provision of the First Amendment. The NAE support of vouchers is consistent with their movement away from government-sponsored initiatives supporting religious expression (such as school prayer amendments) to initiatives that improve the range of choices afforded to religious individuals and groups to exercise the free expression of their beliefs.

The NAE has long been dedicated to addressing the myriad issues related to religion in the schools. Its movement from being a strong advocate in support of embedding Christian values into all aspects of school life to its current emphasis on increasing the opportunities for individual religious expression represents, in part, its recognition of the diversity of voices both within and among religious communities in the United States. Its history of coalition building among its own constituencies as well as with organizations representing the full ideological spectrum has made it an effective voice in public policy discourses over the past five decades regarding religion in the schools. *See also:* Common Ground Documents; Equal Access Act; U.S. Department of Education Guidelines on Religion and Public Education; *Zelman v. Simmons-Harris.*

Further Reading: Joan DelFattore, *The Fourth R* (New Haven, CT: Yale University Press, 2004); *Engel v. Vitale,* 370 U.S. 421 (1962); Edward Felsenthal, "Christian Right Falls out of Unison on School Prayer," *Wall Street Journal,* February 24, 1997, sec. A, p. 24; The Institute on Religion and Democracy, at www.ird-renew.org; National Association of Evangelicals, at www.nae.net; Re:Vision: Broadening Perspectives, Inspiring Action, at www.revision.timberlakepublishing.com/index.asp; Christian Smith, *American Evangelicalism* (Chicago: The University of Chicago Press, 1998); *Zelman v. Simmons-Harris,* 536 U.S. 639 (2002).

Diane L. Moore

National Catholic Educational Association

The National Catholic Educational Association (NCEA) is a voluntary membership organization for professional educators and educational administrators involved in the broad ministry of Catholic education. It serves as an umbrella association, providing a variety of services and networking possibilities for members. The mission statement of the NCEA reads: "Rooted in the Gospel of Jesus Christ, the National Catholic Educational Association is a professional membership organization that provides leadership, direction and service to fulfill the evangelizing, catechetical and teaching mission of the church" (National Catholic Educational Association, 2007, p. 3).

NCEA seeks to serve various constituents and is organized into different departments that represent the various ministries found in Catholic education. Member institutions hold association membership through one of the constitutive departments and access services through the department. Current departments, representing numerous branches of Catholic education, include the Chief Administrators of Catholic Education, Elementary Schools, Secondary Schools, Religious Education, Seminary, and Boards and Councils of Catholic Education.

The Chief Administrators of Catholic Education (CACE) Department includes primarily diocesan central office personnel who serve in some executive capacity under the supervision of the diocesan bishop. Because diocesan offices are structured according to the needs of the local church and the discernment of its bishop, position titles often differ for these executive offices, but typically the chief administrators of Catholic education in a diocese carry such titles as Superintendent of Catholic Schools, Vicar for Education, Secretary of Education, Director of Total Catholic Education, Secretary for Faith Formation and Education, Director of Religious Education, or Secretary for Religious Education. These officers and their staffs are the membership of the CACE department. CACE has a general meeting during the fall every year, gathers as part of the annual NCEA convention every spring during the week following Easter, and sponsors regional meetings across the United States throughout the academic year.

The Elementary Schools Department serves Catholic schools at the elementary level and includes schools organized as K–8, K–6, K–4, and Catholic middle schools. Because Catholic elementary schools are numerous and constitute the most prevalent form of Catholic educational institutions, membership in this department is large. In 2006–2007, Catholic school enrollment in elementary and middle schools was 1,682,412. The total number of Catholic elementary and middle schools during the same period was 6,288 (McDonald, 2007). The Elementary Schools Department provides a regular cycle of professional development opportunities across the United States, often focusing on Catholic identity, educational leadership, curriculum development and enhancement, technology, and issues related to improving human resource and fiscal management.

The Secondary Schools Department serves Catholic high schools. In 2006–2007, there were 1,210 Catholic high schools in the United States, including diocesan schools, private Catholic schools, and those sponsored by religious communities. These schools served a total of 638,239 students during the same period. The department's services are focused on three areas: Catholic identity, leadership development, and institutional advancement.

The Religious Education Department serves those involved in catechetical and religious formation in parishes, schools, and diocesan offices. Because religious education is available and needed in contexts outside of the Catholic school, this department includes a broader community of religious educators. This department sponsors regional and national conferences as well as retreats. A notable service provided by this department is the administration of two religious education assessment tools, the Assessment of Catechetical/Religious Education and Information for Growth. These two tools enjoy widespread use in Catholic schools and parishes as a way to assess the effectiveness of religious education programming.

The Seminary Department consists of those institutions involved with the professional preparation and education of future priests. Seminaries are primarily theologates, or graduate schools of theology, and operate a five–six year program for those preparing for ordained priesthood. Fewer seminaries are found at the college level, and even fewer at the high school level. The Seminary Department hosts an annual convention, a biennial institute for the preparation of seminary formation staff and publishes the *Seminary Journal,* a journal of opinion, research, and praxis in the field of seminary education and formation within the Roman Catholic tradition.

The Boards and Councils of Catholic Education Department works with governance bodies in Catholic educational institutions to support and strengthen their work in service to the educational mission of the Church. These governance bodies often take the form of school boards or councils, commissions of Catholic education, or diocesan school boards. The department offers a variety of on-site consultation and support services to help Catholic educational leaders in such areas as restructuring school governance, starting or jump-starting a school board, strategic planning, and environmental scans.

The most popular event organized and sponsored by the NCEA is the Annual Convention and Exposition, held every year during the week after Easter. This event typically draws in excess of 10,000 Catholic educators and is held in different venues to attract the broadest range of educators possible. The convention follows a standard format, with keynote addresses from significant leaders in the field, followed by hundreds of breakout sessions where participants can explore topics of interest and choice. Conventions also have a regular cycle of common prayer, with daily Masses, and special, celebratory opening and closing liturgies. The Exposition is a major attraction at the convention. The Exposition comprises vendors, publishers, textbook companies, computer hardware and software suppliers, journals, candy companies, and other manufacturers and suppliers who do business with Catholic parishes and schools. The Exposition Hall, usually in the convention center of a major metropolitan area, attracts thousands of teachers, catechists, and administrators looking for new ideas and services that will support their respective ministries.

Another popular service of the NCEA is its publication division, which offers books, monographs, curriculum resources, prayer and liturgical planning materials, self-study tools, and a variety of faculty and staff development programs to support the continuous improvement of Catholic education. The NCEA also publishes a monthly journal, *Momentum,* which serves as its official journal for communicating with its membership and disseminating recent success stories, emerging classroom strategies, public policy developments, book reviews, and relevant advertising.

NCEA has enjoyed a long history of success in serving the needs of Catholic educators in the United States. In the early 1900s, once disparate organizations agreed to unite into a centralized entity that could better serve the needs of the growing church. At a meeting held in St. Louis, Missouri, July 12–14, 1904, three separate Catholic educational organizations—the Education Conference of Catholic Seminary Faculties, the Association of Catholic Colleges, and the Parish School Conference—united to form the Catholic Educational Association (CEA). From 1904 until 1919, the CEA provided the only national voice for Catholic educational concerns and was instrumental in bringing together its various constituencies in shaping Catholic educational policies.

Later on, the U.S. bishops established similar national bodies to serve as a vehicle for mutual support and communication, among them the National Catholic War Council, which evolved into the National Catholic Welfare Council. As an organization of the U.S. bishops, the National Catholic Welfare Council addressed all matters pertaining to the Catholic Church in the United States, including education. The bishop's organization exists today as the United States Conference of Catholic Bishops (USCCB), which still includes a department of education. The USCCB's department of education, while having undergone significant restructuring in 2006, maintains a cooperative working relationship with the NCEA and regularly collaborates on national issues of mutual concern, especially those involving public policy, federal legislation, and federal funding.

The CEA added the word "national" to its official title in 1927 and has served Catholic education as the NCEA ever since. It is the single largest private professional educational organization in the world, counting as its constituents 200,000 Catholic educators serving over 7 million students who attend Catholic elementary, middle, and secondary schools, religious education programs, seminaries, and colleges and universities. *See also:* Catholic Schools.

Further Reading: Michael J. Guerra, *Catholic Education: Gift to the Church, Gift to the Nation* (Washington, DC: National Catholic Educational Association, 1987); Donald C. Horrigan, *The Shaping of NCEA* (Washington, DC: National Catholic Educational Association, 1987); Thomas C. Hunt, Ellis A. Joseph, and Ronald J. Nuzzi, eds., *Catholic Schools in the United States: An Encyclopedia* (Westport, CT: Greenwood Press, 2004); Dale McDonald, *United States Catholic Elementary and Secondary Schools 2006—2007* (Washington, DC: National Catholic Educational Association, 2007); National Catholic Educational Association, *2006 Annual Report: Leadership, Direction, and Service* (Washington, DC: National Catholic Educational Association, 2007); National Catholic Education Association, at www.ncea.org.

Ronald J. Nuzzi

National Committee for Public Education and Religious Liberty

The National Committee for Public Education and Religious Liberty (PEARL), earlier known as the Committee for Public Education and Religious Liberty and as the National Coalition for Public Education and Religious Liberty, was a coalition of separationist advocacy groups focusing on Establishment Clause issues in public education. At its peak, its membership included more than 50 organizations ranging from large national groups such as the American Civil Liberties Union, Americans United for Separation of Church and State, and the National Education Association to smaller organizations such as the City Club of New York and the Michigan Council About Parochiaid.

PEARL was founded in 1967 by renowned First Amendment attorney Leo Pfeffer (1910–1993), who remained at its helm until ill health forced his retirement in 1983. He had earlier served as general counsel to the American Jewish Congress, and during most of his tenure at PEARL, he taught political science at Long Island University. Under his leadership, PEARL took the lead in arguing the separationist side in a series of U.S. Supreme Court cases, such as *Committee for Public Education and Religious Liberty v. Nyquist* (1973) and *Levitt v. Committee for Public Education and Religious Liberty* (1973). In *Nyquist,* PEARL successfully challenged a New York law that offered support to nonpublic education, including religious education, in the form of grants for building maintenance and repair, tuition reimbursement to low-income parents, and a tuition tax deduction for other parents. In *Levitt,* the Supreme Court overturned a New York law that provided per-pupil payments to nonpublic schools, including religious schools, to defray the costs of various forms of testing and record keeping. If the amount allotted exceeded the actual cost of the testing and record keeping, the remainder of the money did not have to be returned.

After Pfeffer's departure from PEARL, first Stanley Geller and then Lisa Thurau (now Thurau-Gray) led the organization in challenging both the use of public funding to support religious education and the promotion of religion through the public schools. Among the post-Pfeffer cases were *Aguilar v. Felton* (1985), in which the Supreme Court declared that public school teachers could not be assigned to teach remedial reading and mathematics to low-income students in religious schools; and *Grand Rapids School District v. Ball* (1985), in which the Court struck down two programs involving a school district's leasing of classrooms in religious schools in order to conduct classes for students in those schools. PEARL also filed *amicus curiae* briefs in numerous other cases.

With the passage of time, PEARL saw some of its victories significantly eroded. In *Committee for Public Education and Religious Liberty v. Regan* (1980), the Supreme Court upheld a New York statute developed in response to *Nyquist.* It allocated to private schools, including religious schools, only the actual cost of administering state-mandated tests and recording the results. In *Agostini v. Felton* (1997), the Supreme Court reversed its 1985 ruling in *Aguilar,* finding it inconsistent with later decisions of the Court. Five years later, in *Zelman v. Simmons-Harris* (2002), the Court further weakened *Nyquist* in upholding a Cleveland program that provided vouchers for religious schools. PEARL went out of business after *Zelman. See also:* American Civil Liberties Union; American Jewish Congress; Americans United for Separation of Church and State; First Amendment Religion Clauses and the Supreme Court; Separation of Church and State/Wall of Separation between Church and State.

Further Reading: *Agostini v. Felton,* 521 U.S. 203 (1997); *Aguilar v. Felton,* 473 U.S. 402 (1985); *Committee for Public Education and Religious Liberty v. Nyquist,* 413 U.S. 756 (1973); *Committee for Public Education and Religious Liberty v. Regan,* 444 U.S. 646 (1980); *Grand Rapids School District v. Ball,* 473 U.S. 373 (1985).Marci Hamilton, *God vs. the Gavel: Religion and the Rule of Law* (New York: Cambridge University Press, 2007); Gregg Ivers, *To Build a Wall: American Jews and the Separation of Church and State* (Charlottesville, VA: University of Virginia Press, 1995); *Levitt v. Committee for Public Education and Religious Liberty,* 413 U.S. 472 (1973); Ronald B. Millar, "Strategy Trumps Precedent: Separationist Litigants on the Wrong Side of Legal Change," *Journal of Church and State* 50 (Spring 2008): 299–329; Leo Pfeffer, *God, Caesar, and the Constitution: The Court as Referee of Church-State Confrontation* (Boston: Beacon Press, 1975); James E. Wood, ed., *Religion and the State: Essays in Honor of Leo Pfeffer* (Waco, TX: Baylor University Press, 1985); *Zelman v. Simmons-Harris,* 536 U.S. 639 (2002).

Joan DelFattore

National Council for the Social Studies

The National Council for the Social Studies (NCSS) is an education association that comprises elementary, secondary, and college level teachers and other educational personnel who work in the broad areas that encompass the social studies: history, geography, economics, political science, sociology, psychology, anthropology, and law. The Council was founded in 1921 and is "the largest association in the country devoted solely to social studies education." Membership is open to individuals and institutions interested in the social studies, and is organized as a network of affiliated local, state, and regional councils. Its mission is "to provide leadership, service, and support for all social studies educators" (National Council for the Social Studies, at www.ncss.org). A national board of directors is elected annually from among its members and a hired professional staff supports the work of the NCSS.

Regarding the study of religion in the schools, the NCSS has issued a set of guidelines on how to address religion in the social studies curriculum. The guidelines were first prepared by the Religion in the Schools Committee and approved by the NCSS Board of Directors in 1984. The Curriculum Committee later revised them, and the Board approved the revised version in 1998.

The guidelines are based on the assumption that the study of religion "has a rightful place in the public school curriculum because of the pervasive nature of religious beliefs, practices, institutions, and sensitivities" (www.ncss.org). They are also rooted in constitutional law as represented in the *Abington v. Schempp* (1963) Supreme Court ruling that banned school-sponsored recitation of the Lord's Prayer and devotional Bible reading as unconstitutional. Central to that ruling are clarifying comments issued by Justices Tom Clark and William Brennan in separate concurring opinions where they highlight the distinction between inculcating religious belief and teaching about religion and its influences. According to Justice Brennan, "it would be impossible to teach meaningfully many subjects in the social sciences or the humanities without some mention of religion."

There are 14 guidelines that together offer a comprehensive overview of how to teach about religion in constitutionally sound ways. They stress the importance for educators to present informed, accurate, fair, and balanced representations of the diversity of religious beliefs and practices that are embedded in various dimensions of the social studies curricula. These guidelines provide an important and useful resource for social studies educators.

In a more recent action, the NCSS issued a position statement on Intelligent Design (ID) to help clarify its proper place in a social studies curriculum. The position statement referenced the guidelines outlined above and used them to develop a more specific set of recommendations for how educators can address this controversial topic in responsible and helpful ways. Given the sustained (but thus far failed) attempts in recent years to legally justify the introduction of ID as an alternative to the theory of evolution in science classrooms, the NCSS Board recognized that many social studies teachers were in the position to teach about these controversies from the interrelated perspectives of history, current events, and cultural studies. Commenting that "the same constitutional issues arise whether religious beliefs are taught in science or in the social studies curriculum," the recommendations are intended to help guide educators in how to "allow for substantive discussion of the issues surrounding intelligent design while avoiding First Amendment problems" (www.ncss.org). The recommendations offer suggestions about how to examine issues related to ID from a social studies rather than a religious perspective and include specific outlines of the following approaches: constitutional, historical, sociological, anthropological, and public issues. The conclusion of the position statement reads as follows:

> The NCSS believes that a free and open discussion of ideas is essential to a healthy democracy. However, the social studies classroom should not and cannot be used for teaching any

specific religious belief, as this is antithetical to the First Amendment. The National Council for the Social Studies recommends analysis, and thoughtful discussion, not indoctrination. (www.ncss.org)

In addition to its own internal engagement regarding religion and education, the NCSS is one of 19 organizations that endorsed "A Teacher's Guide to Religion in the Public Schools" that was published by the First Amendment Center in 1999. This guide promotes the same approach to teaching about religion that is represented in the NCSS guidelines outlined above.

The NCSS has been actively educating its membership and the public at large about the complex issues related to religion and the schools for over two decades. As the largest association of social studies educators in the United States, it has been an influential voice in these discourses. *See also:* Common Ground Documents; Intelligent Design; Religion and the Public School Curriculum.

Further Reading: Charles Haynes, "A Teacher's Guide to Religion in the Public Schools" (Nashville: First Amendment Center, 1999); National Council for the Social Studies, at www.ncss.org; Warren Nord, *Religion and American Education* (Chapel Hill: University of North Carolina Press, 1995).

Diane L. Moore

National Council of Churches

The National Council of Churches (NCC) is an association of more than 35 mostly "mainline" denominations or communions dedicated to ecumenical cooperation among its member congregations, which represent more than 45 million people. It was founded in 1950 as an assembly of about a dozen preexisting organizations, for instance (and relevant here), the American Sunday School Association, active since 1824. NCC's mission declares that "genuine unity demands inclusivity and a respect for diversity," and the association serves a wide spectrum of churches, including Protestant and Orthodox denominations as well as historically African American and immigrant churches. It also engages with Jewish and Roman Catholic leadership and has been particularly focused on interfaith dialogue and cooperation with Muslims in the wake of 9/11. In recent years, it has sought to reinsert its left-leaning voice into the public square in order to counter the political influence of the Religious Right. Some of the focal points of NCC advocacy include global poverty, world peace, global warming, and the improvement of public education. The NCC is governed by a general assembly of 300 delegates from member congregations and a smaller governing board that serves those delegates.

The NCC, through the work of the Education and Leadership Ministries Commission, as well as the Public Education and Literacy Committee, advocates forcefully for the improvement of public schools, which it sees as both an "avenue of opportunity" and a "major cohesive force" in an increasingly plural democracy (National Council of Churches, at www.ncccusa.org). It views the support of the public schools to be a theological imperative based upon a biblical mandate to help "the least of these." While the NCC affirms the right of parents to send their children to private or parochial schools, it demands that public money *only* support public schools and therefore opposes vouchers. It strongly affirms the separation of church and state and sees its mission within the schools as to promote justice and to work on behalf of those who have no power to speak for themselves, rather than to evangelize or raise support for its own theological framework.

The work of the NCC on behalf of public schools has been guided since 1999 by the policy statement "The Churches and the Schools at the Close of the Twentieth Century," which details ways that local congregations can "recover" their historic support for public schools and the children and teachers within them. This document explicitly situates the plight of the schools within the context funding disparities and race and class discrimination. Nationally it calls for member churches to provide forums for local school board candidates, to support equalized funding for all school districts, to advocate smaller, more caring school environments, and to demand better facilities across the system. The statement calls upon churches to honor teachers as role models, support academic freedom for teachers and librarians, to advocate curricula that reflect America's diversity, and to demand "quality, age-appropriate comprehensive health education" to all students. The statement also asks that churches insist upon high-quality science classrooms that study evolution in context. The NCC promotes a holistic vision of the child and the educational process and therefore supports increased funding for arts and recreation as core curriculum in schools. It has also encouraged its member churches to agitate against the federal No Child Left Behind Act, which it sees as morally deficient in its test-based assessment and punitive measures.

Another way that the NCC supports public schools and promotes local church involvement is through its encouragement for church-school collaboration in after-school and extracurricular programming. Here the NCC finds itself aligned with many of the more theologically conservative organizations in the United States, which also advocate for increased church involvement within the schools. In the U.S. Supreme Court case *Good News Club v. Milford Central School* (2001), the NCC supported the successful argument that a religious club must be able to hold meetings after school hours on elementary school property if nonreligious clubs are given that privilege. The NCC has also endorsed the First Amendment Center's "The Bible and Public Schools: A First Amendment Guide," which outlines permissible uses of the Bible within academic classrooms. *See also:* Common Ground Documents.

Further Reading: Alan Cooperman, "Christian Groups Trade Barbs on Their Sources of Funding," *Washington Post,* January 11, 2007, sec. A, p. 3; Bob Edgar, *Middlechurch: Reclaiming the Moral Values of the Faithful Majority from the Religious Right* (New York: Simon and Schuster, 2006); Linda Greenhouse, "The Supreme Court: Religion and Free Speech; Top Court Gives Religious Clubs Equal Footing in Grade Schools," *New York Times,* June 12, 2001, sec. A, p. 1; Michael Lerner, *The Left Hand of God: Taking Back Our Country from the Religious Right* (New York: HarperOne, 2006); John Leland, "One More 'Moral Value': Fighting Poverty," *New York Times,* January 30, 2005, sec. 1, p. 26; National Council of Churches, at www.ncccusa.org.

Shipley Robertson Salewski

National Council on Bible Curriculum in Public Schools

The National Council on Bible Curriculum in Public Schools (NCBCPS) is a Christian Right organization that encourages school districts to teach its high school Bible course. Founded in 1993 by Elizabeth Ridenour, a former paralegal and real estate broker from Greensboro, North Carolina, the council's several dozen members include ministers, evangelists, representatives from conservative religious and political advocacy groups, Christian Right media figures, celebrities, lawyers, and lawmakers from both state legislatures and the U.S. Congress. The group includes few professional educators or scholars trained in religious or theological studies. The council is heavily promoted by Christian Right media outlets, and in the past, its Web site noted cosponsorship by the American Family Association and the Center for Reclaiming America. The NCBCPS claims that its curriculum is taught in over 400 school districts across the United States, though critics have suggested that this number is inflated. Until the recent emergence of the Bible Literacy Project, the council was the sole national organization providing a Bible curriculum for public schools. Its level of influence is reflected by the incorporation of language from its materials in a 2006 Georgia law promoting Bible courses.

The NCBCPS shares a view often found within the Christian Right that the United States has entered into a period of social and moral decline since the cessation of devotional Bible reading in public schools in the 1960s. According to the council, the displacement of the Bible from the center of public education is a departure from the intentions of the nation's Founders. It regards the introduction of its course as a means to help return America to what the council perceives as its Christian heritage.

The only textbook of the council's course is the Bible, preferably the King James Version, though other translations are noted as acceptable. The curriculum consists solely of a teacher's guide, which the council frequently revises. No author is identified. Early editions were named *Bible I–Bible II;* more recent versions are titled *The Bible in History and Literature*. The curriculum contains lesson plans; suggested resources, videos, and readings; background information for lecture content; recommended activities; and quizzes and worksheets. In general, it discusses the biblical material in canonical order, though it devotes little attention to the prophetic literature in the Hebrew Bible.

The NBCPS and its allies characterize its curriculum as academically informed, nonsectarian in approach, and legally appropriate for public school usage. Recent versions have emphasized the importance of presenting the material objectively and of not imposing religious beliefs upon students. Some scholarly evaluations of various editions, however, have raised questions about their quality and suitability, citing factual errors, plagiarized passages, and the presentation of material primarily from a conservative Protestant perspective. As examples of the latter problem, reviewers have pointed to the use of creation science resources and arguments; inattention to the ways in which Jewish, Roman Catholic, and Eastern Orthodox Bibles differ from that of Protestants; an emphasis on the historical accuracy of biblical passages, including stories of miracles and divine intervention such as Noah's Flood and the resurrection of Jesus; a seeming endorsement of biblical inerrancy, the view that the Bible is without scientific, theological, or historical error; and advocacy of a view of American history in which the Founders intended to establish a distinctively Christian nation and the Declaration of Independence and the Constitution were directly inspired by the Bible. The NCBCPS counters that such charges misrepresent its material.

The council claims that its course has never been successfully challenged in court. In 1998, however, a judge issued an injunction prohibiting a Florida school district from teaching the New Testament portion of the curriculum in *Gibson v. Lee County School Board*. When a lawsuit challenging the constitutionality of an NCBCPS course was brought against Ector County School District in Odessa, Texas in 2007–2008, the school district agreed in a mediated settlement to discontinue use of the curriculum. *See also:* American Family Association; Bible Literacy Project; Center for Reclaiming America.

Further Reading: Brennan Breed and Kent Harold Richards, Review of *The Bible in History and Literature,* in *Religion & Education* 34 (Fall 2007): 94–102; Mark A. Chancey, *The Bible and Public Schools: The National Council on Bible Curriculum in Public Schools* (Austin: Texas Freedom Network, 2005); Mark A. Chancey, "A Textbook Example of the Christian Right: The National Council on Bible Curriculum in Public Schools," *Journal of the American Academy of Religion* 75 (September 2007): 554–581; Mark A. Chancey, "'Complete Victory is Our Objective': The National Council on Bible Curriculum in Public Schools," *Religion & Education* 35 (Winter 2008): 1–21; *Gibson v. Lee County School Board,* 1 F. Supp. 2d 1426 (M.D. Fla. 1998); National Council on Bible Curriculum in Public Schools, at www.bibleinschools.net; National Council on Bible Curriculum in Public Schools, *Bible I–Bible II* (Greensboro, NC: National Council on Bible Curriculum in Public Schools, various editions); National Council on Bible Curriculum in Public Schools, *The Bible in History and Literature* (Greensboro, NC: National Council on Bible Curriculum in Public Schools, various editions); Frances R.A. Paterson, "Anatomy of a Bible Course Curriculum," *Journal of Law and Education* 32 (January 2003): 41–65.

Mark A. Chancey

National Council on Religion and Public Education

From its founding in 1971 to its termination in the mid-1990s, the National Council on Religion and Public Education (NCRPE) was the only organization whose sole purpose was the promotion of the objective study of religion in public schools. Its objectives included developing specific curriculum and instructional aids, encouraging teacher preparation institutions to develop certification programs for future educators, and convincing legislators that laws promoting the academic study of religion were a better pedagogical strategy than laws forcing school-sponsored prayer.

It is important to understand the climate in the country following the U.S. Supreme Court decisions in 1962 and 1963 that prohibited state-sanctioned prayer and devotional Bible reading in the public schools, and why NCRPE came into existence. A number of states as well as organizations sought ways to implement the high court's dicta regarding religion studies. The Nebraska, Pennsylvania, and Florida legislatures passed legislation calling for the development of curriculum materials and, in the case of Pennsylvania, teacher education programs. Nebraska published *The God and Man Narratives* in 1968. Pennsylvania produced a book, *Religious Literature of the West.* Florida State University began a curriculum project with funding from the National Endowment for the Humanities.

J. Blaine Fister of the National Council of Churches provided the initiative for a meeting focused on religion in the public schools in 1970. The W. Clement and Jessie V. Stone Foundation provided the support that led to the formational meeting of the NCRPE in 1971, attended by 60 representatives of some 40 organizations. Attendees unanimously adopted a mission statement: "To provide means for cooperative action among organizations concerned with religion as a constitutionally acceptable and educationally appropriate part of a secular program of public education."

Why this approach? In the late 1960s, some conservative Christians and political demagogues, using the media's inaccurate reporting of the 1962 and 1963 decisions, argued that the Court had "kicked God out of the front door of the schools and let communism in the back door." Three weeks prior to the 1971 NCRPE meeting, the U.S. House of

Representatives was considering a First Amendment addition allowing "non-denominational prayers in public schools."

The NCRPE sought to carry out Justice Tom Clark's dicta that religion could be taught "objectively" in public schools, specifically in English classes (the Bible in literature), in social studies courses (the role of religious history), and various courses (comparative religions). In NCRPE's early vision, a federal push was needed to develop curriculum and encourage in-service training of teachers and instruction of future educators. The NCRPE leadership also knew, however, that "education" is not mentioned in the U.S. Constitution, and is therefore a legal responsibility of the states (Tenth Amendment). Its members encouraged meetings of governors and state legislative leaders to promote religion studies. In other meetings, NCRPE urged faculty from humanities departments and colleges of education to prepare teachers. Sadly, such meetings were few and rarely effective. In time, the growing power of religiously conservative forces that favored either school prayer efforts or home-schooling derailed public education religion studies efforts.

Few materials in the first decade after *Schempp* (1963) were of high quality. So the NCRPE supported efforts by such institutions as Wright State, Florida State, and Indiana University to both produce curriculum aids and sponsor teachers' workshops.

By the early 1980s, membership by organizations declined. Annual meetings sometimes had fewer than ten delegates. Those in New York City (1988) and Washington, D.C. (1989) had significant programs. They supported the growing number of "teaching about religion" courses, publishers beginning to include religious events in textbooks, and institutes for teacher preparation students. NCRPE members were instrumental in the production of a question and answer pamphlet, "Religion in the Public School Curriculum." NCRPE was recognized in media reports.

NCRPE revised its mission statement during this time: "To facilitate informed, constitutionally appropriate teaching about religions in history and culture that enables students to participate in a pluralistic and religiously diverse world." Its policy statement became:

> As a forum NCRPE focuses on: academically and constitutionally appropriate study (a) about religions in public schools; (b) relation between religion and government in the United States and elsewhere; (c) accommodation to the religious beliefs and practices of public school students and personnel; (d) better understanding of and sensitivity to one another's religious or nonreligious beliefs and activities among public school students; and (e) protection against religious or antireligious indoctrination in public schools.

The development of the refereed journal, *Religion & Public Education,* rekindled interest in the NCRPE. Its articles were cited in the ERIC database system and a theological database. An NCRPE Distribution Center began at Iowa State University, producing a series of monographs and a book of readings from the successful Bible as/in Literature at Indiana University.

Despite its successes, the NCRPE was not able to sustain its mission. Nicholas Piediscalzi, a long-time supporter of the organization, points to four factors that contributed to the eventual demise of the NCRPE: (1) fewer serious attempts to alter the First Amendment religion clauses; (2) the development of constitutionally acceptable ways of dealing with religion in public school curriculum; (3) declining institutional participation in the organization; and (4) significant political and ideological disputes among member groups. At a pivotal 1991 meeting the executive committee of NCRPE decided to use its limited resources for teacher training efforts and cut journal support substantially. The following year, the executive committee of NCRPE disbanded the organization, a process that took several years.

Despite its demise, the NCRPE's agenda is bearing fruit today. Legislation in several states now requires teaching about either religion or character education in public schools. The journal, stronger than before, is published at the University of Northern Iowa. After several moves, the Distribution Center became the Religion and Public Education Resource Center at California State University at Chico. *See also:* National Council of Churches; *Religion & Public Education.*

Further Reading: Association of School Administrators, *Religion in the Public Schools* (1964); Claire Cox, *The Fourth R: What Can be Taught about Religion in the Public Schools* (New York: Hawthorn Books, 1969), 48–49; National Council on Religion and Public Education, *Religion & Public Education,* various issues 1983, 1988, 1989, and 1991; Theodore R. Sizer, ed., *Religion and Public Education* (Boston: Houghton Mifflin, 1967).

Charles R. Kniker

National Education Association

The National Education Association (NEA) is the largest professional organization in the United States, serving as both a labor union and an advocacy group to further the cause of public education. It has 3.2 million members who work at every level of government to advance the interests of public school teachers and education equality. With a relatively small professional staff of fewer than 600 people, the NEA relies primarily on a vast network of volunteers who serve in 14,000 communities nationally from preschool to graduate level programs in public universities. The following principles "guide our work and define our mission": equal opportunity, a just society, democracy, professionalism, partnership, and collective action. Its vision is "a great public education for every child" and its mission is "to advocate for education professionals and to unite its members and the nation to fulfill the promise of public education to prepare every student to succeed in a diverse and interdependent world" (National Education Association, at www.nea.org). Local and state chapters elect delegates to represent their interests at an annual representative assembly where issues and policy are debated and where officers are elected.

The NEA was founded in 1857 to unite the myriad state educational organizations into a common national movement. Thomas Valentine, president of the New York Teachers Association, wrote a letter to various state leaders in education suggesting the formation of the National Teachers Association (NTA). Its mission was "To elevate the character and advance the interests of the profession of teaching, and to promote the cause of popular education in the United States" (Beyerlein, 2003, p. 162). In keeping with the values represented in the common school movement spearheaded by Horace Mann in the 1830s and 1840s, the NTA promoted "common Christianity" as foundational to its educational mission. Like the membership of the NEA today, members of the NTA believed that education was a moral enterprise aimed at building character and promoting public welfare. Common Christianity was interpreted as the "nonsectarian" bedrock uniting a diverse population of (Protestant) believers. These "nonsectarian" values were championed over and against the "sectarian" interests represented by Roman Catholics and other Protestants who were often perceived as divisive and threatening to the common good.

Common Christianity continued to be the prevailing ideology of the NTA until the latter part of the nineteenth century when it expanded by merging with other national education organizations. In 1870 it changed its name to the National Education Association to better represent its more diverse constituency. These mergers also led to a new organizational structure composed of several relatively autonomous departments. This new structure coupled with the rise of ideologies that defined common democratic values in increasingly secular versus exclusively Protestant Christian terms gradually led to the diminishment of common Christianity as the ideological foundation of the organization. The contemporary NEA is similar to its predecessor in its aim of uniting a diverse membership around a common moral vision of education, but the ideological foundation of that vision is defined now in secular versus religious terms.

The secular foundation of the contemporary NEA has been criticized by some who perceive it as biased against religion. These tensions are especially pronounced in debates regarding the merit of school choice plans that include government-issued vouchers, and a broad range of issues related to education about sexuality in the public schools.

The NEA strongly opposes the use of vouchers as a vehicle to promote school choice because it asserts that vouchers divert public funds for private use in ways that diminish overall public welfare. It also claims that when vouchers are used to fund education in religious schools the practice violates the Establishment Clause of the First Amendment. In contrast, school choice proponents argue that individual liberties are jeopardized when parents are not able to use their tax contributions to choose the educational venues most appropriate for their children in matters regarding both quality and ideology. In relationship to the latter, some religious parents object to the secular worldviews that are espoused by the NEA and promoted in public schools. Specifically, many conservative Christians perceive these values as antireligious and believe that their free exercise rights are compromised in public school settings where secular values prevail.

Similar arguments frame controversies regarding how sexuality is addressed in the schools. According to the NEA, all students (including those who identify themselves as gay, lesbian, bisexual, transgendered, or queer [GLBTQ]) have the right to quality public education in a school setting that is safe and devoid of intimidation and harassment. Toward this end, it advocates for comprehensive curricular and policy related measures toward the goal of ensuring that GLBTQ identified students will be safe and regarded with respect. This position is criticized by some religious conservatives who believe that nonheterosexual forms of sexual expression are sinful and detrimental to individual and collective well-being. Furthermore, many who hold this view claim that their free exercise rights are violated when public schools promote values such as those espoused by the NEA. Recent lower court decisions, however, have supported positions similar to those promoted by the NEA, for example, *Citizens for a Responsible Curriculum v. Montgomery County Public Schools* (2005) and *Morrison v. Board of Education of Boyd County* (2006).

The ideology of the contemporary NEA is based on a secular framework aimed at advancing democracy and democratic values through quality public school education for all. Though it differs from its predecessor the NTA in promoting a secular versus a Protestant Christian ideological foundation, both share the assumption that public education is a moral enterprise intended to strengthen individual and collective well-being.

Perhaps this legacy can serve to shed new light on contemporary controversies that define secular and religious frameworks as fundamentally at odds. *See also:* Secularism; Sex Education and Religion; Vouchers.

Further Reading: Kraig Beyerlein, "Educational Elites and the Movement to Secularize Public Education," in *The Secular Revolution,* ed. Christian Smith (Berkeley: University of California Press, 2003); *Citizens for a Responsible Curriculum v. Montgomery County Public Schools,* F. Supp. 2d (D. Md. 2005); James Fraser, *Between Church and State: Religion & Public Education in a Multicultural America* (New York: St. Martin's Press, 1999); *Morrison v. Board of Education of Boyd County,* F. Supp. 2d (E.D. Ky. 2006); The National Education Association, at www.nea.org; *Zelman v. Simmons-Harris,* 536 U.S. 639 (2002).

Diane L. Moore and Mary Ellen Giess

National Labor Relations Board v. Catholic Bishop of Chicago

After more than a decade of developments in mostly urban and suburban Roman Catholic dioceses in the United States, the question of whether teachers in these schools could organize and bargain collectively came to a head in 1979 in *National Labor Relations Board v. Catholic Bishop of Chicago.* The nascent union movement in Catholic schools, following on the heels of similar developments in public education, received a substantial boost in a pair of companion cases in Catholic secondary schools that originated in the Archdiocese of Chicago, Illinois, and the Diocese of Fort Wayne–South Bend, Indiana, in 1975. At that time, the National Labor Relations Board (NLRB) decided that officials in schools operated by the Roman Catholic Church violated the National Labor Relations Act by refusing to recognize or to bargain with unions representing their lay faculty members. Regardless, officials refused to comply with the NLRB's order directing them to recognize and bargain with the unions. The schools sought further review from the Seventh Circuit Court of Appeals, which agreed that the NLRB improperly exercised its discretion in light of the religious nature of the schools and that related First Amendment considerations precluded the Board from directing school officials to meet with the teachers and their unions. The NLRB, in turn, petitioned the U.S. Supreme Court, which agreed to hear an appeal in February 1978.

More than a year later, the Supreme Court handed down its 5-4 decision in *Catholic Bishop* (1979), the leading case in the history of teachers' labor organizations and labor-management relations in Roman Catholic schools. In *Catholic Bishop,* the Court affirmed that the NLRB lacked jurisdiction to mandate bargaining between teachers and their Roman Catholic secondary school employers.

Writing for the Court, Chief Justice Warren Burger framed two issues for consideration. First, he addressed whether Congress intended to grant the NLRB jurisdiction over teachers in church-operated schools. Second, Burger considered that if Congress did not have such an intention, whether the NLRB's action violated the constitutionally sensitive questions arising from the First Amendment religion clauses. He managed, however, to avoid the difficult First Amendment issue by applying the long-standing principle that the Court first enunciated in *Murray v. Schooner Charming Betsy* (1804), a noneducation case that directs judges not to construe legislation as violating the Constitution if they can resolve disputes on other grounds. As such, Burger reviewed the legislative history of the National Labor Relations Act and its amendments, concluding that Congress did not express an affirmative intent to extend the NLRB's jurisdiction to schools that were operated by religious organizations. In reaching this outcome, Burger clearly was influenced by its desire to avoid having "to resolve difficult and sensitive questions arising out of the guarantees of the First Amendment Religion Clauses."

In a brief dissent, Justice William Brennan was of the opinion that insofar as the majority erred in its interpretation of the National Labor Relations Act, the Supreme Court should have extended NLRB jurisdiction and the National Labor Relations Act to protect lay teachers who are employed in religious schools. Even so, Brennan did not further pursue any constitutional law–based rationale because the majority chose not to do so. *See also:* Catholic Schools.

Further Reading: *National Labor Relations Board v. Catholic Bishop of Chicago,* 440 U.S. 490 (1979); *Murray v. Schooner Charming Betsy,* 2 Cranch. 64 (1804).

Charles J. Russo

National Parent Teacher Association

The National Parent Teacher Association (PTA), originally the National Congress of Mothers (NCM), was founded in 1897 and is "the largest volunteer child advocacy association in the nation" currently composed of 6 million volunteers in over 23,000 local units. Its purpose is as follows:

> To promote the welfare of the children and youth in home, school, community, and place of worship; To raise the standards of home life; To secure adequate laws for the care and protection of children and youth; To bring into closer relation the home and the school...and; To...secure for all children and youth the highest advantages in physical, mental, social, and spiritual education. (National Parent Teacher Association, at www.pta.org)

Since its inception in 1897, the PTA has been a strong advocate for children through the promotion of quality public education for all. It has focused its advocacy efforts in three broad arenas: (1) promoting policies that benefit children directly; (2) educating parents about how they can become advocates for their children; (3) building community coalitions in support of children and education. It has addressed and championed a wide variety of issues over the years ranging from desegregation to arts education to the construction of playgrounds on school grounds. One significant area of focus relates to the proper role of religion in the schools.

As exemplified in a series of documents, resolutions, and public policy statements, the PTA's position on religion in the schools is consistent with a 1995 document entitled "Religion in the Public Schools: A Joint Statement of Current Law" that was issued by a coalition of religious and nonprofit public policy organizations representing a wide range of ideologies. This coalition document served as the basis for a set of guidelines that were distributed by the U.S. Department of Education to educators across the nation. In 1996, the PTA joined with the First Amendment Center to publish a pamphlet entitled "A Parent's Guide to Religion in the Public Schools" that essentially reproduced the information from "Religion in the Schools" into a more accessible, question-answer format. There are other documents and resolutions produced by the PTA itself on these issues that closely parallel the language of the pamphlet and the approach represented in the joint statement. They include a resolution titled "Teaching about Religion in the Public Schools"; a statement outlining the National PTA "position" on religion in the schools; and, in a related document, a strong statement opposing government-issued vouchers for private school tuition, whether in religious or secular contexts.

In its Statement on Principles, the PTA asserts that "religion is fundamental in our American tradition as a basic factor in personal and social behavior and that every child is entitled to the opportunity to develop a religious faith" (www.pta.org). This theme of the importance of faith and spiritual development runs throughout the history of the PTA and reflects its strong Protestant roots. What is distinctive about the PTA, however, is the stated ideal of inclusiveness regarding religion (as well as race and ethnicity) that was present at the founding of the organization and is one of its defining characteristics. Education historian Christine Woyshner asserts that the original 1897 platform of the NCM "was guided by [a] maternalist ideology that maintained women were united across race, class, and religion in the effort to care for all children because of their shared capacity for motherhood" (Woyshner, 2003, p. 526). Though the gender essentialism that informed the founding of the NCM is no longer assumed, the spirit of uniting a diverse constituency toward the shared aim of promoting the well-being of children was a guiding principle throughout much of the history of the PTA and is still apparent today. For example, in the resolution "Teaching about Religion in the Public Schools" the PTA linked its assertion that "every child is entitled to the opportunity to develop a religious faith" with its support of teaching about religion in the schools from a nonsectarian perspective. Similarly, in its position statement on "Religion in the Schools," the PTA asserts that it supports "the right of children to pray but opposes mandatory or organized prayer," while also supporting moments of silence so long as their intent and implementation do not serve to privilege religious over secular expressions. Finally, in this same document, the PTA asserts its opposition to government funding of religious organizations "that discriminate based on religion in employment or delivery of services" (www.pta.org).

In a related position, the PTA strongly opposes voucher initiatives that authorize the use of public funds to subsidize private school tuition costs such as the one in Cleveland, Ohio, that was the focus of the 2002 landmark Supreme Court case *Zelman v. Simmons-Harris*. Though it shares the concern expressed by many that such programs can serve to violate the Establishment Clause when parents choose to send their children to religious schools, the PTA is more concerned about the dangers such programs pose to the vitality of public education itself. Its position is based on the assumption that the nation's "system of universal public education is a cornerstone of our society and has played a vital role in preparing citizens to participate in our democracy, instilling our shared values, and helping children understand and appreciate our nation's diversity" (www.pta.org). The PTA believes that vouchers and other related subsidies are part of a larger effort to privatize education that will, in turn, diminish rather than enhance democratic citizenship and the opportunity for all children to have access to a quality education. According to the PTA: "The way to ensure that every child has an equal and valuable education is to invest in our public school system" (www.pta.org).

Read in isolation, the assertion in the PTA Statement of Principles that "religion is fundamental in our American tradition as a basic factor in personal and social behavior and that every child is entitled to the opportunity to develop a religious faith" could be interpreted to mean that the PTA supports the promotion of Protestant Christian values and practices in public schools. Indeed, the language is similar to that employed by many who maintain that state-sanctioned prayer and devotional Bible reading should be reinstated in the schools as pivotal dimensions of a sound moral education. Considered in its larger context, however, it is clear that the vision of the PTA is a more inclusive one that aims to respect the wide diversity of religious beliefs (or none) that are represented in the nation's schools. Through its affirmation of the importance of faith coupled with its advocacy for policies that aim to ensure that diverse expressions of faith will be respected in the schools, the PTA provides an important and potentially unifying voice regarding the proper role of religion in public education. *See also:* Common Ground Documents; Vouchers.

Further Reading: The National Parent Teacher Association, at www.pta.org; The National PTA and The First Amendment Center, "A Parent's Guide to Religion in the Public Schools" (1996), at www.freedomforum.org; American Jewish Congress et al., "Religion in the Public Schools: A Joint Statement of Current Law" (1995), available from signatories and the U.S. Department of Education; Christine Woyshner, "Race, Gender, and the Early PTA: Civic Engagement and Public Education," *Teacher's College Record* 105 (April 2003): 520–544; *Zelman v. Simmons-Harris,* 536 U.S. 639 (2002).

Diane L. Moore

National School Boards Association

The National School Boards Association (NSBA) is a nonprofit organization operating as a federation of state associations of school boards. The advantages of forming an association for local school boards were recognized as early as 1895, when Pennsylvania became the first state to organize a state association. Many states followed Pennsylvania's example and created their own state associations. The idea for a national association was first considered at the 1938 convention of the National Education Association. At these discussions it was entitled the National Association of Public School Boards. The national association was formally organized as National Council of State School Boards Association in 1940. The name was later changed to the National School Boards Association. For many years the main office was located outside of Chicago, Illinois. In the 1970s there was a recognized need for a greater presence in Washington, D.C., for the purpose of national connections, exposure, and lobbying. It was then that the offices were moved to the greater D.C. area, first in Georgetown, and now in Alexandria, Virginia.

NSBA's publicly stated mission is "to foster excellence and equity in public education through school board leadership." NSBA achieves that mission by representing the school board perspective before federal government agencies and with national organizations that affect education, and by providing information and services to state associations of school boards and local school boards. NSBA supports each local school board, acting on behalf of and closely with the people of its community. The Association sees each community as holding the future of education—the community holds the structure and environment that allows students to reach their maximum potential.

NSBA and its federation members are dedicated to educating every child to his or her fullest potential and are committed to leadership for student achievement. This commitment has coalesced into a strategic vision for the NSBA as a powerful, united, energetic federation; as an influential force for achieving equity and excellence in public education;

and as a catalyst for aligning the power of the community on behalf of education. Underlying this shared vision are certain fundamental convictions:

- belief that effective local school boards can enable all children to reach their potential;
- conviction that local governance of public education is a cornerstone of democracy;
- belief in the power of local school boards to convene the community around education issues;
- conviction that together, local school boards can influence education policy and governance at the state and national levels;
- commitment to the principle that through collaboration comes impact; and
- belief that the strength of local school board leadership arises from the board's capacity to represent the diversity of students and communities.

Central to NSBA's vision is the "Key Work of School Boards" initiative. The "Key Work of School Boards" is NSBA's framework for raising student achievement through community engagement. It is designed to give school boards the concrete action tools to be even more effective in the role of school board member and community leader and is based on the premise that excellence in the classroom begins with excellence in the boardroom. The "Key Work" initiative is framed around eight key areas: vision, standards, assessment, accountability, alignment, climate, collaborative relationships, and continuous improvement. It means engaging the community, identifying priorities, and setting standards for student performance. It requires establishing assessment and accountability measures, demanding student data to drive decision making, and aligning district resources to support priorities. All of this involves setting the right climate for learning, forming collaborative relationships, and always continually improving performance. Through these goals and its long-standing commitment to excellence and equity in public education through school board leadership, the NSBA is a powerful force in public education policy.

The National School Boards Association offers an array of resources that help school boards and school attorneys to understand the legal environment, to keep up to date with new and emerging legal developments, and to anticipate, prevent, and overcome legal challenges. To further its legal advocacy, NSBA's Office of General Counsel houses the Council of School Attorneys. With over 3,000 members currently, the Council was formed in 1967 to provide information and practical assistance to attorneys who represent public school districts. In direct legal advocacy, NSBA files more *amicus* briefs to the Supreme Court each year than all education associations combined (National School Boards Association, at www.nsba.org).

Today, NSBA represents the 95,000 local school board members that govern 14,890 local school districts across the United States. Its current executive director is Ann Bryant. NSBA has a 150-member delegate assembly of local school board members that determine NSBA policy. There are also 25 members of the Board of Directors who are responsible for turning the policies into actions. Programs and services are executed by the NSBA executive director and a 140-person staff. The Delegate Assembly annually enacts policy statements, including *Resolutions* and *Beliefs & Policies*. NSBA's lobbying and legal advocacy positions are dependent on these policy statements. The following NSBA policy statements relate to religion and schools.

Student Prayer

NSBA supports an individual student's constitutional right to engage in religious activity. However, in accordance with the U.S. Constitution, school officials when acting in their official capacity, should not solicit, encourage, or discourage religious activity.

Vouchers/Tuition Tax Credits

NSBA urges Congress to oppose any efforts to subsidize tuition or expenses at elementary or secondary, private, religious, or homeschools with public tax dollars. Specifically, NSBA opposes the creation of vouchers, tax credits, and tax subsidies for use at nonpublic K–12 schools. Rather than diverting scarce tax dollars away from our public school classrooms, NSBA urges Congress to support improvements in our public schools, where nearly 90 percent of America's children are being educated.

Recent cases involving religion in schools (at the Supreme Court level) in which NSBA was involved include:

- *America Civil Liberties Union of Kentucky v. McCreary County, Kentucky* (2005)—display of Ten Commandments on courthouse property;
- *Elk Grove U.S.D. v. Newdow* (2004)—school district policy requiring teachers to lead classroom in Pledge of Allegiance;
- *Locke v. Davey* (2004)—state law prohibiting use of state college/university scholarship funds for students seeking pastoral degrees; and
- *Zelman v. Simmons-Harris* (2002)—vouchers for parents to send their children to private schools in Cleveland, Ohio.

NSBA also consulted with the Department of Education in the development of the guidance document on school prayer as part of the federal statute *No Child Left Behind,* and NSBA was one of the 18 co-signers of the document, *The Bible & Public Schools: A First Amendment Guide* (1999), which represents accord on the general approach to religion in the public schools. *See also:* Common Ground Documents; Tuition Tax Credits; Vouchers.

Further Reading: Benjamin Dowling-Sendor, "A Troubling Religion Case," *American School Board Journal* 185 (September 1998): 18–19; Benjamin Dowling-Sendor, "When It's Safe to Talk about Religion," *American School Board Journal* 184 (March 1997): 9–10; Lawrence Hardy, "Bible Story," *American School Board Journal* 185 (April 1998): 34–37; National School Boards Association, at www.nsba.org.

Julie Underwood

Nativism

Nativism, as John Higham states, is a term that is difficult to precisely define. The word itself is distinctly American, the result of a specific chain of events in some eastern American cities in the late 1830s and 1840s. It also applies when inhabitants of a given area oppose strangers in their midst. Here it will apply to the former description, in which the majority of attention will be devoted to the late 1830s and early-to-mid 1840s. Prejudice against foreigners, often expressed in hostility toward ethnic-related schools sponsored by churches (Catholic and Lutheran) present in subsequent movements in the nineteenth century, due to the Know-Nothing Party and the American Protective Association, and in the twentieth century under the auspices of the Ku Klux Klan, are covered in other entries, but will receive some consideration.

Originating in England, anti-Catholicism ("No Popery") was grounded in colonial America. The prejudice was fueled by England's conflicts with Catholic France and Spain. As the authoritative work on Nativism, written by Ray Allen Billington, *The Protestant Crusade, 1800–1860* makes clear, after the Revolutionary War as the nineteenth century progressed, tensions increased between the dominant Protestants and Catholic immigrants, many of whom settled in the eastern cities. The trustee controversy that occurred in the Catholic Church in Philadelphia and elsewhere, and the Catholic position on Scripture exacerbated the tensions. In the 1830s books on the evils of convent life appeared. Violent sermons by Protestant ministers, such as the Reverend Lyman Beecher, increased the tensions. On August 11, 1834, the Ursuline convent in Charlestown, a suburb of Boston, was burned by Nativists. Other assaults on Catholic churches occurred. Books that were virulently anti-Catholic, such as the *Downfall of Babylon,* appeared. At first directed entirely against Roman Catholics, later in the 1830s the belief spread that an alliance between immigrants and Roman Catholics had been forged with the intent of destroying the United States.

Nativist tactics changed somewhat as the nation entered the decade of the 1840s. Catholicism was regularly portrayed as the enemy of the Bible and of the public schools. Public school practices that focused on the devotional reading of the King James Version of the Bible became a leading battleground. New York City witnessed a major battle over practices in its schools. Allegedly nonsectarian, the Public School Society fostered the devotional reading of the King James Version and used textbooks that were offensive to Catholics in its public schools, ones, for example, that were opposed to "Popery." Archbishop John Hughes of New York City took up the cudgels on behalf of his flock, challenging books that contained passages that claimed that the United States would become the "common sewer" of Ireland unless immigration were limited. Ultimately, Hughes defeated the Public School Society but failed to obtain governmental financial assistance for Catholics for their schools.

Nativists continued in their verbal assault on Catholicism. For instance, convents were accused of being "one vast brothel"; the pope was referred to as "Anti-Christ" and as "The Man of Sin and the Son of Perdition." The purpose of the American Protestant Union, headed by Samuel F. B. Morse, founded in 1841, was to oppose subjugation of the country to the control of the pope. Protestant churches denounced the Vatican, with the Presbyterian General Assembly leading the way in 1841, followed by the Congregationalists in 1843, and then the Methodists in 1844. They formed a united front by the mid-1840s.

The scene turned from words to action in Philadelphia in the summer of 1844. The Philadelphia School Board had accepted Bishop Kenrick's request, made in January 1843, that Catholic children in Philadelphia's public schools be allowed to read the Douay (Catholic) Version of Scriptures in that city's schools. Nativists protested the school board's decision, and a year later in 1844 the trouble began. Following conflict with some Irish Americans, Nativists rioted, burned Catholic Church property, including churches, and destroyed homes of Irish Americans. Mob rule prevailed until public officials restored order. As a result of the three days of rioting, 13 persons had been killed and more than 50 wounded. Thousands of Catholic families fled the area. In subsequent anniversaries of the uprising, Nativist sentiment claimed that "The Papists deserve all this and much more," and "It were well if every Popish church in the world were leveled with the ground." Meanwhile, in New York City, Archbishop Hughes had publicly stated that "If a single Catholic Church were burned in New York, the city would become a second Moscow." Unable to obtain protection from government sources for Catholic property, Hughes stationed armed guards outside Catholic churches and not one was touched by Nativists.

It is well to note that Nativists, while denouncing immigrants, and especially the supposed alliance of Catholics and immigrants (since many of the immigrants were Catholic, especially the Irish) that "threatened" the republican form of government in the United States, also took offense at the presence of Catholic parochial schools that were supposedly teaching "un-American" beliefs and values to their children. It is also important to note that the violence advocated by Nativists, and their hatred of all things Catholic, led to the erection of Catholic schools by the Catholic hierarchy and their support by many lay Catholics as the nineteenth century progressed. These schools, and their Lutheran counterparts, were often motivated by ethnic heritage, particularly German, as well as religious reasons. They, and their adherents, were often looked upon as "un-American" and a threat to the republic. Tensions in the United States were perhaps influenced by the conflicts between the Catholic Church and several European governments in the 1840s and 1850s, which included the control of schooling. These conflicts were highlighted by the controversial "Syllabus of Errors" authored by Pope Pius IX.

By the mid-1840s the furor had generally subsided, sidetracked by the Mexican-American War. It was to resurface, however, with a vengeance in the 1850s under the guise of "Know-Nothingism."

The Know-Nothing Party became a major player in the nation in the early 1850s and was a staunch advocate of things "American." Their influence ended with the growth of regional tensions that resulted in the Civil War. After the War, however, persons like President Ulysses S. Grant and Representative James G. Blaine were among the leaders of those who were both staunch advocates of the virtues of public schooling on behalf of the republic and bitter opponents of parochial schools, in the main operated by the Catholic Church. Legislative efforts to regulate and perhaps destroy these schools were made by several states in the 1880s, most notably Illinois and Wisconsin, on the grounds that they placed old world ethnic and religious heritages ahead of "good American citizenship." Conflicts between Nativists and the alleged "disloyalty" of these schools, supposedly mired in their attachment to ethnic and religious heritage, continued as the nation entered the twentieth century. They led to the famous decision by the Supreme Court of the United States in the *Pierce* case from the state of Oregon, in which the Court ruled that parents, not the state, were the primary educators of their children and that attendance at public schools was not a necessary condition for citizenship. *See also:* American Protective Association; Anti-Catholicism in Education; Know-Nothing Party; Ku Klux Klan.

Further Reading: Ray Allen Billington, *The Protestant Crusade, 1801–1860* (New York: Macmillan, 1938); John Higham, *Strangers in the Land, Patterns of American Nativism, 1850–1925* (New York: Atheneum, 1970); Gustavus Myers, *History of Bigotry in the United States* (New York: Random House, 1943); Diane Ravitch, *The Great School Wars in New York City, 1805–1925* (New York: Basic Books, 1974); William G. Ross, *Forging New Freedoms: Nativism, Education, and the Constitution, 1917–1927* (Lincoln: University of Nebraska Press, 1994).

Thomas C. Hunt

New York v. Cathedral Academy

The New York legislature authorized reimbursement to nonpublic schools for the cost of state-mandated record keeping and testing services (1970 N.Y. Laws, Ch. 138). A federal district court ruled that the legislation was unconstitutional (*Committee for*

Public Education and Religious Liberty v. Levitt). This legislation included reimbursement for expenses that the nonpublic schools had previously incurred. The federal district court permanently "enjoined any type of payment under the Act, including reimbursement for expenses already incurred in the last half of the 1971–1972 school year." A federal appellate court affirmed this decision. Shortly after the decision ruling Ch. 138 unconstitutional in June 1972, the New York Legislature passed Ch. 996 (1972 N.Y. Laws Ch. 996). The legislation said that the state had a moral obligation to pay schools for expenses included prior to June 13, 1972. This new act stated that since nonpublic schools had relied on Ch. 138 and therefore incurred expenses they should be reimbursed. This legislation authorized what the federal court had prohibited, namely reimbursement for expenditures by religious schools for state-mandated services through the 1971–1972 school year.

Cathedral Academy sued under Ch. 996 to obtain reimbursement for expenses it had incurred. On appeal from the New York Court of Appeals, the U.S. Supreme Court stated that "the depositive question is whether the payment it (under Ch. 996) authorizes offends the First and Fourteenth Amendments." The Court ruled that to monitor all previous expenses and to parcel out secular versus sectarian expenses in order to provide reimbursement would result in excessive entanglement between church and state, therefore a violation of the entanglement prong of the *Lemon* test. Furthermore, the Court asserted that Ch. 996 had the primary effect of aiding religion and "Ch. 996 amounts to a new and independently significant infringement of the First and Fourteenth Amendments." *See also: Levitt v. Committee for Public Education and Religious Liberty.*

Further Reading: *Committee for Public Education and Religious Liberty v. Levitt,* 342 F. Supp. 439 (1972); *New York v. Cathedral Academy,* 434 U.S. 125 (1977).

M. David Alexander

P

People for the American Way

People for the American Way (PFAW) is a self-described progressive advocacy organization, "an energetic advocate for the values and institutions that sustain a diverse democratic society...threatened by the influence of the radical right and its allies who have risen to political power" (People for the American Way, at www.pfaw.org). PFAW was founded by television producer Norman Lear (*All in the Family, Maude, The Jeffersons,* etc.) in 1981 specifically to counter the efforts of the so-called "Religious Right." According to the PFAW Web site, Lear was particularly concerned with the growing clout of televangelists such as Pat Robertson and Jerry Falwell. Co-founders included Barbara Jordan, Andrew Heiskell, and other leaders from the political, religious, business, and entertainment communities. PFAW continues to maintain its ties to each of those communities today, with such figures as actress Kathleen Turner and the Rabbi David Saperstein sitting on its boards. Each year, PFAW holds "Spirit of Liberty" awards dinners, which usually honor such prominent figures from the various communities as well. Recent recipients have included Sharon Stone (entertainer), Peter Lewis (businessman), and Reg Weaver (president of the National Education Association).

When it was first formed, PFAW was broadly bipartisan after Norman Lear had changed his voter registration to the Republican Party and endorsed John Anderson's campaign, as an independent, for president in 1980. Former Republican President Gerald Ford also served for a number of years as co-chairman. The former presidents of PFAW are Anthony Podesta (1981–1987), Arthur Kropp (1987–1995), and Carole Shields (1996–2000). Soon after its founding, PFAW launched an affiliated 501(c)(3) organization, PFAW Foundation, for the purpose of conducting more extensive educational and research activities. Later, the PFAW Voter Alliance was launched as a political action committee, which, as opposed to its sister organizations, has the legal capacity to endorse candidates for office.

Today PFAW has over 1 million members nationwide. PFAW is an independent nonprofit advocacy organization dedicated to maintaining equal rights, freedom of speech, religious liberty, and equal justice under the law for every American. The current president of PFAW is Ralph Neas. He states, "we're fighting to maintain and expand fifty years of legal and social justice progress that right-wing leaders are trying to dismantle. We won't let them turn back the clock on our rights and freedoms."

The national headquarters of PFAW and PFAW Foundation is in Washington, D.C., and smaller regional offices are located in New York, Los Angeles, San Francisco, Austin, Chicago, Tallahassee, and Miami. Various organizers are also employed in "battleground" states such as Pennsylvania and Ohio. The organizations share field, policy, research, communications, legal, Internet strategy, and administrative departments.

PFAW is prominent within the liberal political movement for monitoring right-wing activities, conducting rapid response, political lobbying, and volunteer mobilization. In addition, PFAW's affiliated foundation runs programs designed for voter education and progressive infrastructure building. PFAW Foundation programs include Mi Familia Vota, which conducts Hispanic civic engagement, and several African American outreach programs such as the African American Ministers Leadership Council. It is also an active antigun organization.

In 2005, PFAW Foundation initiated a fellowship program, called Young People For, to identify, train, and support future progressive leaders. In 2006, Young People For spun off the Young Elected Officials Network, which was created to identify and support progressive elected officials from around the country who are under the age of 35. Its publicly stated mission is as follows:

> In times of hardship, in times of crises, societies throughout history have experienced wrenching dislocations in their fundamental values and beliefs.... We are alarmed that some of the current voices of stridency and division may replace those of reason and unity. If these voices continue unchallenged, the results will be predictable: a rise in "demonology" and hostility, a breakdown in community and social spirit, a deterioration of free and open dialogue, and the temptation to grasp at simplistic solutions for complex problems. PFAW was established to address these concerns. (www.pfaw.org)

PFAW communicates and educates the public, and lobbies and litigates at the state and national levels. It is prominent within the progressive political movement for monitoring conservative activities and providing rapid national responses to counter such activity. The issues identified as focal points by PFAW include civic participation, an independent judiciary, constitutional liberties, civil rights, religious freedom, and public education.

Regarding religious issues in the context of public education, PFAW advocates against public funding of religious schools and vouchers. Its position is based on the following principle: People for the American Way Foundation believes that well-educated children are critical to our society and that public schools are vital to our communities. PFAWF works to track publicly funded voucher programs, which it believes threaten both the funding and the goals of America's public education system. For example, PFAW unsuccessfully opposed the Cleveland, Ohio, voucher program in the U.S. Supreme Court (*Zelman v. Simmons- Harris,* 2002). PFAW has also been involved in issues regarding teaching religion in the public schools. It supports teaching students about religion. Most authorities agree that teaching students about religion is part of a good education. Such instruction can and does take place appropriately in courses such as comparative religion, the history of religion, world history, and American history. Efforts to inculcate students with sectarian beliefs, however, have no place in the public schools. According to the organization: "Teaching religious subjects from a sectarian viewpoint is not simply unsound education. Such instruction violates the constitutional requirement that public schools must remain neutral toward religion and not endorse religion generally or any particular faith specifically" (www.pfaw.org). PFAW has been involved in litigation on using the Bible to teach in the public schools, and it was successful in ending a number of courses where the Bible was used to inappropriately teach history. PFAW was also instrumental in the Florida Department of Education removing religion classes from their approved curriculum.

PFAW was one of the 18 cosigners of the document, *The Bible & Public Schools: A First Amendment Guide* (1999). This document represents widespread accord among a broad spectrum of religious, educational, and political groups regarding the general approach to religion in the public schools:

> On one end of the spectrum are those who advocate what might be called the "sacred public school" where one religion (theirs) is preferred in school practices and policies. Characteristic of the early history of public education, this unconstitutional approach still survives in some school districts. In more recent decades, there are those on the other end of the spectrum who push for what looks to some like a "religion-free zone" where religion is largely ignored in public schools.
>
> The sponsors of this guide reject both of these models and offer another approach—one in which public schools neither inculcate nor inhibit religion but become places where religion and religious conviction are treated with fairness and respect. In this third model, public schools protect the religious-liberty rights of students of all faiths or none. And schools ensure that the curriculum includes study *about* religion as an important part of a complete education. This is a vision of public education that is both consistent with First Amendment principles and broadly supported by many educational and religious organizations. (First Amendment Center, at www.firstamendmentcenter.org)

See also: Common Ground Documents; Vouchers.

Further Reading: First Amendment Center, at www.firstamendmentcenter.org; J. Helms and B. Lynn, "Should a School Prayer Constitutional Amendment be Approved by Congress?" *Congressional Digest* 74 (January 1995): 19–31; People for the American Way, at www.pfaw.org.

Julie Underwood

Pierce v. Society of Sisters

In *Pierce v. Society of Sisters* in 1925, the U.S. Supreme Court unanimously invalidated an Oregon statute that required all children between the ages of 8 and 16 to attend public school. In an opinion that has become the cornerstone for constitutional protection of parental rights, the Court held that the statute unduly interfered with the liberty of parents to direct the upbringing of their children. "The child," the Court declared, "is not the mere creature of the State; those who nurture him and direct his destiny have the right, coupled with the high duty, to recognize and prepare him for additional obligations." The Court also held that the law unduly interfered with the property rights of parochial schools.

The *Pierce* decision terminated a nationwide campaign by Nativists to destroy parochial education by mandating compulsory public education. Part of a surge of hostility toward Roman Catholics and ethnic Americans that arose out of the hyperpatriotism of the First World War, the compulsory public education movement reflected fears that parochial schools threatened national cohesion and imperiled the nation's security by impeding the assimilation of immigrants and their children. The movement received the support of some prominent educators and many powerful fraternal lodges, including various Masonic organizations. It also had many advocates among members of the Ku Klux Klan, which attracted millions of members throughout the United States during the early 1920s and which outside the South directed its primary animus against Roman Catholics rather than African Americans.

In 1920, Michigan voters by a margin of two to one defeated a compulsory public education referendum that encountered vigorous opposition from a broad coalition of religions that operated schools, including Roman Catholics, Lutherans, Seventh-day Adventists, Dutch Reformed, and Episcopalians. Two years later, however, voters approved a similar referendum in Oregon by a margin of 55 to 45 percent. In contrast with Michigan, Oregon had relatively few Roman Catholics and Lutherans, the religions that had the most extensive networks of parochial schools in the nation. Although the homogeneity of this predominately white Protestant state had prevented ethnic tensions in the past, many Oregonians had begun to fear that the growing influx of immigrants and their children into the state would threaten the traditions of rugged individualism, egalitarianism, direct democracy, and honest government for which the state was known. The public school was a potent symbol of public probity and social cohesion.

Proponents of the referendum argued that the compulsory public education would promote assimilation and would discourage snobbery and bigotry by enabling children from different economic, cultural, and religious backgrounds to mingle during their formative years. At a time when the physical facilities of parochial schools often were inferior to those of the public schools, advocates of the measure also argued that the law would improve the quality of education. Less scrupulously, many advocates of the measure also alleged that parochial schools sought to destroy public education.

Opponents of the referendum emphasized that the transfer of the state's 12,000 nonpublic parochial school students into public schools would impose an enormous burden on taxpayers. They also argued that the state had no right to require parents to send their children to public school, provided that parochial and private schools met the requirements of state certification. Although most opponents of the referendum were motivated primarily by their desire to educate their children in a religious environment, they did not claim that the law would violate their religious freedom because the Court had not yet incorporated the free exercise clause of the First Amendment into state law.

As in Michigan, Roman Catholics and Lutherans led a well-financed and highly organized campaign against the compulsory education bill. Lacking significant numbers, they enlisted vocal support from many educators and some Protestant clergy. Mindful of the threat to minority rights, Jews spoke out against the referendum, as did some members of the state's tiny African American community.

The approval of the referendum had national significance insofar as it encouraged advocates of compulsory public education in other states. Shortly after its approval, the Grand Dragon of the Ku Klux Klan predicted that Congress would approve a national compulsory education law.

The National Catholic Welfare Conference commenced a legal challenge in federal court. Since the law was not scheduled to take effect until 1926, no schools were closed during the pendency of the litigation. The prospects for the challenge were greatly enhanced in June 1923, when the U.S. Supreme Court in *Meyer v. Nebraska* sustained a constitutional challenge by parochial schools to laws that prohibited the teaching of foreign languages in private, parochial, and public schools. Like the Oregon statute, the laws challenged in *Meyer* were intended to encourage assimilation of ethnic Americans and promote social cohesion. In holding that the statute violated the economic rights of schools and teachers and the personal liberties of parents, *Meyer* strongly suggested that the Oregon law was unconstitutional. In June 1924, a federal court held that the law violated the Due Process Clause of the Fourteenth Amendment. Five months later, voters in Michigan once again rejected a compulsory public education measure, as did voters in Washington State.

In its appeal to the U.S. Supreme Court, Oregon argued that the statute was within its inherent power to protect the safety and welfare of its citizens because it was intended to facilitate social cohesion and ameliorate religious prejudices, political subversion, and juvenile crime. The state also, without evidence, contended that parochial schools sought to destroy public education. Although the state admitted that the statute would have the practical effect of shutting down every full-time parochial school in Oregon, the state argued that the statute would not interfere with religious instruction since parents could arrange for children to receive such instruction when they were not attending public school.

Opponents of the law argued that the state failed to demonstrate any need for so drastic a measure. While the schools conceded that the state could regulate nonpublic schools, they disputed the state's contention that nonpublic schools interfered with assimilation or exacerbated economic and cultural tensions.

The Court's decision, announced on June 1, 1925, held that the statute's interference with the property rights of the schools and the personal liberties of parents violated the due process clause of the Fourteenth Amendment. The Court's opinion, written by Justice James C. McReynolds, was based on the same doctrinal foundation as the Court's decision in *Meyer*.

The Court pointed out that the schools owned costly buildings that were specially constructed for educational purposes and that the schools had a valuable economic interest in the goodwill of the parents. The state, the Court explained, had failed to demonstrate that any circumstances or emergency excused a law that "would seriously impair, perhaps destroy, the profitable features of [the schools'] business and greatly diminish the value of their property." Indeed, the court observed that the schools were "engaged in a kind of undertaking not inherently harmful, but long regarded as useful and meritorious."

In holding that the statute unduly interfered with parental rights, the Court explained that parents have a right to control the education of their children unless the state can demonstrate a strong need to abridge that right. "A fundamental theory of liberty," the Court explained, "excludes any general power of the state to standardize its children by forcing them to accept instruction from public teachers only." In declaring that the "child is not the mere creature of the State," the Court provided a forceful response to the question "Whose Is the Child?," a slogan coined by Lutherans in opposing the 1920 Michigan referendum and repeated during the campaign against the Oregon law.

The Court's decision in *Pierce* effectively ended the national campaign against parochial education, although the *coup de grace* did not occur until two years later, when the Court in *Farrington v. Tokushige* nullified a Hawaiian law that imposed restrictions on part-time Asian language schools. During recent years, *Pierce* has served as a significant legal precedent in support of the constitutionality of school vouchers and the rights of parents to educate their children at home. *See also:* Anti-Catholicism in Education; *Farrington v. Tokushige;* Ku Klux Klan; *Meyer v. Nebraska;* Nativism; State Regulation of Religious Schools.

Further Reading: *Farrington v. Tokushige,* 273 U.S. 283 (1927); *Meyer v. Nebraska,* 262 U.S. 290 (1923); *Pierce v. Society of Sisters,* 268 U.S. 510 (1923); William G. Ross, *Forging New Freedoms: Nativism, Education and Constitution, 1917–1927* (Lincoln: University of Nebraska Press, 1994); Barbara Bennett Woodhouse, "'Who Owns the Child?': Meyer and Pierce and the Child As Property," 33 *William and Mary Law Review* (Summer 1992): 995–1122.

William G. Ross

The Pledge of Allegiance

The Pledge of Allegiance, recited daily by most schoolchildren across America, became a topic of controversy from the time that the U.S. Congress added to it the phrase "under God" in 1954. Despite many court challenges that the Pledge violates church-state separation, only one court, the Ninth Circuit Court of Appeals in 2002, has ruled any part of the Pledge unconstitutional. Considering a case brought by a father of a third-grade student in California who objected to his daughter being subjected to the daily ritual, the court ruled that

> A profession that we are a nation "under God" is identical, for Establishment Clause purposes, to a profession that we are a nation "under Jesus," a nation "under Vishnu," a nation "under Zeus," or a nation under "no God," because none of these professions can be neutral with respect to religion, which is what the Constitution requires.

When the case was appealed to the U.S. Supreme Court, a unanimous High Court in 2004 nullified the lower court's ruling but sidestepped the constitutional issue by holding that the student's father had no formal custody of his daughter and thus should never have been permitted to file the case. In the days following the decision, surveys of Americans, according to the *Washington Post,* showed that 87 percent support retaining the phrase "under God" in the Pledge.

The Pledge indeed has an interesting history. In 1892, a Baptist pastor, Francis Bellamy, wrote the Pledge of Allegiance for *Youth's Companion,* a national family magazine for youth with one of the largest national circulations of its day, about 500,000.

One authority (Baer, 2007) relates that in 1891 one of the magazine's owners had the idea of using the celebration of the 400th anniversary of Christopher Columbus's discovery of America to promote the use of the flag in the public schools. At the time, the American flag was rarely seen in the schools. The magazine decided to try to change that. In 1888, the magazine began a campaign to sell American flags to the public schools and, by 1892, had sold American flags to more than 26,000 schools. The magazine then hired Bellamy to assist. Bellamy, who frequently lectured and preached on the virtues of socialism and the evils of capitalism, had been forced to resign from his Boston church, the Bethany Baptist Church, due to his socialist leanings.

By February 1892, Bellamy had lined up the National Education Association to support the *Youth's Companion* as a sponsor of the national public schools' observance of Columbus Day along with the use of the American flag. By June, they had arranged for Congress and President Benjamin Harrison to announce a national proclamation making the public school ceremony the center of the national Columbus Day celebrations for 1892. Bellamy wrote the program for this celebration, including its flag salute, the Pledge of Allegiance. His version was, "I pledge allegiance to my flag and to the Republic for which it stands—one nation indivisible—with liberty and justice for all." On October 12, 1892, the quadricentennial of Columbus's arrival, more than 12 million children recited the Pledge of Allegiance, thus beginning a common ritual in the nation's schools.

The original Pledge, recited while giving a stiff, uplifted right-hand salute, was criticized and discontinued during World War II because of the resemblance of the salute to the Hitler salute. At the first National Flag Conference in Washington, D.C., on June 14, 1923, the words "the Flag of the United States" replaced, for sake of clarity, "my flag." A year later, the words "of America" were added. It was not until 1942 that Congress officially recognized the Pledge of Allegiance. One year later, in June 1943, in *West Virginia v. Barnette,* the Supreme Court ruled that schoolchildren could not be forced to recite the Pledge if their religious beliefs did not allow it.

The addition of the words "under God" to the Pledge began as a campaign of the Knights of Columbus in 1951. The Knights, a Catholic fraternal organization well known for its patriotism, believed that adding the phrase would acknowledge the "dependence of our nation and its people upon the Creator of the Universe." The Knights began pitching the idea to members of Congress. The idea caught on, and among its proponents was President Dwight Eisenhower, who was looking for ways to certify communism as inconsistent with American ideals. On Flag Day, June 14, 1954, President Eisenhower signed the measure into law. Eisenhower proclaimed,

> From this day forward, the millions of our schoolchildren will daily proclaim…the dedication of our nation and our people to the Almighty. To anyone who truly loves America, nothing could be more inspiring than to contemplate this re-dedication of our youth, in each school morning, to our country's true meaning.

The Pledge was now both a patriotic oath and a public prayer.

Since its inception in the late nineteenth century, the Pledge of Allegiance has become a major centerpiece in America's civil religion, which is a shorthand term for the nation's religious dimension and is generally recognized as distinct from a private person's faith. In addition to the Pledge of Allegiance, the most common symbols of American civil religion are the national motto, "In God We Trust," which also appears on U.S. currency; the Declaration of Independence, which has four references to God; observance of a national day of prayer; and the utilization of government-paid chaplains in the military, U.S. Congress, and state legislatures. Some scholars suggest that accommodating these religious expressions takes the rough edge off the separation of church and state, and helps to maintain the American government's fundamental credibility (Bellah, 1967).

All of these practices are violations of a strict notion of the separation of church and state. Yet they form a rich tradition of practices that are culturally and judicially accommodated. That the judiciary continues to validate these practices without elevating them to constitutionally protected status is an indication that the Court wishes not to pursue a rigid principle of church-state separation, and, in fact, sanctions civil religion as a kind of middle ground between a too-strict separation and a too-lenient public accommodation of religion.

American civil religion is not tied to any particular faith, even Christianity, although the distinction between civil religion and personal faith is lost on many people of faith. Civil religion acknowledges a somewhat deistic God. Thus, the God invoked in the Pledge of Allegiance is simultaneously the God of Christianity, Judaism, Islam, or any other religion that gives credence to a monotheistic god. It is not Jesus, Jehovah, or Allah that is invoked, but the generic "God." As the Ninth Circuit Court stated, it might even be Vishnu or Zeus that is invoked. One can merely "fill in the blank" in terms of the precise order of faith to which the God of the Pledge belongs. It is, in fact, this nondiscriminatory aspect of the Pledge's reference to God that makes it acceptable as a "national" ritual.

The Pledge of Allegiance is indeed a rather unique ritual. Among the nations of the world, only the United States of America and the Philippines, imitating the United States of America, have a pledge to their flag. Not even in the Soviet Union was there such a pledge to the flag. There was a similar practice utilized by the Soviets, an oath taken when children, upon becoming nine years of age, would enter the Pioneer Youth. The "Pioneer" program, of which Soviet children were members until becoming age 14, represented the Soviet effort to institutionalize commitment to a political idea. It was similar to the Boy Scouts or Girl Scouts, but more universal and a bit more militaristic. Children were proud to utter the oath of induction:

> I, (name), entering the ranks of the All-Union Pioneer Organization named after Vladimir Ilyich Lenin, solemnly promise before my comrades: to love my motherland fervently; to live, study, and fight as the great Lenin bequeathed us, as the Communist Party teaches us. I promise always to observe the laws of the pioneers of the Soviet Union.

Whereas the Soviet oath was to an ideal, the American Pledge is to an ideal as well as to that ideal's chief symbol, the American flag. The combination perhaps makes pledging allegiance to the American flag doubly potent as a revered practice.

The Pledge of Allegiance has today achieved a status as one of America's most sacred traditions. There are few indications that this status will change anytime soon. *See also:* Civil Religion and Education; *Elk Grove Unified School District v. Newdow; West Virginia State Board of Education v. Barnette.*

Further Reading: John Baer, *The Pledge of Allegiance: A Revised History* (Annapolis, MD: Free State Press, Inc., 2007); Robert N. Bellah, "Civil Religion in America," *Daedalus* 96 (Winter 1967): 1–21; Richard Ellis, *The Unlikely History of the Pledge of Allegiance* (Lawrence, KS: University Press of Kansas, 2005).

Derek H. Davis

Plenary Councils of Baltimore

In 1852, 1866, and 1884, the American Catholic bishops met in plenary council to discuss the issues affecting the Catholic Church in America. The resulting pastoral letters were meant to guide both the temporal and the spiritual lives of American Catholics. As was the custom in such letters, most of the advice was very general, reflecting the bishops' concern for various social problems but offering no specific solutions.

The message on education, however, was quite clear. Catholic parents had a moral responsibility to provide for the spiritual lives of their children, and the best means of providing that spiritual life was through parish schools. Catholic parents were never required to send their children to parish schools until 1884, but not to do so was to incur the displeasure of the organized Church.

The bishops first spoke to the Catholic population through pastoral letters that were issued at the close of periodic provincial councils. Beginning in 1829 and continuing until 1849, the Catholic hierarchy met every two years to discuss the issues affecting the Catholic Church in America. The resulting pastoral letters were meant to guide both the temporal and the spiritual lives of American Catholics. It was left to the Catholic press to interpret what the bishops wanted done.

The pastoral letters on education warned Catholic parents about the dangers of public schooling. Throughout the 1830s, the messages from the councils were very similar; in 1833, and again in 1837, the bishops reminded the laity of their duties as parents and implied that their only possible choice was Catholic education. In the 1840s, the bishops complained about the response of the laity and were particularly alarmed at the large number of Catholic children who attended public schools or no schools at all. The bishops were not so much concerned with illiteracy as they were religion—parents must protect the spiritual lives of their children.

The Catholic bishops first met in plenary (national) council at Baltimore in 1852 to address the state of Catholicism in the nation. It was a historic occasion for the American Church. Growth in the number of communicants and growth in the number of dioceses and provinces meant that by 1852 American Catholicism was truly national—from the Archdiocese of Baltimore in the East to the Archdiocese of Oregon City in the West. The pronouncements of this first national council had a more substantial impact than the previous messages of the provincial councils.

One message that certainly came through clearly was the firm resolve of all the bishops to support and establish parochial schools. "Listen not to those who would persuade you that religion can be separated from secular instruction," the bishops warned. "Encourage the establishment and support of Catholic schools; make every sacrifice which may be necessary for this object" (McCluskey, 1964, p. 80).

The next plenary council came 14 years later. The development of Catholic parochial education after the Civil War caused serious concerns within the Catholic community. Many Catholic leaders were pleased with the rapid growth of parish schools, but some Catholics were angry that many of their brethren spurned these institutions. In fact, conservatives were appalled with the large number of Catholic parents who continued to send their children to public schools.

They looked for a way to force reluctant pastors to build more schools and require recalcitrant Catholic parents to send their children to these schools. The intervening years between the plenary councils of 1866 and 1884 did little to resolve the conflict within Catholic education. To be sure, Catholic schools continued to grow at unprecedented rates, but in spite of this growth, hundreds of thousands of Catholic children continued to attend public schools. What could be done to change this latter trend?

Much of the discussion of parochial schools at the Third Plenary Council was tactical. How can the laity be convinced of the vital importance of parish schools? Should the council take a clear-cut stand and require pastors to build parish schools? Should they require recalcitrant parents, under the pain of sin, to send their children to parish schools? It was clear to all the bishops present that the tone of their message would be as important as the content.

The result was an effort to take the middle ground. The pastoral letter on the "education of youth" was gentle. "No parish is complete," concluded the letter, "till it has schools adequate to meet the needs of its children and the pastor and the people of such a parish should feel that they have not accomplished their entire duty until the want is supplied" (McCluskey, 1964, p. 93). There were no harsh words in the pastoral concerning pastors and parents who did not agree with the bishops or follow their advice.

The decrees of the council were another matter, however, and reflected a firm commitment to the belief that every Catholic child belonged in a Catholic school. The first decree stated bluntly that a parish school must be built near every Catholic Church. The second decree provided for the removal of parish pastors who were "gravely negligent" in erecting parish schools. The third decree promised spiritual "punishment" for any parish that failed to support its pastor's effort to build a school. A final decree stressed that "all Catholic parents are bound to send their children to parochial schools unless at home or in other Catholic schools, they provide sufficiently and fully for their Christian education" (McCluskey, 1964, p. 94). The implementation of the four decrees was reserved for the bishops themselves.

The decrees were a setback for some prelates who wanted to encourage Catholic parents to send their children to parish schools but stopped short of imposing sanctions on those parents who chose not to follow. But other prelates had argued persuasively that decades of "encouragement" had not stopped the tide of Catholic children from attending public schools. It was time, they argued, to require these fair-weather Catholics and recalcitrant pastors to build and support parish schools.

Yet there was a vast chasm between this new policy and its implementation, and the education decrees had only limited impact on the pattern and rate of parochial school development during the balance of the century. In sum, the education decrees of the Third Plenary Council failed to face the clear fact that the American Church lacked the economic resources to provide a Catholic education for every child.

The decrees did, however, have a significant impact on the organizational structure of parochial schools. For more than a century the Catholic schools had been administered at the parish level by pastors and trustees. Most dioceses were patchworks of semiautonomous parish schools as different from one another as the cultures that made up American Catholicism itself. But the educational discussions of the Third Plenary Council gave momentum to an effort to coordinate parish schools through diocesan school boards. The establishment of boards in most dioceses in the years from 1885 to 1920 was the first major step in the long campaign to standardize and establish centralized control over parochial schools. *See also:* Catholic Schools.

Further Reading: Harold A. Buetow, *Of Singular Benefit: The Story of U.S. Catholic Education* (New York: Macmillan, 1970); Neil G. McCluskey, ed., *Catholic Education in America: A Documentary History* (New York: Teachers College Press, 1964); Bernard Julius Meiring, *Educational Aspects of the Legislation of the Councils of Baltimore, 1829–1884* (New York: Arno Press, 1978); Hugh J. Nolan, ed., *Pastoral Letters of the American Catholic Hierarchy,* 4 vols. (Huntington, IN: OSV, 1971); Timothy Walch, *Parish School: American Catholic Parochial Education from Colonial Times to the Present* (Washington DC: National Catholic Educational Association, 2003).

Timothy Walch

Poughkeepsie Plan

The Poughkeepsie Plan was a cooperative effort between Catholic parishes and local public schools to educate Catholic children at little or no cost to their parents or the parishes. The plan, as manifested in a number of different forms, generated the most controversy and educated the fewest students of any of the efforts to educate Catholic children in the United States.

From 1831 to 1916, Catholics in at least 21 communities in 14 states attempted to bridge the gap between parochial and public education. The specific terms of agreement between parishes and school boards varied slightly. In almost every community where the experiment took place, the school board leased a school from a local parish for a small sum and paid the salaries of teachers in those schools. The teachers were selected jointly by the school board and the parish pastor. The board regulated the curriculum, selected the schoolbooks, and conducted periodic examinations, but the parish pastor had the right to ensure that all of the elements of the curriculum were acceptable to the Catholic Church. Most important, however, was the fact that the school day at these publicly supported Catholic schools was the same as at any other public school. No religious instruction was conducted until after classes were dismissed.

These schools were experimental and in most communities the experiment was short-lived. But in three communities—Lowell, Massachusetts, from 1831 to 1852; Savannah, Georgia, from 1870 to 1916; and Poughkeepsie, New York, from 1873 to 1898— publicly supported parochial schools educated several generations of Catholic children. Even though the number of Catholic children educated in these schools was small, the publicly supported Catholic school was an important grassroots effort to resolve the outstanding differences that separated many Catholics from public education.

The publicly supported parish school in Poughkeepsie is worthy of closer attention not only because of its longevity but also because it received national attention as the representative example of cooperative education efforts in other communities. The "Poughkeepsie Plan," as cooperative efforts came to be known, began when the Reverend Patrick F. McSweeney, pastor of St. Peter's parish in Poughkeepsie, informed the local school board in the spring of 1873 that his parishioners could no longer afford to maintain St. Peter's two schools. Starting in the fall, McSweeney noted, the 800 children who attended St. Peter's two schools would enter the public school system.

But Father McSweeney not only precipitated the problem, he also had a solution. With the permission of Archbishop John McCloskey of New York, McSweeney proposed that the school board lease his parish buildings to conduct public school classes for the children of St. Peter's parish. Religious instruction would not be part of the public school curriculum, but would be conducted in the building after normal school hours. Participation in religious exercises would be completely voluntary for all students.

The new public schools were to be staffed by teachers selected, employed, and paid by the board. But McSweeney made it clear that the board should hire Catholic teachers for the schools so long as they met school board requirements. The board agreed to McSweeney's terms and further agreed that the parish school would retain unrestricted use of the building outside of regular school hours. A lease agreement was signed on August 21, 1873.

Not everyone was happy with this arrangement, however. Protestant ministers objected to the plan and to the board's decision to abandon Bible reading in these schools. The ministers appealed to the board for a return to the "secular education" that emphasized religion and morality as taught in the Bible.

But local criticism of the plan faded in the face of the community-wide goal of assimilating the foreign-born into American society. The agreement between the school board and St. Peter's parish continued year after year without further criticism from the general public.

The eventual termination of the plan in 1899 was precipitated by factors far beyond the Poughkeepsie city limits. Throughout the 1890s, particularly after the Third Plenary Council of Baltimore in 1884, the plan came under attack by conservative Catholic newspapers. Even though these attacks—and scattered criticism from Protestant journals—did not undermine the agreement, they did create an air of tension and controversy throughout the period.

The agreement held fast until the late 1890s when New York State School Superintendent Charles Skinner ordered the Poughkeepsie school board to break the agreement or lose state aid. Skinner based his actions on two grounds: the wearing of religious garb by the nuns who taught in St. Peter's school, and the long-term rental of parish buildings for the purpose of public education. Thus ended in January 1899 the most innovative and visible effort to bridge the gap between parochial and public education. *See also:* Catholic Schools; Faribault-Stillwater Plan; Lowell Plan.

Further Reading: Clyde and Sally Griffin, *Natives and Newcomers: The Ordering of Opportunity in Mid-Nineteenth Century Poughkeepsie* (Cambridge, MA: Harvard University Press, 1978); Daniel Reilly, *The School Controversy, 1891–1893* (New York: Arno Press, 1969); Timothy Walch, *Parish School: American Catholic Parochial Education from Colonial Times to the Present* (Washington, DC: National Catholic Educational Association, 2003).

Timothy Walch

Prayer in the Public Schools

Colonial Times

For most of educational history, from the days of Plato onward, school leaders viewed moral education as even more salient than academic instruction. Given this fact, from the days of Christ early Christians regarded the state of one's relationship with God as the foundation of efficacious education. Most of the early European settlers who came to America carried with them this orientation. Moreover, they viewed an intimate relationship with God established through prayer not only as foundational, but the gateway to other facets of knowledge. According to the Puritans, Pilgrims, Quakers, and myriad other settlers, a strong relationship with God enabled an individual to gain access to the truth that God had to offer. Hence, they emphasized prayer as an important component of schooling. Surely, a large part of this truth was spiritual in nature, but most early settlers believed that it also applied to academic truth. With this instructional philosophy in mind, it is vital that one understand that the early settlers did not view prayer as disparate from the schooling process but inextricably intertwined with successful education (Ulich, 1968).

Many of the early settlers were very religious and maintained daily family devotional times, in addition to attending church regularly. The Puritans, Pilgrims, and Quakers, who were among the most religious groups, also influenced the foundation of American schooling considerably more than others. These settlers more than any of their European counterparts focused on the salience of prayer as part of this family devotional time. This daily expression of family piety not only possessed a definite religious orientation but also was designed to be educational in nature. It consisted of a time of usually about an hour in which people prayed and read the Bible, but also engaged in reading the newspaper and perusing a classic book. During this period, life was not as compartmentalized as it is in contemporary society. That is, although prayer was clearly an expression of piety, so were the other literary expressions. New England and Mid-Atlantic settlers, in particular, viewed literacy as a high priority. First and foremost, literacy enabled people to read the Bible, which facilitated salvation, even though it was not necessary for salvation. It was literacy that enabled a person to understand the truths of the Bible. Second, literacy was an individual's responsibility before God because it enabled one to understand the wonders of salvation. Parents therefore encouraged their children to pray soon after these young learned to talk, and well before the schooling years (Fleming, 1969; Mintz and Kellogg, 1988).

In the colonial era, whether elementary school education took place at home or in a dame school, church-sponsored school, town school, or subscription school setting, the school day usually began with prayer. This action was designed to serve as both an example to students and a means of instructing students that placing Jesus Christ as first in one's life was of utmost importance. Kent Greenawalt explicated it well when he said, "Education in the early American colonies was almost entirely private and substantially religious" (Greenawalt, 2005, p. 13).

The majority of the schools of the 13 colonies were church-sponsored schools, and therefore there was usually a considerable overlap between the church curriculum and the school curriculum. Even the town schools of New England were strongly influenced by religious traditions. The populace of the time believed that prayer should have a prominent role in town schools as well. Consequently, at that time, there was almost no difference between the practice of prayer in town- and church-sponsored schools. In addition, students frequently prayed for the needs of people in the church and in their community. The school day in both public and private schools nearly always started and ended with prayer (Fenwick, 1989; Fleming, 1969). School days often provided a time when students could share their prayer needs, pray for one another, and share about God's answers to their prayers (Fleming, 1969).

Revolutionary War until the Early 1900s

Many school textbooks throughout the late 1700s, 1800s, and early 1900s placed a special emphasis on God's providence in a full gamut of situations, which patently encouraged people to pray (Henry, 1964; Jeynes, 2007). Although this fact may be hard for contemporary Americans to fathom, it is quite consistent with the general American perspective held at that time that, as Alfred Whitehead expressed it, "The essence of education is that it be religious" (Eavey, 1964, p. 54). The primary task of education in the minds of most Americans was to produce moral, civic, and intelligent human beings. The teacher, therefore, was to serve as a model in prayer and in other aspects of piety. By the mid-1800s when Americans began to more frequently accept the notion of government-run schools, the leaders of the common school movement were often religious. Common schools arose as an outgrowth of the Protestant establishment. It is this fact that largely gave birth to the parochial school movement. As Virginia Brereton observes: "Beginning in the 1830s and 1840s many Americans from the common schools...often felt that their religious, cultural, and ethnic survival in predominantly Anglo-Saxon Protestant America depended on the establishment of parochial schools" (1982, p. 45). Part of the reason that Catholics wanted their own schools was so that they could pray according to Catholic, rather than Protestant, custom.

Given that Americans of the 1700s and 1800s believed that school textbooks should include passages about God's providence, it probably comes as no surprise that the two most published school textbooks in American history both include copious references to God's providence. Noah Webster's series of schoolbooks and McGuffey's *Readers* together sold about 200 million copies. Their contents reflect the national beliefs at the time that schools and textbooks should teach children about God's providence to stimulate their faith and prayer life. Prayer was frequently practiced, particularly at the beginning of each day in charity schools and common schools (Kaestle, 1973; Ulich, 1968).

Statements of the leading educators of the 1700s and 1800s suggest the extent to which educators saw piety and education as inextricably connected. Horace Mann, called the father of the common schools, claimed that the most vital focus that educators should have is "best expressed in these few and simple words from Proverbs 22:6 in the Bible: 'Train up a child in the way he should go, and when he is old he will not depart from it'" (Cremin, 1957, p. 100). He also asserted, "The more I see of our present civilization and of the only remedies for its evils, the more I dread intellectual eminence when separated from virtue. We are in a sick world, for whose maladies, the knowledge of truth, and obedience to it, are the only healing" (Filler, 1965, p. iii). Mann, a Unitarian who was skeptical of many orthodox Christian doctrines, believed prayer should be present in the schools as long as it was nonsectarian in nature (Fraser, 1999). Friedrich Froebel, the founder of the kindergarten, declared, "All things have come from the Divine Unity, from God, and have their origin in the Divine Unity, in God alone" (Von Bulow, 1849, p. 211). These educators believed that various religious and moral expressions facilitated character development, including prayer, reading the Bible, and singing hymns. The most common time that students prayed was during the beginning of the school day. Schools of this era generally had a period just prior to the commencement of classes or what in contemporary terminology would constitute a homeroom class, in the urban high schools, in which teachers would either lead the class in prayer or a student or succession of students would lead the class in prayer (Dierenfield, 1962).

The religious orientation of many of the education leaders of the 1800s ensured that prayer would have a continued presence in American public schools. Friedrich Froebel founded the kindergarten in 1839 and asserted that the purpose of the kindergarten was to produce a garden of children who would grow up to experience unity with God and with each other. Froebel was a minister and a son of a minister. Therefore, not surprisingly, he established the kindergarten to have a definitively Christian orientation. He also believed that a major purpose of the kindergarten was to provide a moral foundation that would prepare youth to become strong students and citizens in the future. Consequently, in Froebel's kindergarten prayer, hymns and Bible reading played prominent roles (Jeynes, 2003). J. P. Slight notes that in the United States educators applied the Froebel kindergarten model even more than in Europe because of its "religious emphasis" (Slight, 1969, p. 178). In myriad American kindergartens prayer was practiced several times during the day.

Virtually all of the major figures in mid-nineteenth century education advocated a central place for religious education and prayer in the schools. Horace Mann, Johann Pestalozzi, Calvin Stowe, and others all saw the exercise of piety in the classroom as key to personal development. The *McGuffey Readers,* clearly the most popular school textbook from the second half of the nineteenth century into the early twentieth century, included both prayers and exhortations to pray. McGuffey especially quoted the Lord's Prayer in his books and would remind children of the need to pray to God first thing in the morning.

Surges in church attendance during the Great Depression, World War II, and the Cold War contributed to a belief among early- and mid-twentieth century Americans that prayer had a salient role in the public schools.

According to a nationwide study by Dierenfield, who likely conducted the most extensive study of religion in the public schools just prior to 1962, prayer in the public schools was widespread at that time. For example, among communities with a population of over 100,000, Dierenfield found that 63 percent of school districts had "homeroom devotional services" in their schools. These devotional services included Bible readings and prayer, but also sometimes included "devotional teachings" and the singing of hymns. Prayer occurred in nearly 50 percent of the nation's school districts (Dierenfield, 1962).

U.S. Supreme Court Decisions of 1962–1963 and Their Aftermath

School prayer and other religious practices were common parts of the school day throughout American educational history until three combined U.S. Supreme Court decisions in 1962 and 1963. As Tricia Andryszewski notes,

> Religious exercises were regularly conducted in many, perhaps most, public schools across the country. The most common religious exercises were the reading of Bible passages by a designated student or students, and either in each classroom or school wide, over the public address system, and the recital of the Lord's prayer (usually by all students in unison, with their heads bowed). (Andryszewski, 1997, p. 21)

Furthermore, she claims, "Most people approved of these practices in their public school" (Andryszewski, 1997, p. 21).

These practices changed dramatically with three U.S. Supreme Court decisions, first of which was *Engel v. Vitale* (1962). In that decision the Court declared that, "State officials may not compose an official state prayer...even if the prayer is denominationally neutral and pupils who wish to do so may remain silent or be excused from the room while the prayer is being recited."

Two other Supreme Court decisions in 1963 affirmed and expanded this decision. *Murray v. Curlett* involved a Maryland case in which Madeline Murray, later known as Madeline Murray O'Hare, filed a complaint on behalf of her son, Bill, over the practice of school prayer in her son's school. She later gained a great deal of fame in the country as the nation's most outspoken atheist, founded an organization called the American Atheists, and via articles in *Life* and *Fact* magazines became known in many circles as "the most hated woman in America."

The combination of *Murray v. Curlett* (1963) and *Abington Township v. Schempp* (1963) affirmed that teacher-led prayer and Bible reading without comment in the public schools violated the no establishment clause in the First Amendment. Ironically, Bill Murray, the student involved in the *Murray v. Curlett* decision, became thoroughly disillusioned with his mother's atheistic lifestyle. According to Bill Murray, his mother's incessant obscene language and her unethical behavior, including her use of funds given to the American Atheists, caused him to conclude that he did not want to be an atheist. Much to his mother's chagrin, Bill later not only became a Christian but also went into the ministry. He then dedicated his life to attempting to put government-sponsored prayer back into the schools. He inaugurated this mission by writing a letter to the *Baltimore Sun* apologizing for his role in removing prayer from the public schools. In essence, he stated that he was merely a child when the U.S. Supreme Court removed teacher-led prayer from the schools. Since then he came to the realization that this decision had removed a valuable practice out of the schools for which, he believed, the United States was paying a considerable price (Murray, 1982).

Justice Potter Stewart filed the lone dissent in these cases, using words that proponents of Bible reading and freedom of religious expression often use to bolster their case. In the *Schempp* dissent Stewart asserted:

> As a matter of history, the First Amendment was adopted solely as a limitation upon newly created National Government. The events leading to its adoption strongly suggest that the Establishment Clause was primarily an attempt to insure that Congress not only would be powerless to establish a national church, but would also be unable to interfere with existing state establishments.

Furthermore, Stewart averred:

> If religious exercises are held to be an impermissible activity in schools, religion is placed in an artificial and state-created disadvantage...And a refusal to permit religious exercises thus is seen, not as the realization of state neutrality, but rather as the establishment of a religion of secularism, or at least, as governmental support of the beliefs of those who think that religious exercises should be conducted only in private. (*Abington Township v. Schempp,* 1963)

Some legal experts objected to the Supreme Court's decisions on the basis of not only the decisions themselves but also the unusual dearth of judicial experience of the justices. In nearly every case, the justices were appointed to the Supreme Court following a long history of political rather than judicial experience (Michaelsen, 1970). Chief Justice Earl Warren had served as governor of California for ten years before his appointment; Justice Hugo Black had been a U.S. senator for ten years; Justice Arthur Goldberg served as secretary of labor; Justice William Douglas was chairman of the Security and Exchange Commission; and Justice Felix Frankfurter was an assistant to the secretary of labor and served as a founding member of the American Civil Liberties Union (ACLU). Ironically, the only justice with extended federal constitutional experience before he began his service on the Supreme Court, Justice Potter Stewart, was also the only justice to object to the removal of prayer and Bible reading.

The three Supreme Court decisions resulted in an immediate backlash among the American public and many of its leaders, which led to an effort to pass a constitutional amendment to put prayer back into the schools. The initial response by the American public and their leaders to the 1962 and 1963 decisions was immediate and powerful. Following the decisions, many political leaders and the general public condemned the Court's rulings. Congressional representatives adamantly opposed the Court's decision. In the *Congressional Record* for day following the *Engel v. Vitale* decision, there was not one member of Congress who defended the Court's decision. Some congressional leaders initiated a movement to impeach the Supreme Court Chief Justice Earl Warren. Senator Eugene Talmadge declared that, "the Supreme Court has set up atheism as a new religion" (Committee on the Judiciary, 1962, p. 140). Congressman Frank Becker, a Catholic, called the *Engel* decision, "the most tragic in the history of the United States." A Gallup Poll in 1963 indicated that Americans were opposed to the *Engel, Murray,* and *Schempp* decisions by a three to one margin. Nevertheless, efforts to reintroduce state-sponsored prayer in the public schools have failed to gain traction.

Subsequent court cases also altered the place of prayer in the schools and in some cases went to the extremes. One case, *Reed v. Van Hoven* (1965), did not reach the U.S. Supreme Court, but nevertheless had considerable influence. In this Michigan Supreme Court case, the court averred that saying grace over one's lunch at school was permissible only if one did not move his or her lips. Both the American Center for Law and Justice and the ACLU now agree that saying grace over one's meal is permissible.

Although there was Supreme Court activity regarding religion in the schools during the 1970s, politicians did not aggressively address the issue again until Americans elected Ronald Reagan as president and he assumed that office in 1981. Reagan made it a major priority of his administration to protect religious liberty in the public schools, and he urged the passage of a constitutional amendment to allow prayer in the schools. Although Reagan's attempt to get an amendment passed failed, the effort made it clear that most Americans and their political leaders favored increased religious liberty in the schools.

The momentum that emerged during the Reagan administration yielded a new venture to reduce discrimination against people of faith called the Equal Access Act. Eventually enacted by Congress in 1984, it established a law that extended the principle of a U.S. Supreme Court case from 1981, *Widmar v. Vincent* (Andryszewski, 1997). In the *Widmar* case the U.S. Supreme Court ruled that a *university* could not explicitly deny the equal use of its facilities to religious groups and that to do so would discriminate against people of faith. The congressional Equal Access Act extended the *Widmar* principle to include public secondary schools (Andryszewski, 1997). The act made it possible for prayer and Bible clubs and other religious groups to have the same access to school facilities during nonclass hours as nonreligious groups. Although technically the legislation amounted to a victory for religious liberty advocates, the fact that this initiative should be the subject of debate demonstrated to advocates how much some educators and government officials had impinged upon religious liberty.

Given that the U.S. Supreme Court had declared unconstitutional state-authorized teacher-led and student-led prayer in the schools, a considerable number of people thought that the Court would prove more amenable to the idea of a moment of silence in the schools. A number of states adjusted their classroom practices to the 1962 and 1963 U.S. Supreme Court mandates by allowing a moment of silence. This practice might have remained rather uncontroversial had it not been for Alabama's decision to make the directions for this practice more specific by an assertion that a teacher could announce a period of silence for "meditation or voluntary prayer." The U.S. Supreme Court ruled in *Wallace v. Jaffree* (1985) that the moment of silence needed to be distinguishable from oral prayer. The Court concluded that the particular directions given to teachers for the moment of silence appeared to encourage prayer. Given this declaration, many people believe that a moment of silence in the public school classroom is acceptable as long as prayer is not specifically mentioned. Indeed, a majority of states now have moment-of-silence statutes.

Over the years the decision to remove government-sanctioned prayer and Bible reading from of the schools has produced a considerable level of consternation for especially two reasons. First, many people believe that the United States has paid a considerable moral price for excising prayer and Bible reading from the public schools. When the Supreme Court removed state-sanctioned prayer and Bible reading from the schools, many schools also avoided explicit moral education in the public schools as well because they were afraid that a few civilians might interpret moral instruction as religious inculcation. Many individuals believe that the removal of moral education contributed to the sudden surge that occurred in criminal and socially destructive behavior that emerged beginning in 1963, including fivefold increases in juvenile and pre-juvenile murder arrest rates (U.S. Department of Health and Human Services, 1998; U.S. Department of Justice, 1999). They believe that the removal of explicit moral education, in conjunction with increased divorce rates and other cultural and economic factors all worked concurrently to produce these social trends. Others concur that family dissolution and other changes in the American social fabric produced these trends, but do not view the de-emphasis on moral education as particularly salient.

Second, many citizens believe that either the Court's decisions themselves or a misapplication of them have led to blatant discrimination against students' attempts to practice their faith. Further clarity will come to this debate once the court rules definitively on the constitutionality of a moment of silence. According to the Gallup poll, three out of four Americans support the practice of a moment of silence in the public schools.

Recent Developments

In recent years, the Supreme Court has addressed several prayer-related cases. The 1990 case *Board of Education of the Westside Community Schools v. Mergens* involved a Nebraska school district's decision to block the students' efforts to form a Christian club in their high school. The district decided that the club could not have a faculty sponsor, which was a requisite for all after-school clubs, because such sponsorship was the equivalent of endorsing a religion. In response, the students claimed that the district's action violated the Equal Access Act that stated that groups seeking to express "religious, political, philosophical, or other content" messages could not be denied the freedom to form after-school clubs. The Supreme Court voted eight to one that the students had the right to establish their Christian club, since the school had created a forum in which other clubs were allowed to meet.

Lee v. Weisman (1992) involved Daniel Weisman's objection to a Jewish rabbi's prayer delivered at a 1989 graduation ceremony of his daughter, Deborah Weisman. The Supreme Court voted five to four in support of Daniel Weisman's objections. The close vote was particularly interesting because Justice Anthony Kennedy switched his vote during the deliberations even though the prayer itself was nonsectarian. He affirmed that the Establishment Clause forbade any government-sponsored prayer in schools, not only those representing a particular religious tradition. Justice Antonin Scalia dissented, claiming that the Supreme Court was engaging in "social engineering" and that there are countless examples of American leaders calling on divine guidance.

The U.S. Supreme Court ruled similarly in the case of *Sante Fe Independent School District v. Doe* (2000). It ruled that a school policy permitting student-initiated and student-led prayer at football games violated the Establishment Clause of the First Amendment. Previous to this time, the Sante Fe School District in Texas permitted students to read prayers over the public address system at football games and also during graduation ceremonies. An elected student chaplain read these prayers.

Some leaders and social scientists have contended that Americans tend to place too much emphasis on what staff and students cannot do in terms of prayer and religious expression rather than focusing on what is permissible. Therefore one should note that such activities as praying at the school flag pole and saying grace over one's meal are allowed as long as these activities do not disturb others. *See also: Abington School District v. Schempp* and *Murray v. Curlett; Engel v. Vitale;* Moments of Silence; *Wallace v. Jaffree.*

Further Reading: *Abington Township v. Schempp,* 374 U.S. 203 (1963); Tricia Andryszewski, *School Prayer: A History of the Debate* (Springfield, NJ: Enslo, 1997); Paul Blanshard, *Religion and the Schools* (Boston: Beacon Press, 1963); Virginia. L. Brereton, "The Public Schools are not Enough: The Bible and Private Schools," in *The Bible in American Education,* ed. D.L. Barr and Nicholas Piediscalzi (Philadelphia: Fortress Press, 1982); Lawrence A. Cremin, ed., *The Republic and the School: Horace Mann on the Education of Free Men* (New York: Teachers College, Columbia University, 1957); Richard B. Dierenfield, *Religion in American Public Schools* (Washington, DC: Public Affairs Press, 1962); Charles Benton Eavey, *History of Christian Education* (Chicago: Moody Press, 1964); *Engel v. Vitale,* 370 U.S. 421 (1962); Lynda B. Fenwick, *Should the Children Pray?* (Waco, TX: Baylor University Press, 1989); Louis Filler, *Horace Mann on the Crisis in Education* (Yellow Springs, OH: Antioch Press, 1965); Sandford Fleming, *Children and Puritanism* (New York: Arno Press and the New York Times, 1969); James W. Fraser, *Between Church and State* (New York: St. Martin's Press, 1999); Carl F.H. Henry, "The Secularization of American Life," in *An Introduction to Evangelical Christian Education,* ed. J. Edward Hakes (Chicago: Moody Press, 1964); William Jeynes, *American Educational History: School, Society, and the Common Good* (Thousand Oaks, CA: Sage Publications, 2007); William Jeynes, *Religion, Education and Academic Success* (Greenwich, CT: Information Age Publishing, 2003); Carl F. Kaestle, ed., *Joseph Lancaster and the Monitorial School Movement* (New York: Teachers College Press, 1973); *Lemon v. Kurtzman,* 403 U.S. 602 (1971); Robert Michaelsen, *Piety in the Public School* (London: Macmillan, 1970); Steven Mintz and Susan Kellogg, *Domestic Revolutions: A Social History of American Family Life* (New York: Macmillan, 1988); William Murray, *My Life Without God* (Nashville, TN: Thomas Nelson Publishers, 1982); *Murray v. Curlett,* 374 U.S. 203 (1963); *Reed v. Van Hoven,* 237 F. Supp. 48 (W.D. Mich. 1965); J.P. Slight, "Froebel and the English Primary School of Today," in *Froebel and English Education: Perspectives on the Founder of the Kindergarten,* ed. Evelyn May Lawrence (London: Routledge, 1969); Robert Ulich, *A History of Religious Education* (New York: New York University Press, 1968); U.S. Department of Health and Human Services, *Statistical Abstracts of the United States* (Washington, DC: U.S. Department of Health and Human Services, 1998); U.S. Department of Justice, *Age-specific Arrest Rate and Race-specific Arrest Rates for Selected Offenses* (Washington, DC: U.S. Department of Justice, 1999); Baroness Von Bulow, *Reminiscences of Froebel* (Boston: Lee & Shephard, 1849); *Wallace v. Jaffree,* 472 U.S. 38 (1985).

William Jeynes

Presbyterian Schools

On May 31, 1847, the General Assembly of the Presbyterian Church, U.S.A. (Old School) adopted a resolution that said that:

> the interests of the church and the glory of our Redeemer, demand that immediately and strenuous exertions should be made, as far as practicable, by every congregation to establish within its bounds one or more primary schools, under the care of the session of the church, in which together with the usual branches of secular learning, the truths and duties of our holy religion shall be assiduously inculcated. (Minutes of the General Assembly of the Presbyterian Church in the U.S.A., 1847, p. 3)

Coming as it did some 40 years before the nation's Catholic bishops' 1884 proclamation that every Catholic parish should open its own school; this resolution could easily be seen as the Presbyterian version of a much better-known Catholic Church policy. However much the Presbyterian resolution may, or may not, have influenced the Catholic bishops (and there is virtually no evidence of such influence), the fate of the two efforts could not have been more different.

By the 1840s large numbers of American evangelicals—Presbyterians, Congregationalists, Methodists, Baptists—as well as more diverse denominations including Unitarians and Episcopalians, had become enthusiastic, indeed almost uncritical, supporters of the nation's emerging public school system. Calvin Stowe, a professor at Lane Theological Seminary, a Presbyterian school in Cincinnati, Ohio (and husband of Harriet Beecher Stowe), was one of the many evangelical advocates for public education. As part of the campaign to expand public schools in Ohio, Stowe wrote a pamphlet, "The Religious Element in Education," arguing that religious instruction, "without violating any of the rights of conscience," was possible in the schools as long as they contained the common elements of all Christian faiths and excluded only that which was unique to each. Thus Stowe and his evangelical allies argued moral education in Ohio and across the country could have a strong religious foundation while remaining strictly undenominational. The fact that Stowe's definition of the common elements of Christianity might be offensive to some, not only Roman Catholics who saw a different set of core beliefs, but non-Christians or nonbelievers and also other Protestants who took the particular doctrines of their denomination with special seriousness, was something that Stowe simply dismissed.

It was in large part because of the success of an "evangelical united front" that the Presbyterian Church itself came to be divided. In 1838, after more than a decade of infighting, the Presbyterian Church formally split into two denominations known as the New School and the Old School. The former tended to be more influenced by New England Congregationalism, more ecumenical in outlook, more committed to religious revivals, and at least moderately antislavery. The latter, with stronger ties to Presbyterianism's Scotch-Irish roots in the Middle States and the South, distrusted anything that might undermine the historic, Reformed theological heritage of the denomination, including emotional revivals and ecumenical religious societies. A minority of the Old School was pro-slavery but many more adherents simply preferred to ignore the issue. The Old School criticized the New for the latter's willingness to modify doctrine for the sake of pan-Protestant unity. In the public school movement they believed such modifications would only be extended. Thus as early as 1844 the Old School General Assembly began considering "the expediency of establishing Presbyterian Parochial Schools . . ." (Minutes of the General Assembly of the Presbyterian Church in the U.S.A., 1844, p. 376). Three years later they went from considering the possibility to making the establishment of such schools denominational policy.

In *Presbyterian Parochial Schools*, Lewis J. Sherrill provided an excellent study of the experiment. For over 20 years the independent Presbyterian school system persisted. In the 1850s there were over 100 such schools, each under the direct control of a specific Presbyterian church and its Session (or governing board) in 26 states. Princeton theologian Charles Hodge and Cortlandt Van Rensselaer, who led the Old School Board of Education, were both tireless advocates of these schools. For these defenders of the Presbyterian schools, teaching the common elements in public school Monday through Friday and the unique elements of Presbyterian doctrine in Sunday school was an insufficient compromise. Presbyterian doctrine and the daily teaching of school subjects needed to be melded as thoroughly as possible.

Ultimately, however, the Presbyterian system of parochial schools faded from the scene and disappeared. From the beginning many Old School ministers who attacked New School ministers in Presbytery meetings joined with their adversaries in supporting public schools. And while the Presbyterian schools were plagued by curricular and administrative problems, that was not the primary issue in their demise. Ultimately too few Presbyterian parents saw anything sufficiently unique about their parochial schools to support them. In the end the common elements of Christianity that still remained in the fast-growing system of public schools seemed quite sufficient to most parents. And whatever was left out could easily be covered in an hour on Sunday morning. In the decades after the Civil War, as most Presbyterians, north and south, saw themselves as part of a single Christian America, they did not want to separate themselves from the mainstream and saw far too little reason to do so. By the early 1870s virtually all traces of the Presbyterian schools had disappeared. *See also:* Common School; Dabney, Robert L.; Hodge, Charles.

Further Reading: *Minutes of the General Assembly of the Presbyterian Church in the U.S.A., (Old School)* 1844 and 1847; Lewis Joseph Sherrill, *Presbyterian Parochial Schools, 1846–1870* (New Haven, CT: Yale University Press, 1932).

James W. Fraser

R

Released Time for Religious Instruction

Released time is a particular program in which public school students are excused from their secular classes to attend religious instruction during the school day according to their parents' wishes. It has faced particular opposition because it raises First Amendment concerns regarding the proper separation of church and state as well as the free exercise of religion in public schools. Local legislatures generally enact such programs either at the request of parents or religious authorities, and students who choose not to participate continue with their secular studies.

With the secularization of public schools in the late nineteenth and early twentieth centuries came a great deal of concern for the moral upbringing of America's youth. Many expressed the sentiment that Sunday school, that is, religious training that occurred merely once a week, was not enough to meet the moral needs of adolescents. William Wirt, superintendent in Gary, Indiana, first suggested a coalition between public schools and religious institutions in 1913. Religious instruction took place in the public schools, but it was conducted in its entirety by local religious officials. The program did not see widespread growth, however, until Protestant sponsors were able to garner Catholic support. After 1923, released-time programs took hold in 48 states, particularly in urban centers with larger Catholic populations. Generally, organized religious bodies would offer their services at the beginning of each school year, and parents provided permission for their children to take part. Religious instructors came into the schools for one hour weekly, and students who did not take part would retire to separate rooms to continue their secular studies. Curricula were generally altered so that no new material was taught during released time. By 1947, an estimated 2 million students were in released-time programs across 48 states.

The two Supreme Court cases that give legal precedent to released time are *Pierce v. Society of Sisters* (1925) and *Everson v. Board of Education* (1947). In *Pierce,* the State of Oregon passed a law demanding that all students attend compulsory public education. Two private schools in the area challenged the law, and the Court found in their favor due to the parental right of choice. Though *Pierce* did not only refer to religious choice, it is often used in defending the rights of parents to choose religious instruction for their children, a crucial starting point when considering the legitimacy of released-time programs. *Everson,* on the other hand, concerned federal support for religious schools. While the Court decided that governmental aid to religious schools was constitutional so long as it was disbursed for a secular reason, this case was the first to advocate for "strict separation" between church and state. The theory of "strict separation" advocates for an impenetrable wall that should lie between governmental and religious institutions, leading to a strict separation between the two. Clearly, the Supreme Court's articulation of this theory has great implications for released-time programs.

In 1948, the first case challenging the constitutionality of released time, *McCollum v. Board of Education,* reached the Supreme Court. Vashti McCollum, the mother of a child in public schools in Champaign, Illinois, claimed that the released-time program violated the First Amendment due to a breach of the Establishment Clause. The Supreme Court agreed. The opinion delivered by Justice Hugo Black found several things wrong with the program as enacted in Champaign. First, the instruction took place on public school grounds, which means that tax-supported property was used for religious purposes. Second, there was close cooperation between the school administrators and religious officials, as the administrators had to approve both the teachers and the content of the religious education. With these two situations in tandem, Black found a "utilization of the tax-established and tax-supported public school system to aid religious groups to spread their faith" (*McCollum v. Board of Education,* 1948). Thus, relying on strict separation as articulated in *Everson,* the released-time program in Champaign was ruled unconstitutional. Concurring opinions articulated an unwillingness to disregard released-time programs across the board. Certain justices argued that should crucial elements be changed, released-time programs could very well be constitutionally viable. This critical statement opened the door for subsequent released-time cases.

Zorach v. Clauson (1952) was just such a case regarding released-time programs in New York City. Several parents of public school children claimed that the public school was impermissibly supporting religious education programs. The parents argued that both tracking the attendance of children in released-time programs and stopping the educational process of those who did not attend released-time activities were unconstitutional. The Court decided against the parents given that (1) the classes were taught on off-campus sites, in local churches and synagogues, where attendance was recorded and reported to the school; and (2) parents had to request that their children take part, rather than merely consent. Justice William Douglas articulated the necessity of governmental support for religious institutions due to the inherently religious nature of the American people, a stance commonly called religious accommodation. According to Douglas, cooperation between the schools and parents is entirely appropriate and necessary to maintain free exercise liberty as stringently as possible. This accommodation is also necessary so as not to privilege nonreligion over religious belief. Therefore, if parents request religious instruction for their children, the state is right in granting that request, so long as the program is not explicitly supported by tax dollars.

Zorach faced harsh criticism as it was a sharp deviation from the Court standard of strict separation and *McCollum.* Supporters maintained, however, that there are distinct differences between *Zorach* and *McCollum.* In *McCollum,* the religious education took place on school grounds, with parental consent, monitored by school officials. *Zorach,* on the other hand, took place at religious institutions, by parental request, with no public administrative interaction beyond assuring attendance. Therefore, *Zorach* attempted to fulfill the promises of parental autonomy made in *Pierce,* while *McCollum* leaned towards the emphasis placed on separation by *Everson.* The clash between accommodation of religious belief and the need for separation is one that continues today.

Other released-time cases decided by lower state and federal courts have helped specify further requirements to maintain constitutionality. *Smith v. Smith* (1975) specified that schools may not solicit students for released-time programs. *Lanner v. Wimmer* (1981) demanded that school officials find the least entangling way of managing attendance, and continued to mandate separation between curricula (as the program in question here offered credit towards graduation for released-time courses). *Doe v. Shenandoah County School Board* (1990) asserted that students cannot be penalized for attending released-time classes; that is, teachers cannot teach new material during released time at the risk of harming the education of students engaged in the program.

Though the prevalence of released-time programs has sharply declined in recent years, the religious pluralism of those that remain has increased to include Muslim, Hindu, and other non-Christian communities. The issue also remains relevant for those Protestant communities that wish to establish Bible study classes during the school day. Current programs are no less controversial than the original released-time cases of the 1940s and 1950s as the issues regarding the appropriate balance between parental rights and the separation of church and state continue to be negotiated. *See also: McCollum v. Board of Education of School District No. 71, Champaign County; Zorach v. Clauson.*

Further Reading: Perry Oswin Chrisman, "The Released Time Program in Public Schools," *Baylor Law Review* 11 (Summer 1952): 252–305; *Doe v. Shenandoah County School Board,* 737 F.Supp. 913 (W.D. Va. 1990); *Everson v. Board of Education,* 330 U.S. 1 (1947); *Lanner v. Wimmer,* 662 F.2d 1349, 1361 (10th Cir. 1981); *McCollum v. Board of Education,* 333 U.S. 203 (1948); James D. McWilliams, "Released Time," from www.firstamendmentcenter.org; *Pierce v. Society of Sisters,* 268 U.S. 510 (1925); *Smith v. Smith,* 523 F.2nd 121 (4th Cir. 1975); Jonathan Vinson, "Religion in the Public Schools: Released Time Reconsidered," in *Gateways to Spirituality,* ed. Peter W. Cobb (New York: Peter Lang Publishing, 2005); *Zorach v. Clauson,* 343 U.S. 306 (1952).

Mary Ellen Giess and Diane L. Moore

Religion and Academic Achievement

Religion in the United States has a long history of influencing academic achievement at several levels of social life. At the individual level, the importance of reading the Bible has been credited with increasing literacy rates in the eighteenth century. At the school level, Protestant religious organizations established the dominant educational institutions in early America, emphasized the importance of an educated public, and were primary movers behind the incredible expansion of public schools in the mid-1800s. Later, religious dissenters from the public school system, including the Catholic Church, the Christian Reformed, and Lutheran Church–Missouri Synod religious denominations, built schools that became the focus of research on the effect of religion at the school level on academic outcomes. More recently, the fundamentalist and evangelical Protestant movements have played significant roles in challenges to public school curriculum and the expansion of what are now called Christian schools. Some academics and educational leaders are concerned that conservative religious families and schools harbor an anti-intellectualism that has detrimental effects on public educational institutions and individual learning. For example, many scientists have voiced concerns that skepticism regarding Darwinian evolution has diminished the quality of science education in the United States. Are these concerns legitimate? What is known about the effect of religion at the individual, family, and school levels on academic achievement?

Most scholarship shows that general aspects of religion have positive effects on academic achievement at the individual level, but there are important differences by religious tradition. At the primary and secondary school levels, academic achievement is typically defined by scores on standardized tests, grades, staying on track in high school (measured, for example, by extent of skipping school and discipline problems), and graduation from high school. On these scores, religious involvement predicts higher educational expectations, higher standardized test scores, more time spent on homework, less truancy, and a lower likelihood of dropping out of high school. These beneficial effects of religious participation extend to the verbal ability among girls and to the grades of teenagers in rural areas and of immigrant children. These religious effects are particularly important for disadvantaged adolescents, especially those in high poverty neighborhoods and urban areas, and for Hispanic and African American children.

There are several reasons why religion would influence academic achievement. At an individual level, religious involvement develops skills and character traits that tend to improve outcomes at school. For example, through involvement in congregations children may learn the discipline of sitting quietly or listening to a speaker, which may translate into improved behavior, grades, or learning at school. By structuring children's everyday life routines, religious participation may contribute to a disciplined lifestyle that enhances educational success. It may also contribute to a strong work ethic and the moral fortitude necessary for persistence in the schooling task.

The practice of religion appears to have positive effects on academic achievement, especially in primary and secondary grades, but some scholarship on educational attainment argues that religious beliefs dampen motivation for learning. Research has shown that conservative Protestants, at least as measured by biblical literalism, tend to have lower levels of educational attainment compared to Catholics and mainline Protestants. Some conservative Protestants, especially fundamentalists, have lower interest in education since they are skeptical of the scientific method and of humanistic or antireligious sentiment in public educational institutions. Thus, research shows that fundamentalists tend to have lower levels of educational attainment, especially when compared with Jews, who have the highest level of educational attainment among religious traditions. While there is conflicting evidence on whether educational attainment for Catholics was significantly lower in the past, Catholic educational attainment has converged with mainline Protestants.

Recent research has narrowed the extent of the negative relationship between conservative religion and academic success. The negative effect of fundamentalism on educational attainment is concentrated among girls. Further, the key juncture for fundamentalist boys is the decision to go to college, while for fundamentalist girls it is the decision to complete the college degree. This research argues that fundamentalist gender norms emphasize marriage and childbearing over career advancement, which leads girls to drop out of college or to have lower educational expectations. Besides gender differences, important research has further isolated the denominational effect to Pentecostals, who tend to experience conflict between the organizational culture of public schooling and Pentecostal worldviews and organizational practices. These results raise the question of whether any negative effect of conservative Protestant traditions on educational attainment should be seen as an outcome of anti-intellectualism, or institutional discrimination against forms of cultural capital dominant among some conservative religious families. Moreover, it seems likely that the negative effects of conservative religion on educational outcomes may be further limited to earlier generations.

Though public educational institutions are seen by some conservative Protestants as a key battleground in a cultural war, the practice of religion has many practical benefits for educational success. Most contemporary congregations send explicit messages that learning is important, that "getting a good education" is an important goal. And most congregations spend a good deal of organizational resources tying youth to the church. They do so in part by highlighting, announcing, and celebrating success in school, including ceremonies during religious services that recognize recent graduates. Religious organizational involvement offers opportunities for student accomplishments to be celebrated publicly, which is likely to have the effect of increasing educational expectations and effort.

Even if the importance of education is not always reinforced by messages from the pulpit, academic success is higher for children in religious families because religious involvement is a form of conventional behavior that reinforces the authority of the school. It connects children to an adult world, and this increases motivation and expectations for doing well in school. In general, integration into a religious community facilitates integration into a school community, since both require some level of submission to organizational and adult authority.

More specifically, religious involvement provides forms of social capital that contribute to academic achievement. Social capital is defined here as the emergent properties of social networks marked by trust and mutual obligation that create collective resources available to individuals in the network. Religious involvement shapes the peer networks of children, reducing contact with deviant peers and increasing contact with children who are more academically focused, who have more "pro-school" values. Congregations are likely to provide opportunities for teenagers to meet and develop friendships with teenagers who have conventional values. Religious involvement, then, reduces the likelihood that children are influenced by peers who are connected to an oppositional school culture, which constructs identity in opposition to the values and organization of schools.

Another example is the effect of religion in intergenerational closure. Religious participation increases the extent that children have strong social ties to adults. Congregations increase the opportunities for adolescents to regularly interact with adults outside of the family. Church activities can provide a context in which parents get to know their children's friends as well as parents of those friends. And adults in congregations may be influenced by religious norms that encourage intergenerational closure as part of a commitment to socializing children into the faith. For these reasons, it is not surprising that research shows that religious involvement leads to peer networks with higher educational values, which in turn enhance educational expectations, time spent on homework, regular class attendance, and taking advanced math credits.

The effect of religious participation on networks extends to extracurricular participation. Teens who are more involved in their congregations are also more likely to be involved in nonsports extracurricular activities at school, and this in turn leads to better grades and a greater likelihood that teens will stay on track in school. Congregational participation may combine socialization into conventional norms with the recruitment networks that lead to greater academically oriented extracurricular participation.

At the school level, there is much more controversy over whether religion per se has any effect on academic outcomes. James Coleman argued most famously that Catholic schools were better able to encourage academic achievement than public schools because of the overlapping ties of parish, family, and school. This created network closure, since the parents of a child knew the parents of their child's friends. The result of network closure is increased social control over the child and enhanced socialization into prosocial values. Whether in fact Catholic schools have a positive impact on learning, especially for the disadvantaged, has been hotly contested. Even the claim that network closure enhances academic achievement is not settled. Some have argued that religious schools have strong norm-reinforcing, or bonding, social capital, but that these kinds of insular networks are actually detrimental to academic achievement. In comparison to religious schools, other types of schools provide the horizon-expanding social capital that offers the information and contacts that are beneficial to academic success. For example, horizon-expanding social capital would help students gain access to information about colleges that may not be available in religious school contexts.

Still, most research shows some advantage or no disadvantage of religious schools on academic achievement. Catholic schools seem to promote academic achievement, even if this is not due to differences in network closure. Anthony Bryk and colleagues have put forward the most explicit and widely accepted argument that religion per se matters at the school level. Catholic schools are communal organizations as a direct result of their religious beliefs and practices. Their communal form of organization grew out of a post-Vatican II theology, which emphasized that all people are created in the image of God and that organizations must be decentralized in order to maintain a personalism that respects individual dignity. The school ethos in a communal organization includes a strong sense of shared mission and commitment to the collective goals of the school by parents, teachers, and administration. This form of organization benefits academic achievement, especially for the disadvantaged. For example, the best teachers are assigned and willing to teach both the higher and lower division classes out of a commitment to the religious mission of the school. A disciplined environment emerges that increases time spent on learning tasks. Academic tracking is weaker in Catholic schools, since the school maintains commitment that every child has God-given capacities for learning. The general educational tracks in Catholic schools, therefore, are quite rigorous academically.

This Catholic school advantage is perhaps short-lived. Demographic changes, including increasing residential segregation by race and income, have made it difficult for inner-city Catholic schools to remain financially viable. Further economic pressures have emerged as the supply of priests and nuns who are available to teach at the schools declines. Some research has seen in these trends the likely outcome that Catholic schools will lose any religiously based academic advantage, and that they will be molded into the image of elite, private schools.

What about conservative Protestant schools? Social capital and communal organization arguments should generalize to some non-Catholic religious schools. We would expect that the greater network closure generated in conservative Protestant religious communities, which unites school, church, and family, would improve academic outcomes for children. Some have argued, however, that conservative Protestant schools harbor an anti-intellectualism, dogmatism, and separatism that is antithetical to quality education. But other research has argued that conservative Protestant schools are not radically isolated from dominant educational practices or values in America. There is little systematic and nationally representative data on conservative Protestant schools, in part because the best available data tend to conflate all non-Catholic religious schools into one category, ignoring obvious differences between mainline Protestant, Jewish, and conservative Protestant schools. Recent analyses, however, reveal lower levels of math but not reading achievement at conservative Protestant schools at the primary school level. But there is evidence using longitudinal data that conservative Protestant schools are more effective in boosting reading achievement in early childhood, though this does not extend to other subjects.

Moving forward, we would not expect consistent and strong negative effects of conservative religious traditions on most educational outcomes. The religious barriers that arise in latter stages of the educational career, such as the lower number of advanced placement classes taken by fundamentalists, are likely to mitigate as education continues to play a dominant role in identity and stratification processes in the United States, and religious groups, through visible on-campus ministries, an increasing number of conservative religious faculty, and the expansion of religious colleges and universities, find new ways to negotiate educational careers and religious careers. The emphasis on homeschooling among some conservative religious groups may have a positive effect on the importance of education among religiously conservative women. And most studies show that homeschooling, which is dominated by conservative Protestants and Catholics, is not detrimental to academic achievement. In addition, it seems more likely that the general advantages of religious participation for academic achievement will only become more important. Religious families and communities may become more significant for a child's academic achievement in a context where education is linked to social mobility strategies and educational institutions are less successful in creating a functional community that embeds a shared mission and provides effective value socialization. *See also:* Catholic Schools; Christian Day Schools; Homeschooling.

Further Reading: David Baker, "The 'Eliting' of the Common American Catholic School and the National Education Crisis," *Phi Delta Kappan* 80 (September 1998): 16–23; Carl Bankston and Min Zhou, "Social Capital and Immigrant Children's Achievement," *Research in Sociology of Education* 13 (2002): 1–39; Kraig Beyerlein, "Specifying the Impact of Conservative Protestantism on Educational Attainment," *Journal for the Scientific Study of Religion* 43 (December 2004): 505–518; Henry Braun, Frank Jenkins, and Wendy Grigg, "Comparing Private Schools and Public Schools Using Hierarchical Linear Modeling," NCES 2006-461 (Washington, DC: U.S. Government Printing Office, 2006); Anthony Bryk, Valerie E. Lee, and Peter Blakeley Holland, *Catholic Schools And the Common Good* (Cambridge, MA: Harvard University Press, 1993); James Coleman and Thomas Hoffer, *Public and Private High Schools: The Impact of Communities* (New York: Basic Books, 1987); Alfred Darnell and Darren E. Sherkat, "The Impact of Protestant Fundamentalism on Educational Attainment," *American Sociological Review* 62 (April 1997): 306–315; Jennifer L. Glanville, David Sikkink, and Edwin I. Hernandez, "Religious Involvement and Educational Outcomes: The Role of Social Capital and Extracurricular Participation," *The Sociological Quarterly* 49 (Winter 2008): 105–137; William H. Jeynes, *Religion, Education, and Academic Success* (Greenwich, CT: Information Age Publishing, 2003); William H. Jeynes, "The Effects of the Religious Commitment of Twelfth Graders Living in Non-Intact Families on Their Academic Achievement," *Marriage & Family Review* 35 (2003): 77–97; Evelyn L. Lehrer, "Religion as a Determinant of Educational Attainment: An Economic Perspective," *Social Science Research* 28 (December 1999): 358–379; John W. Meyer, "Public Education as Nation-Building in America: Enrollments and

Bureaucratization in the American States, 1870–1930," *American Journal of Sociology* 85 (November 1979): 591–613; Stephen L. Morgan, "Counterfactuals, Causal Effect Heterogeneity, and the Catholic School Effect on Learning," *Sociology of Education* 74 (October 2001): 341–374; Chandra Muller and Christopher G. Ellison, "Religious Involvement, Social Capital, and Adolescents' Academic Progress: Evidence from the National Education Longitudinal Study of 1988," *Sociological Focus* 34 (May 2001): 155–183; Toby L. Parcel and Laura E. Geschwender, "Explaining Southern Disadvantage in Verbal Facility Among Young Children," *Social Forces* 73 (March 1995): 841–874; Alan Peshkin, *God's Choice: The Total World of a Fundamentalist Christian School* (Chicago: University of Chicago Press, 1986); Mark D. Regnerus, "Shaping Schooling Success: Religious Socialization and Educational Outcomes in Metropolitan Public Schools," *Journal for the Scientific Study of Religion* 39 (September 2000): 363–370; Mark D. Regnerus and Glen H. Elder, "Staying on Track in School: Religious Influences in High- and Low-Risk Settings," *Journal for the Scientific Study of Religion* 42 (December 2003): 633–649; Darren E. Sherkat and Alfred Darnell, "The Effect of Parents' Fundamentalism on Children's Educational Attainment: Examining Differences by Gender and Children's Fundamentalism," *Journal for the Scientific Study of Religion* 38 (March 1999): 23–35; David Sikkink, "The Social Sources of Alienation from Public Schools," *Social Forces* 78 (September 1999): 51–86; David Sikkink, "Speaking in Many Tongues: Diversity Among Christian Schools," *Education Matters* 1 (Summer 2001): 36–45; Melinda Bollar Wagner, "Generic Conservative Christianity: The Demise of Denominationalism in Christian Schools," *Journal for the Scientific Study of Religion* 36 (March 1997): 13–24.   *David Sikkink*

Religion & Public Education

Religion & Public Education (R&PE) is the only journal devoted exclusively to cover the significant matter of teaching about religions in the public schools and higher education. Later changed to *Religion & Education,* its articles include historical analyses, legal interpretations, and reports of classroom instruction.

The focus on religion in the public school context is most especially linked to court cases beginning in the post–World War II period. In 1962 a New York Board of Regents' prayer was found to be unconstitutional (an establishment practice). Literally hundreds of attempts in Congress were made to modify the First Amendment to permit school-sponsored prayer over the next several decades.

In 1963, a Pennsylvania school district case (*Abington School District v. Schempp,* 374 U.S. 203) and a related Maryland case (*Murray v. Curlett,* 374 U.S. 203) focused on mandatory reading of Bible verses. The Supreme Court's carefully worded decision found the Bible reading practice in the district unconstitutional because it was devotional in intent. Justice Tom Clark's dicta, nonetheless, prescribed what would be an acceptable public school religion studies curriculum:

> In addition, it might well be said that one's education is not complete without a study of comparative religion or the history of religion and its relationship to the advancement of civilization. It certainly may be said that the Bible is worthy of study for its literary and historic qualities. Nothing we have said here indicates that such study of the Bible or of religion, when presented objectively as part of a secular program of education, may not be affected consistently with the First Amendment. (*Abington v. Schempp,* 1963)

Teaching about religion did not have success immediately. Some school districts tried to use Sunday school curriculum, which the lower courts repeatedly rejected. Slowly, curriculum that was constitutionally appropriate and pedagogically sound appeared. Faculty at Wright State University's Public Education Religion Studies Center coordinated curriculum projects and established teacher-training programs beginning in 1972. Florida State University faculty did some similar work. Underwritten by the Lilly Endowment, Indiana University offered eight-week programs ten years in a row for secondary school English teachers.

Concerned about legal issues, the American Association of School Administrators (AASA) produced resources as early as 1964; these, however, were more helpful to administrators than classroom teachers. The American Jewish Committee published materials and the National Conference of Christians and Jews developed a calendar on ethnic and religious holidays. Slowly, publishing companies began to produce history textbooks that earlier had rightly been criticized for inaccurate and incomplete data on religious events and peoples.

The most prominent voice for teaching about religions, however, was the National Council on Religion and Public Education (NCRPE). Sensing the need for curricular implications of legal cases and model teaching examples, it began *Religion & Public Education*. Using each letter of NCRPE to outline its scope (News, Commentaries, Reviews, Perspectives, and Events), *R&PE*'s managing editor, Thayer Warshaw, and editor in chief, Charles Kniker, covered religion and education news from the 50 states as well as international settings. Commentaries evolved into pro and con essays on topics ranging from creationism to vouchers. In one issue, for example, an ACLU representative debated a representative of Pat Robertson's law center over whether Mississippi state textbooks were or were not espousing secular humanism.

The journal evolved from a nine-volume newsletter that Thayer S. Warshaw had created to a refereed journal. Charles Kniker, Iowa State University, became editor of the journal. With the help of Lynn Taylor at the University of Kansas, and financial assistance from the Graduate College at Iowa State University, *Religion & Public Education* began in 1983. The response to the journal was positive and broad. An outstanding editorial board, including Martin Marty, church historian, Father Robert Drinan, Catholic priest and U.S. Congressman, Warren Nord (University of North Carolina), and Randall Balmer (Barnard College, Columbia University), wrote articles, solicited a new generation of contributors, and inspired new curriculum. The editorial board included liberals and conservatives from many faiths who held various educational positions—administrative, classroom teachers, professors, and lawyers. Subscription income and Lilly Endowment funding enabled NCRPE to begin a resource center at Iowa State University for books, articles, pamphlets, etc., in the field of teaching about religion(s).

When Kniker left Iowa State University to become president of Eden Seminary, the journal's headquarters moved to Webster University, across the street from Eden in Webster Groves, Missouri. The faculty in Webster's Religion and Philosophy Department covered personnel costs while funds from Lilly Endowment covered publication costs. Charlie Russo, then of the University of Kentucky, became the new editor in chief in 1993.

By the late 1990s, the journal needed a new home. It moved to the University of Northern Iowa, under Michael Waggoner's leadership. With new artwork, editorial board, and Web site (www.uni.edu/jrae), the journal continues to have a significant role in regarding teaching about religion and spirituality matters in PK–12 and higher education.

These are a few of the issues that the journal has dealt with and will treat in the years to come: the neutrality of government regarding religion(s); the debate regarding evolution/creationism/intelligent design; displays of religious art in public schools; school concerts that feature religious music; distribution of religious materials by students; student rights, relating to religious practices such as diet, dress, prayer, and holiday observances as well as religious clubs meetings on school grounds; and vouchers. *See also:* National Council on Religion and Public Education.

Further Reading: American Association of School Administrators, *Religion in the Public Schools* (Arlington, VA: AASA, 1986); Charles Haynes, *Finding Common Ground: A First Amendment Guide to Religion and Public Education* (Nashville: Freedom Forum, First Freedom Center at Vanderbilt, 1994); Thomas C. Hunt and James C. Carper, eds., *Religion and Schooling in Contemporary America: Confronting Our Cultural Pluralism* (New York: Garland Publishing, 1997).

Charles R. Kniker

Religion and Public Education Resource Center

Located at the University of California at Chico in the Religious Studies Department, the Religion and Public Education Resource Center (RPERC) was founded in 1995 to provide resources and to promote education about the world's religious traditions in public schools within First Amendment guidelines. It is also the home of materials formerly housed at the National Council on Religion and Public Education Distribution Center that was located at the Indiana University of Pennsylvania in Indiana, Pennsylvania. The philosophy of the Center is based on the "conviction that the academic study of the world's religions in public elementary and secondary schools not only makes an indispensable contribution to historical and cultural literacy, it is also an integral part of education for citizenship in a pluralistic democracy" (Religion and Public Education Resource Center, at www.csuchico.edu/rs/rperc/). In addition to providing resources for teachers and administrators in the form of curriculum guides, sample lesson plans in a variety of subjects, and literature on the legal issues related to religion in the schools, RPERC coordinates the "Project on Religion and Public Education" at California State University, Chico. This ongoing project has three components: (1) Professional Development for Classroom Teachers; (2) Pre-Service Teacher Education; and (3) regional coordination of the "California 3 Rs Project."

For in-service teachers, faculty in the religious studies department at the University of California at Chico offer workshops and seminars for educators on the religious clauses of the First Amendment and on a variety of topics in the study of religion itself. For preservice teachers enrolled in the school's teacher education program, the faculty offers a course titled "Teaching about Religions in American Public Schools" that provides an overview of the world's religious traditions as well as information about First Amendment principles and guidelines for teaching about religion in constitutionally sound ways. The California 3 Rs Project was launched in 1993 as a joint venture sponsored by the California County Superintendents Educational Services Association and the Freedom Forum First Amendment Center. The project brings together teachers, administrators, and school board officials to learn about the "shared civic principles of the Religious Liberty clauses of the First Amendment to the U.S. Constitution" (www.csuchico.edu/rs/rperc/proj.html). The three Rs are presented as essential elements of democratic citizenship and represent rights, responsibilities, and respect: the right for "people of all faiths or none" to be entitled to religious liberty; the responsibility to honor the religious liberty rights of others; and the necessity to respect religious differences in civil discourse and debate. *See also:* Religion and the Public School Curriculum.

Further Reading: Bruce Grelle, "The Religion and Public Education Resource Center," *Spotlight on Teaching* 17 (March 2002): 6; Religion and Public Education Resource Center, at www.csuchico.edu/rs/rperc/; "The Project on Religion and Public Education at CSU, Chico," at www.csuchico.edu/rs/rperc/proj.html.

Diane L. Moore

Religion and the Public School Curriculum

The role of religion in the public school curriculum has long been controversial. Conflicts over evolution, sex education, the Bible, and literature and history texts flare up with regularity. This being the case, it is perhaps surprising that there is now widespread consensus about the role of religion in the curriculum *in principle, at the national level.* No doubt, some educators in the trenches and many parents remain unaware of this consensus—and, of course, the devil is often in the details.

Among the topics discussed below are the following: (1) the secularization of the curriculum; (2) the Supreme Court's ruling in *Abington v. Schempp* and the new consensus about religion and the curriculum; (3) arguments for including religion in the curriculum; (4) objections to including religion in the curriculum; (5) arguments over whether there should be *religion in courses* or *courses in religion*—or both; (6) the role of religion in various subjects; and (7) issues relating to *teaching about religion* in ways that are constitutionally and pedagogically sound.

Secularization of the Curriculum

In the nineteenth century, the Bible and Protestant Christianity played an important role in textbooks and the public school curriculum. The Bible was viewed as essential to moral education—a major task of public schools. America's history was often viewed through a religious lens, and religious (often biblical) stories were commonplace in readers and literature anthologies. Science texts and courses taught that nature was the handiwork of God and provided evidence of his existence.

By the end of the nineteenth century the formal curriculum had become largely secular. Why? As America grew more pluralistic, especially with Catholic immigration, battles were fought over the Protestant ethos of public education and the funding of sectarian schools. Eventually, *Americanism* replaced Protestantism in providing the *common values* that shaped schooling, though the former was heavily influenced by the latter. The economic and vocational purposes of schooling gradually displaced the traditional conception of education rooted in the Bible and the classics. Perhaps most important, post-Darwinian scientific interpretations of physical and human nature led to the marginalization of religion. As scientists and secular scholars (rather than ministers) began to write textbooks, shape curricula, and develop educational theories, the older religious context for making sense of physical and human nature, and the purposes and content of education, gave way, and education became largely a secular enterprise (though government-sanctioned prayer and devotional Bible reading continued in many schools until they were ruled unconstitutional by the U.S. Supreme Court in 1962 and 1963, and in some schools after the Court had spoken). The curriculum had become almost entirely secular long before the Supreme Court first addressed the place of religion in public schools in 1948.

Recent textbook studies and surveys of state and national content standards confirm that textbooks and curricula give scant attention to religion apart from the context of history. And while history texts and standards, and literature anthologies (if organized historically), include a good deal about religion, religious themes, movements, and texts receive less and less attention as we move past the seventeenth century. Not surprisingly, several recent studies have confirmed what most teachers know: most students are religiously illiterate.

Common Ground

A *new consensus* about religion and the curriculum gradually grew out of the Supreme Court's seminal ruling in *Abington Township v. Schempp* (1963), in which the Court distinguished *devotional* reading of the Bible, which is unconstitutional, from *academic* study of the Bible (and of religion generally), which is constitutional so long as it is carried out "objectively as part of a secular program of education." Because devotional Bible reading is a religious exercise, it violates the Establishment Clause, which requires that government—and therefore public schools—*"maintain strict neutrality, neither aiding nor opposing religion."* To pass muster, academic study of religion—*teaching about religion*—must be conducted *neutrally.* In his majority opinion, Justice Tom Clark added that "it might well be said that one's education is not complete without a study of comparative religion or the history of religion and its relationship to the advancement of civilization" and "it certainly may be said that the Bible is worthy of study for its literary and historic qualities."

Because it has proven relatively uncontroversial in the long run, the ruling has provided the framework for a broad coalition of supporters of *public education religion studies* that gathered first under the banner of the National Council for Religion and Public Education (1971–1994), and then coalesced around a series of *common ground* statements on religion and public education. These statements, developed under the leadership of Charles Haynes and the First Amendment Center, were endorsed by a broad spectrum of national religious (Christian, Jewish, and Islamic), educational, and civil liberties organizations. The first of the statements, "Religion and the Public School Curriculum: Questions and Answers" (1988), made several important claims: it is constitutional to teach about religion; teaching about religion must be done neutrally; it is important to teach about religion; and textbooks are deficient in their treatment of religion. (This last claim is not to be found in the Court's opinion, but came to be widely accepted as the result of a series of textbook studies conducted by scholars in the late 1980s.) Other common ground statements, followed, including *The Bible in Public Schools* and *A Teacher's Guide to Religion and Public Schools.* Hundreds of thousands of copies of these documents have been distributed, and in 1999, President Bill Clinton had several of them sent to every public school in the country. Cumulatively, the statements have established a *new consensus* in dealing with religion in public schools. They have helped provide a "safe haven" for teachers and administrators in schools that offer course work in religion, often without controversy.

Arguments for Religion in the Public School Curriculum

In our post-9/11 world the claim that students should learn about religion has acquired new legitimacy and urgency. In fact, however, there are a *variety* of reasons for studying religion. The first common ground statement says:

Because religion plays a significant role in history and society, study about religion is essential to understanding both the nation and the world. Omission of facts about religion can give students the false impression that the religious life of humankind is insignificant or unimportant. Failure to understand even the basic symbols, practices and concepts of the various religions make much of history, literature, art and contemporary life unintelligible. Study about religion is also important if students are to value religious liberty, the first freedom guaranteed in the Bill of Rights. Moreover, knowledge of the roles of religion in the past and present promotes cross-cultural understanding essential to democracy and world peace. (Haynes and Thomas, 2007, p. 98)

It will be helpful to disentangle the arguments in this short statement, and mention others that have been given by scholars. They include:

1. *Literacy and Liberal Education.* Perhaps the most common argument is that without knowing something about religion students cannot understand *other subjects*—history, literature, art, or civics (including, as the common ground statement notes, religious liberty, the first freedom in our Bill of Rights). This is the least controversial argument for studying religion. It might be called the argument for *weak* religious literacy.

   There is also an argument for *strong* religious literacy: it is important to study religion not just to understand other subjects, but because *religion itself* is important. The common ground statement notes that without the study of religion, students will acquire "the false impression that the religious life of humankind is insignificant or unimportant." One need not believe that any particular religion is true or good to acknowledge that religion has been, and continues to be, an important part of culture and the human experience.

   The argument for strong religious literacy is often framed in terms of liberal education. An education is liberal if it is not *narrowly* specialized or vocational, if it provides students a *broad* understanding of history and culture, and introduces them to a variety of ways of making sense of the world, *religious ways included*.

2. *Critical Thinking.* The value of a liberal education is often taken to be that it nurtures critical thinking by giving students *perspective* on their studies and their lives. Some critics have argued that because of the practical thrust of much education—the focus on basic skills, vocationalism, and exclusively secular approaches to their school subjects—students must be exposed to religious alternatives if they are not to be uncritically socialized (perhaps even indoctrinated) in secular ways of thinking and living.

   Advocates of this kind of argument often draw on the idea of *worldviews*. In teaching secular history and science and sex education we do not just teach students various facts about the world, we teach them to *interpret* the subject matters of their various courses in ways that often marginalize or even discredit religious interpretations, and in so doing, we uncritically nurture a secular mentality or worldview. One important implication of this position is that religion should not be taught in isolation from other subjects. If critical thinking is to be encouraged, religious and secular ways of understanding the world must be compared and contrasted. Education must nurture a conversation rather than just a series of disciplinary monologues.

3. *Religious Neutrality.* Some conservative religious critics and attorneys have argued that schools teach the *religion of secular humanism*—a comprehensive secular view of the world that is conveyed across the curriculum, uncritically, as a matter of faith. If schools teach this secular religion, they must provide some balance with traditional religion if they are to be *neutral among religions* as the Establishment Clause requires.

   Most scholars reject the claim that schools teach the religion of secular humanism, but some have argued that in uncritically teaching secular ways of interpreting the various subjects of the curriculum schools privilege secular over religious ways of making sense of the world and our lives, and this is not neutral *between religion and nonreligion,* as the Establishment Clause also requires. The question is whether ignoring or marginalizing religion is *neutral*—or whether it favors those who do not believe over those who do believe.

4. *Civic Arguments.* First, the common ground statement on religion and the curriculum notes that it is important to understand *religious liberty,* the first freedom of our First Amendment, a defining principle of the constitutional framework of America. Second, in a society and a world where religion has so much influence and is so much in the news (not least after 9/11), one cannot be a good citizen, a thoughtful voter, if one does not understand a good deal about religion. Third, because we live in a religiously pluralistic society and world, we must respect and understand each other (with our respective beliefs and values, cultures and traditions) if we are to live together peacefully. As the common ground statement puts it, study of religion "promotes cross-cultural understanding essential to democracy and world peace." (Of course, mutual understanding does not require that we agree with each other.) It has become part of the conventional wisdom of educators that the curriculum must be sensitive to the multicultural nature of our society and students, but the multicultural movement has been almost entirely silent regarding religious identities and values, even though they are often more important to people than their ethnic, racial, class, or gender identities and values.

5. *Arguments Regarding Morality and Meaning.* First, it is often claimed that it is a task of schooling to locate students in *traditions* that provide moral guidance and nurture virtue. It is sometimes argued that some study of religious history and literature is essential to this task (as well as to avoid teaching the controversial lesson that our moral traditions have nothing to do with religion). Second, the curriculum inevitably and properly addresses controversial moral questions in a variety of courses. Some scholars argue that to exclude religious answers and ways of thinking about these questions is both illiberal and not religiously neutral. Third, many people believe that modern culture encourages materialism, self-interest, technological fixes, professional specialization, and insensitivity to the moral and spiritual dimensions of life. Consequently, it is sometimes argued, students should be exposed to various moral, philosophical, *and religious critiques of modern culture.*

Finally, some scholars have argued that education should be responsive to the *need of students* to explore the existential (aesthetic, moral, spiritual, and religious) dimensions of their lives—the ways in which people find *meaning* in their lives. This is sometimes called exploring the *Big Questions.* Education, as such, is a search for *wisdom,* not just knowledge. It is implausible and illiberal to argue that this search can be conducted apart from religion and alternative worldviews. There is overlap between this argument and the argument based on critical thinking; arguably, students can only think *critically* about the world, their lives, and the subjects of the curriculum, if they have some understanding of the Big Questions and the worldviews in terms of which answers are framed.

Most of these arguments are complementary. They all purport to be secular arguments, as they must be to pass constitutional muster.

Objections to Religion in the Public School Curriculum

Critics have raised a number of objections to including religion in the curriculum. At least seven common objections have been put forth. They have, in turn, usually prompted a response:

1. It is often claimed that it is the right and responsibility of parents, not schools, to teach children about religion. No doubt it is the right of parents to raise their children *within a religious*

tradition, but it is a quite different thing to *educate* students (neutrally) about a variety of religious traditions, which is the task of schools.

2. Some conservative religious parents object to having their children learn about religious traditions other than their own; some fear that neutral study of various religions encourages relativism or even agnosticism. This is, of course, only one example of a more general concern: schools teach students about cultures, political parties, and moral values different from those of their parents. Religion raises no *new* problem in this regard; exposure to new ideas and different traditions is inherent in education. Teachers do need to be clear that learning about different cultures and traditions, treating them with respect, does not require relativism (the view that no values or religion is any better or more reasonable than others). Some of these parents would not object to their children learning about traditions other than their own if they believed their own religion was taken seriously.

3. Teaching about religion can be controversial, and many school administrators see it as an open invitation to fundamentalists or civil liberties groups to bring lawsuits against them. Schools already deal with *many* controversial subjects (such as politics, gender, race, and sex education) other than religion. Religion has been taught in many schools without controversy. If schools have strong religion policies (as they should), they can minimize the risk of controversy. Moreover, leaving religion out of the curriculum is *also* controversial; it is because many schools do not take religion seriously that some parents desert them for private schools or homeschooling.

4. If teachers are going to teach about religion they should stick to *the facts* (in history courses, for example) and avoid theology and controversial religious interpretations of various subjects. But why, one might wonder, should we treat religion differently from politics? Although politics is controversial, we do not just teach the facts about our political life; we teach students something about political theory and ideologies, about how people think politically, and about the resulting controversies. Theology and religious interpretations of various subjects can be taught neutrally (that is, we can teach *about* them) just as political thinking can be taught neutrally. It *is* essential to convey to students that theology (like politics) is controversial and to give them some sense of the diversity of alternatives.

5. A few critics take a stronger position, arguing that religion should not be taken seriously because it is not open to scientific verification or falsification, or because it is a matter of faith rather than reason, or because it is not intellectually respectable. Any such suggestion, however, would appear to discriminate against religion, violating constitutional neutrality between religion and nonreligion. Of course, what counts as intellectually respectable is a matter of considerable controversy, and if we take seriously only what is scientifically respectable, then the arts, history, and literature also become problematic. Moreover, as we have seen, some scholars argue that too often students are taught to accept *much of what they learn* (including science) as a matter of faith rather than truly critical thinking, which requires some study of alternative worldviews; some study of religion is necessary for critical thinking.

6. It is difficult to teach about religion well: many teachers feel insecure in addressing religions other than their own; many parents from minority religious traditions fear that teachers will misunderstand *their* traditions or privilege the teacher's own tradition; many liberals fear that the line between proselytizing and academic teaching about religion is difficult to draw, and teachers will not be able to observe it in practice. No doubt most teachers try to be fair, but it is also true that most teachers do not have the educational background to teach about religion competently. Indeed, teacher education has been largely tone-deaf to the need for preparing teachers (and administrators) for this task. Clearly, schools must proceed with caution in phasing in serious study of religion. Teachers must be given the training (in schools of education and in-service workshops) and the resources they need to teach well.

7. There is not time to take religion seriously in an already overcrowded curriculum. It is no doubt true that those who set educational policy typically value the more utilitarian goals of society and the economy over religion (and over the humanities more generally) at least in their role

as educators. This suggests that policy makers need themselves to be liberally educated and rethink the purposes of education.

Some of these objections are substantial and are not easily addressed in practice. A constant aggravating factor is that too often discussion of religion in the curriculum gets caught up in the polarizing rhetoric of our culture wars, pitting religious conservatives (who sometimes wish to have only their own religion taught) against secular liberals (who sometimes wish to make schools into religion-free zones). Of course, there are also secular conservatives and religious liberals and many people in the middle. More important, there is, as we have noted, a broad position of common ground on which educators can stand in taking religion seriously in ways that are constitutionally acceptable and pedagogically sound.

Religion in Courses or Courses in Religion—or Both?

It is usually easier to incorporate some study of religion into existing courses (especially history and literature courses) than to create new courses in religion. Moreover, if religion is necessary to make sense of the subject at hand (as is often the case in history or literature) or for critical thinking in dealing with moral controversies or in addressing the Big Questions, it should be included in the courses where these matters come up. This is often called *natural inclusion.* Indeed, to leave religion *out* of courses where it is relevant may be illiberal and not neutral.

Some scholars argue, however, that natural inclusion is inadequate. Any study of religion in (nonreligion) classes will inevitably be superficial, both because there will be little time devoted to it, and because many teachers are not prepared to discuss religion with much sophistication. Because of the importance and the complexity of religion, there should be courses in religion taught by teachers certified to do so. More than a third of public universities now have curricula or departments of *religious studies;* a parallel field should be created in public education.

According to one recent survey, about 8 percent of high schools offer elective Bible courses. Some schools, probably fewer, offer courses in world religions. Some scholars have argued for other courses that are essentially *introductions* to religion (paralleling introductory religion courses in universities). Yet others have argued for courses in philosophy, worldviews, or ethics, which take religions seriously. While most advocates of courses in religion argue that they should be elective, a few have argued that such courses are sufficiently important that they be required (perhaps a single high school course, perhaps with an excusal policy).

Critics of religion courses worry that such courses may have a religious agenda and be taught by teachers unqualified to teach them. This is a particular concern with Bible courses.

The Curriculum

Religious topics, controversies, and Big Questions may come up in any course. (Nel Noddings has proposed several that might relevantly be discussed in mathematics courses.) Indeed, the role of religion raises issues in history, literature, economics, and science courses, in moral education, and in Bible courses.

1. *History.* It is uncontroversial that history textbooks and courses should address religion. A series of studies have concluded that textbooks often slight religion, although there has been some incremental improvement over the past several decades. Of course, teachers may supplement the texts and standards, but they often are not prepared to do so or provided the resources they need. In any case, the shortcomings of the texts suggest some of the issues to consider in teaching history.

   First, the brief introductions to the world religions found in world history texts (three pages, on average) are not adequate for actually making sense of the religions. Second, religion largely disappears from both the world and U.S. history texts (and content standards) as students page past the seventeenth century, in part, at least, because social, political, and military history are thought more important than religious or cultural history. Third, the treatment of religion in the twentieth century focuses primarily on wars, conflict, and violence. According to one study, the five twentieth century religious topics receiving the most coverage in world and U.S. history texts are the following: the Holocaust; Islamic fundamentalism; religious conflict in the partition of India; anti-Semitism in turn of the century Europe; and Malcolm X and the Nation of Islam. Fourth, the texts pay little attention to theologians or religious thinkers over the past several centuries. They largely stop discussing Christianity with the Puritans, and freeze other religions into their classical forms, saying little about how they have developed intellectually and theologically, particularly in response to modernity. They almost completely ignore liberal theology and movements. Finally, all of the great Western religions teach religious interpretations of history, which are ignored in the texts (and standards). The conventional view of historical periodization, conceptions of historical causation, and interpretations of the *meaning* of history are exclusively secular and are never put into critical religious perspective. A reasonable conclusion is that we cannot rely on history texts and courses to give students any substantive understanding of religion, particularly in the modern world.

   It should be acknowledged that the intense pressure often put on textbook publishers by religious special-interest groups (as well as nonreligious special interest groups) makes both fairness and integrity challenging. One way to defuse some of these controversies is to acknowledge them in texts and in courses. We are long past the time when anyone could say that history texts should just teach "the facts." All history is interpretative and the interpretations are often controversial (though some interpretations are, no doubt, better than others).

2. *Literature.* Because literature is taught through primary sources—poems, plays, film, short stories, and novels—rather than narrative textbooks as in history, literature courses can give students a deeper understanding of religious traditions. Literature often addresses the Big Questions in imaginatively powerful ways, enabling students to get *inside* the hearts and minds of people in those traditions.

   No doubt because of this, literature can be controversial, not least on religious grounds. Particular literary texts have been challenged for advocating magic or witchcraft, New Age religion, or secular humanism. Teachers need to be sensitive to deep-felt religious objections to literature, and sometimes alternative reading assignments may be appropriate (though for constitutional reasons religious critics cannot be given a veto over the curriculum). Literature teachers also need to understand when classroom activities such as dramatizations and role-playing may be offensive within some traditions or cross the constitutional line and become religious activities.

   While anthologies that approach literature historically often include a good deal of religious literature (including, sometimes, Scripture) there is often little, if any, religious literature (or literature with religious themes) in anthologies that are organized thematically or in terms of genre, which focus primarily on the past several centuries. Arguably, it is important (for many of the reasons given above) to ensure that a variety of religious as well as secular literature is included in the literature curriculum. Teachers should be familiar enough with the religious contexts and interpretations of novels, stories, and poems to draw out their religious (or antireligious) meaning and significance.

A particularly important question is whether to include some study of the Bible in high school literature courses. Many would say it should be included; after all, the Bible is the most influential book in history and its influence on literature has been immense. It is, however, challenging to deal with literature that also serves as Scripture within a religious tradition, for there will inevitably be contending interpretations of such literature, they will often be controversial, and they will be passionately held. At the least, teachers need to be sensitive to various religious as well as secular interpretations of the Bible, and this requires considerable sophistication.

3. *Economics.* There have been no public controversies over religion and economics in the curriculum, although the national economic standards and economics textbooks ignore religion. They also largely ignore morality, moral controversies, and matters of justice. Why? Because both the standards and the texts hold that economics is a *value-free social science.* Within the framework of the *neoclassical economic theory* that shapes the standards and the texts, persons are essentially self-interested social atoms with unlimited wants, who compete for limited resources. Moral values are subjective preferences, and value judgments are matters of cost-benefit analysis. It is hard to reconcile this with any religious view of human nature and the economic domain of life.

The economics texts and standards provide a good deal of economic information and analysis relevant to moral problems and questions of justice, but they provide no moral context—political, philosophical, or religious—for assessing various economic and policy alternatives. They are unlikely to say anything about moral and spiritual problems relating to poverty, justice, consumerism, charity, work, the environment, individualism, or the meaning of our lives.

A few critics have argued that virtually all of the reasons mentioned above for including religion in the curriculum apply to economics texts and courses. Unless we have a very narrow view of the economic domain of life we will recognize that we cannot divorce economic from moral, philosophical, and religious questions having to do with ethics, human nature, work, and public policy. Arguably, to fail to include religious perspectives on these Big Questions is to make critical thinking all but impossible.

4. *Science.* Over the past several decades a new science/religion dialogue has led to a great deal of interdisciplinary discussion among scholars about areas in which science and religion make overlapping claims, their respective limitations, methodological and philosophical naturalism, disciplinary conflicts and tensions, and ways in which science and religion might be integrated. In addition to these controversies, a short list of topics in the new science/religion discussion would include the following: the Big Bang; cosmological fine-tuning; the origins of life; biological evolution; the origins of consciousness (and whether it makes sense to talk of a soul); determinism and free will; the evolutionary origins of altruism, morality, and religion; the nature, causes, and extent of our environmental crisis and responses to it; the relationship of prayer and spirituality to health and healing; the technological ethos of modern culture; and a cluster of moral and religious questions (some having to do with what it means to be a person) that revolve around embryonic stem-cell research, cloning, germ-line genetic engineering, nanotechnology, and robotics. This is an area of lively discussion that goes well beyond the old culture wars over evolution.

Most of these issues are not discussed anywhere in the curriculum, although some of them are clearly related to the Big Questions, while others are caught up in important moral and policy debates. The science establishment has usually held that any discussion of religion should take place elsewhere in the curriculum than science courses, which should be reserved for teaching science. (Of course, students are likely to learn little, if anything, about the relationship of science and religion elsewhere in the curriculum.) Studies have shown that many science texts say nothing about religion, while others may devote several paragraphs to explaining that science and religion have nothing to do with each other (a controversial position). Biology texts may acknowledge the controversy over evolution, but usually without providing any context for understanding it.

The *National Science Education Standards* say nothing about religion, but they do require that science courses address social and personal issues (the seventh content standard) and that science should be taught in historical perspective (the eighth content standard). Arguably, it is hard to do either apart from some consideration of religion. Some critics have argued that science texts and courses should provide historical, cultural, and philosophical context for thinking about science (perhaps by way of introductory chapters in textbooks). If this is done, some substantive discussion of the relationship of science and religion, and controversies that have a religious dimension, should be included.

The Supreme Court has ruled on religion and science courses twice: it held that schools cannot ban evolution from the curriculum (*Epperson v. Arkansas,* 1968) or require the teaching of religion in science courses on the pretension that it is science (*Edwards v. Aguillard,* 1987). In both cases the Court discerned a religious *purpose* behind the relevant state laws; they were not religiously *neutral.*

There would appear to be no constitutional reason, however, why science courses cannot teach *about* religion, perhaps in the context of providing historical and cultural perspective for the fully secular purpose of providing a good liberal education, just as this can be done in secular history or literature courses. Some scholars have gone further, arguing (more controversially) that *neutrality between religion and nonreligion* requires that when there are deep disagreements about how to interpret nature, or controversies over the relationship of science and religion, students must at least be introduced to the controversies.

If religious interpretations of nature and controversial issues are to be discussed, courses and curricula cannot privilege conservative or fundamentalist Christianity. Schools must be neutral among religions, and a variety of religious views must be included. Of course, as the new science/religion dialogues makes clear, there are more than two positions (science and biblical creationism) on all the major issues; in fact, there are *many* positions and dealing with them adequately requires some sophistication. The politics of our culture wars have focused almost entirely on evolution, however, and have so polarized public understanding that it is difficult to consider what is at issue educationally, much less find common ground.

5. *Moral Education.* There are a variety of ways in which the curriculum addresses moral education—and a variety of ways in which religion may be relevant to moral education. They include:

Character Education. Because of concerns about controversy, character education programs typically ignore religion. Some critics have argued, however, that religious stories and history must be included if character education is not to be superficial or convey the deeply controversial idea that character and morality are independent of religion.

History and Literature Courses. These courses locate students in traditions, particularly in the narratives of American history or Western Civilization that shape their moral identities and values. The plot lines of those narratives are informed, in part, by religion. Critics of the traditional Western canon have argued that this can be a conservative, even oppressive, educational practice. Of course, students can also be located in a multicultural anthology of narratives (a more liberal view). On either view, leaving religion out of these narratives will be illiberal and, almost certainly, bad history.

Moral Controversies. Many courses—in social studies, literature, economics, and sex education—address moral controversies. Arguably, religious voices, positions, and texts should be included in the discussion if schools are to encourage critical thinking and avoid privileging secular views. Too often economics and sex education courses avoid overt discussion of moral controversies (such as abortion or homosexuality), particularly when they involve religion.

Meaning. Literature courses more than any enable students to think deeply about their values and the meaning of their lives, by addressing moral and existential issues (often the Big Questions) in imaginative and emotionally powerful ways. But teachers in all courses (including science courses) should be sensitive to the Big Questions relating to their subjects, and the context they provide students for thinking about their values and how they make sense of their lives.

Ethics Courses. Some scholars have argued that students should be required (or least have the opportunity) to take a course in ethics or moral philosophy that provides substantive context for assessing and critiquing the moral dimension of lives and culture. It is striking that for all of the importance we attach to morality, we require no serious, systematic study of it. Any such course should include religious texts and perspectives.

6. *Bible Courses.* As the Supreme Court has made clear, the purpose of studying the Bible cannot be *religious or devotional* (as some parents would like) but there are also secular reasons for studying the Bible. It is hard to understand Western history, art, literature, and culture without some understanding of it; and many people believe that understanding the Bible is critical to understanding (or providing critical perspective on) morality and the Big Questions. It is almost certainly the most influential book in all of history.

Should schools offer elective Bible *courses?* There are two reasons commonly given for not doing so: such courses may privilege Christianity; and they are extremely difficult to teach well. Offering *complementary* courses in world religions may address the first concern. The second is more problematic without some broadly acceptable way of certifying teachers in the field. There is a good deal of suspicion that many existing Bible courses are little more than glorified Sunday school courses that would be found unconstitutional if challenged.

It is essential that Bible courses be neutral (an admittedly difficult task), that they not privilege a particular religious tradition. Fortunately, there is a widely endorsed, common ground statement, *The Bible and Public Schools* (1999), which offers helpful guidelines. Different religious traditions and denominations have different Bibles and favor different translations; these differences must be respected so that no particular religion is privileged. More important, and more difficult, different traditions *interpret* the Bible in different ways, sometimes emphasizing different parts of the Bible; students must be made aware of the more important differences. (Just teaching the text is often viewed as a conservative Protestant approach to the Bible.) The common ground statement suggests that approaching the *Bible as history* is likely to prove problematic because claims about the Bible's historical accuracy are deeply controversial; it instead suggests approaching the *Bible as literature*—though as noted above, many religious traditions wish to read the Bible not *simply* as literature, but *theologically* as their tradition interprets it. (Teaching *about* theological interpretations of the Bible need not be unconstitutional so long as students are introduced to a variety of interpretations and none is privileged.) Clearly, teaching the Bible requires a great deal of sophistication.

Many scholars have argued that instead of Bible courses, schools should offer courses in world religions, which are less likely to privilege Christianity and are more likely to serve the broad purposes of a liberal education. Such courses might include some study of the Bible along with other Scriptures.

A possible limitation of Bible courses and world religions courses is that because they often focus on the historical context of the Bible and the classical form of the great world religions, they convey the idea that religion is a historical artifact rather than a living tradition. If one purpose of studying religion is to understand it as a *live* alternative for students, it is important to understand *contemporary* understandings of the Bible and world religions.

Teaching about Religion

How does a teacher teach about religion in ways that are constitutionally permissible and pedagogically sound? (For further discussion of some of these and other issues see the common ground document, *A Teachers Guide to Religion and Public Schools* (in *Finding Common Ground,* 2007.) Suggestions frequently offered include:

1. Teachers (and curriculum planners) must be sensitive to age appropriateness. While study of the Big Questions and religious controversies may be appropriate for high school students, the elementary school curriculum should be limited to developing a measure of factual literacy regarding religious holidays, symbols, practices, and history.

2. The First Amendment requires that teachers be *officially neutral;* they must not take sides in matters of religious controversy. Teachers should be wary of expressing their *personal* views, except with the most mature students who can distinguish between personal and official views.

3. Neutrality and liberal education both require that students be exposed to a diversity of views, especially when there are controversies. Sometimes diversity and neutrality are only possible in the curriculum as whole, not in a particular course. An American history or literature course will necessarily give much more attention to Christianity than to other religions, but the curriculum as a whole (including world history and literature courses) should give serious attention to other religious traditions.

4. Some scholars argue that *neutrality between religion and nonreligion* imposes an obligation to teach students about religions as a way of balancing or providing critical perspective on secular ways of thinking and living that are controversial. This is perhaps a matter more for curriculum planners than individual teachers, though teachers must be sensitive to secular approaches to their subject matter that are religiously controversial.

5. It is not enough to mention *facts* about religion as history texts typically do. To *understand* a religion (like any culture or worldview that may be foreign to students) requires imagination, and is helped immensely if students can get *inside* that religion or worldview by way of primary sources (literature, art, film, autobiographies) written or created *within* those traditions. This may be difficult or impossible given constraints of time and resources, but it remains the ideal (as in any humanities course).

6. It has sometimes been argued that if religion is to be taken seriously students must understand *contemporary* religions (or *live* religions), not just religion in distant historical contexts.

7. Teachers must be sophisticated enough about the religions they teach about to convey to students something of the internal complexity of different religions, avoiding simplistic generalizations and stereotypes. (After all, not all Christians agree; nor do all Muslims—or Jews or Buddhists or Hindus.) They must also recognize the great differences among religions and resist conveying any personal *theological* opinion that all religions are basically alike. Whether we all believe in the same God is controversial; indeed, it is not always appropriate to use the word "God" for what is ultimate or transcendent within a religious tradition. Or, to note another difference, most religions do not place the emphasis on doctrines and beliefs that Christianity does, but may emphasize ritual or tradition or religious experience much more.

8. Some scholars have argued that education should be a *conversation* rather than a series of *monologues,* particularly if critical thinking is to be possible. Teachers should encourage and help *mature* students to compare and contrast various religious and secular positions (while refraining from taking any position themselves).

9. Teachers must be sensitive to the beliefs of students (whether or not they are religious) as well as to their existential concerns, interests, and insecurities. If religion is to be discussed, it is critical to establish trust in the classroom, treat students with respect, and allow considerable latitude for student religious expression (while not allowing proselytizing or harassment).

10. If a (secondary school) teacher is to deal adequately with moral controversies, critical thinking, worldviews, and the Big Questions, the *role* of the teacher must be broadened beyond that of technician or disciplinary specialist. Teachers need to be sensitive to, and concerned and informed about, ways in which they can address cultural diversity, justice, morality, the public good, and concerns about how we find meaning in our lives; they need to be sensitive to, and informed about, interdisciplinary controversies and the Big Questions that cut across disciplines.

11. This requires that teachers themselves be *liberally educated*. Clearly, schools of education must give substantive attention to the role of religion in education (for administrators as well as for teachers). Some critics have argued that teachers should take at least one course in religious studies as it relates to their subject(s).

12. All schools should have religion policies that provide guidance and protection for teachers in dealing with potentially controversial material.

See also: *Abington School District v. Schempp* and *Murray v. Curlett;* The Bible in the Public Schools; Bible Literacy Project; Common Ground Documents; First Amendment Center; Haynes, Charles C.; Moral Education; National Council for the Social Studies; National Council on Bible Curriculum in Public Schools; Released Time for Religious Instruction; Science and Religion.

Further Reading: Ronald Anderson, *Religion and Spirituality in the Public School Curriculum* (New York: Peter Lang, 2004); Stephen Bates, *Battleground* (New York: Poseidon Press, 1993); James Frazer, *Between Church and State: Religion and Public Education in a Multicultural America* (New York: St. Martins, 1999); Barbara B. Gaddy et al., *School Wars: Resolving Our Conflicts Over Religion and Values* (San Francisco: Jossey-Bass, 1996); Perry Glanzer, "Taking the Tournament of Worldviews Seriously in Education," *Religion and Education,* 31 (Spring 2004); Kent Greenawalt, *Does God Belong in Public Schools?* (Princeton, NJ: Princeton University Press, 2005); Charles Haynes and Oliver Thomas, *Finding Common Ground: A Guide to Religious Liberty in Public Schools* (Nashville: First Amendment Center, 2007); Charles Kniker, "Religious Pluralism in the Public School Curriculum," in *Religion and Schooling in Contemporary America,* ed. Thomas C. Hunt and James C. Carper (New York: Garland Publishing, 1997); Martin Marty with Jonathan Moore, *Education, Religion, and the Common Good* (San Francisco: Jossey-Bass, 2000); Robert J. Nash, *Faith, Hype, and Clarity: Teaching About Religion in American Schools and Colleges* (New York: Teachers College Press, 1999); Warren A. Nord, *Religion and American Education: Rethinking a National Dilemma* (Chapel Hill, NC: The University of North Carolina Press, 1995); Warren A. Nord and Charles C. Haynes, *Taking Religion Seriously Across the Curriculum* (Alexandria, VA: ASCD, 1998); Steven Prothero, *Religious Literacy* (San Francisco: HarperSanFrancisco, 2007); James T. Sears with James C. Carper, eds., *Curriculum, Religion, and Public Education* (New York: Teachers College Press, 1998); Stephen Webb, *Taking Religion to School* (Grand Rapids, MI: Brazos Press, 2000).

Warren A. Nord

Religious Accommodation

Religious accommodation is a theory regarding the interaction between religion and government that advocates for government recognition or support of religious belief and practice. Religious accommodation usually occurs in the form of government exemption to religious individuals from state regulation that infringes upon or prohibits religious practice. Religious accommodation, however, has also come to mean a certain amount of government support of religious activities through funding of religious groups. Religious accommodation is grounded in the belief that the best and most historically consistent way to ensure religious liberty is by protecting and even encouraging religious belief and practice.

Supreme Court Justice William Douglas first promoted religious accommodation as a constitutional ideal in his *Zorach v. Clauson* (1952) decision. Having stated that Americans are a religious people by nature, Douglas argued that it is only appropriate that the government acknowledge and support that religiosity. While *Zorach* was the first time the Court acknowledged it formally, religious accommodation has been a recurring theme throughout U.S. history. Many religious activists at the time of the founding of the country advocated for the religious freedom articulated in the Constitution simply because it allowed for as much religious expression as possible. George Washington himself assured a group of Quakers that he wished to provide as much religious accommodation as the law would permit. While some founding fathers (such as James Madison) expressed anxiety at too much interaction between religion and government, it was commonly felt that the purpose of the Free Exercise Clause and the Establishment Clause was to further religious liberty (often in the form of accommodation).

With the 1940 application of the First Amendment to states, there was a sharp rise in religious liberty cases before the Supreme Court, particularly those in the realm of public and religious education. Individual free exercise accommodation saw its first great success in *West Virginia State Board of Education v. Barnette* (1943), which permitted Jehovah's Witnesses to refuse the flag salute. Cases such as this, however, were not without dissent. Opponents of religious accommodation believed that concerns of government establishment of religion should overrule the demands of the Free Exercise Clause, a stance often called "strict separation." The Court, however, maintained that free exercise principles could trump establishment concerns. It demonstrated this opinion through several cases that furthered free exercise via religious schools. These opinions allowed for various forms of federal aid to private schools, including subsidized bussing (*Everson v. Board of Education,* 1947), lending secular textbooks (*Board of Education v. Allen,* 1968), and even allowing religious training during the school day outside of the schools themselves (*Zorach v. Clauson,* 1952). Advocates of religious accommodation see this sort of establishment accommodation as a natural complement to free exercise accommodation.

Free exercise accommodation reached its own peak in the 1960s and 1970s with "strict scrutiny," a judicial test that demanded religious accommodation for free exercise claims barring any compelling state interest. *Wisconsin v. Yoder* (1972) set the highest standard of religious accommodation in public schools by permitting Amish parents to withdraw their students from mandatory schooling past the age of 16. Simultaneously, however, the theory of "strict separation" for establishment clause issues rose in popularity. Therefore, despite the liberal free exercise accommodation, establishment accommodation became a rarity. This era of strict separation produced several pivotal Supreme Court cases, including *Engel v. Vitale* (1962) that prohibited school-endorsed prayer, *Abington v. Schempp* (1963) that disallowed school endorsed Bible reading and recitation of the Lord's Prayer, *Epperson v. Arkansas* (1968) that overturned the law that prohibited teaching about evolution, and *Lemon v. Kurtzman* (1971) that banned government sponsored aid to religious schools in the form of purchasing textbooks, paying the salaries of secular teachers, and other forms of funding.

Strict separation receded once again in the early 1990s, however, which allowed for renewed establishment accommodation. *Agostini v. Felton* (1997) overturned previously decided *Aguilar v. Felton* (1985) and permitted federally funded social workers to aid disabled students in religious schools. Additionally, public schools were permitted to loan educational materials to religious institutions (*Mitchell v. Helms,* 2000). While separation language began to disappear from establishment clause decisions, the landmark *Employment Division v. Smith* (1990) rejected strict scrutiny in free exercise cases. In its place, the Court adopted a much less rigorous free exercise test, that of "general applicability."

General applicability determined that any neutral, generally applicable law must be followed by religious and nonreligious citizens alike, thus disallowing any special exemptions for religious belief. This case nearly obliterated accommodation as allowed by the Free Exercise Clause and has been highly criticized from both ends of the political spectrum.

These competing interpretations lead to a broader question about the nature of accommodation itself. Is it something required, or merely permitted by the Constitution? The "strict scrutiny" test used by the Supreme Court in evaluating free exercise claims lends itself to an understanding of mandated religious accommodation. Therefore, under this test, certain religious accommodations are required under the Constitution. "Permissive accommodations," on the other hand, ask what religious accommodations are allowed (but not required) by the Constitution. Permissive accommodations are much more controversial and highly debated as to their constitutionality. While a strong Free Exercise Clause would certainly permit such accommodations, the Establishment Clause very well may limit their enactment. The distinction between these two types of religious accommodation often raises issues regarding which governmental branch is responsible for defining the parameters of enactment. Should permissive accommodations be left to the legislative or executive branch of the government, leaving the judiciary to determine which accommodations are constitutionally mandated? Are judges required to grant permissive as well as mandated accommodations?

These various issues beg the very fundamental question: what is the purpose of religious accommodation? Accommodations granted to individuals and those to institutions have different implications. When an accommodation is granted to an individual, such as to a Jehovah's Witness regarding the flag salute, the purpose is to relieve that believer of some conflict between the demands of society and the demands of religious belief. Religious liberty is at risk if one must choose between a government mandate and a religious mandate. Individual accommodations can be denied, however, if they impose a substantial burden on the government or if they require compromising core values. Therefore, some religious claims will be stronger than others (claims of religiously mandated action as opposed to religiously motivated action) and some governmental claims will be stronger than others (such as the ability to promote multicultural ideals in public schools as opposed to disallowing individual students to opt out of particular lessons). Institutional accommodation, on the other hand, strives to grant as much institutional autonomy as constitutionally possible. When religious schools receive federal tax exemption, the purpose is to disengage government from religious entities. Religious schools that receive limited government funding, however, often must submit to certain government monitoring, which may limit religious autonomy. Therefore, accepting government aid means adhering to certain democratic ideals as outlined by the government. This was clearly seen when Bob Jones University (*Bob Jones University v. United States,* 1983) lost its tax-exempt status by forbidding interracial dating. Thus, the government attempts to allow space for religious organizations to operate, but they must maintain certain state ideals. Allowing for accommodation to religious institutions can both cause and mitigate church-state conflict depending on the circumstances.

Current jurisprudence allows for some accommodation while maintaining a certain amount of distance between church and state. This movement, generally called "neutrality," seeks to be a middle way for the Court. In cases regarding free exercise, accommodations are permitted when no generally applicable law would be compromised in the execution of free exercise liberties. If nonreligious exemptions to the law are granted, however, religious exemptions are required as well. In establishment cases regarding funding, government aid is permitted for religious schools so long as it is nonpreferentially given and used for a secular purpose. In this way, religious groups are given "equal access" to public funds. This accommodation, now termed "neutrality," allows for religious cooperation in delivering charity, education, and many other social services. Therefore, while "accommodation" is no longer a catchphrase used by the Court as in ages past, it has by no means disappeared from political practice. Rather, accommodation is used in a limited capacity. Certainly accommodation remains a powerful theory in discussing appropriate relations between church and state. *See also:* First Amendment Religious Clauses and the Supreme Court; Jefferson, Thomas; Madison, James; Separation of Church and State/Wall of Separation between Church and State.

Further Reading: *Abington School District v. Schempp,* 374 U.S. 203 (1963); *Agostini v. Felton,* 521 U.S. 203 (1997); *Board of Education v. Allen,* 392 U.S. 236 (1968); *Bob Jones University v. United States,* 461 U.S. 574 (1983); *Employment Division v. Smith,* 494 U.S. 872 (1990); *Engel v. Vitale,* 370 U.S. 421 (1962); *Epperson v. Arkansas,* 393 U.S. 97 (1968); *Everson v. Board of Education,* 330 U.S. 1 (1947); *Lemon v. Kurtzman,* 403 U.S. 602 (1971); Ira C. Lupu, "The Trouble with Accommodation," *George Washington Law Review* 60 (March 1992): 743–781; Michael McConnell, "Accommodation of Religion," *Supreme Court Review* 1 (1985): 1–59; *Mitchell v. Helms,* 530 U.S. 793 (2000); *West Virginia State Board of Education v. Barnette,* 319 U.S. 624 (1943); *Wisconsin v. Yoder,* 406 U.S. 205 (1972); John Witte, *Religion and the American Constitutional Experiment,* 2nd ed. (Boulder, CO: Westview Press, 2005); *Zorach v. Clauson,* 343 U.S. 306 (1952).

Mary Ellen Giess and Diane L. Moore

Religious Holidays

The treatment of religious holidays in public schools, especially in December, has been a perennial source of conflict in many school districts during the decades following the U.S. Supreme Court decisions prohibiting school-sponsored religious practices in the early 1960s. These fights have become so common that they are sometimes referred to as the "December dilemma."

The vast majority of public schools ended the practice of teacher-led prayer and devotional Bible reading after the Court's decisions in *Engel v. Vitale* (1962) and *Abington v. Schempp* (1963). At the same time, however, many have continued their long-standing tradition of celebrating the Christmas holiday with assembly programs and other activities in the month of December. Most of these programs reflect the Christian faith of the majority, with a mixture of the explicitly religious (e.g., Christmas carols, Nativity scenes) with the secular (e.g., "Jingle Bells," "Frosty the Snowman"). Some schools go further and hold assembly programs with such elements as Nativity reenactments and candle-lighting ceremonies during the singing of sacred music. Until recently, most attempts to balance programs with music or symbols from other traditions have been mostly limited to brief references to Hanukkah.

The Supreme Court has not issued a definitive ruling on religious holidays in public schools. The Court has, however, let stand a federal appeals court decision stating that schools may recognize religious holidays as long as the purpose is to educate students about the holiday and not to promote religion (*Florey v. Sioux Falls School District,*

1980). This ruling is consistent with *Schempp* and other Supreme Court decisions that draw a sharp distinction between school officials promoting religion, which is unconstitutional, and objective teaching about religion, which is not.

The widespread confusion and conflict over December programs in the 1970s and 1980s led a broad coalition of religious, civil liberties, and educational groups to draft consensus guidelines on how to address religious holidays in schools. After four months of negotiation, the coalition published "Religious Holidays in the Public Schools: Questions and Answers" in 1989. Among the 17 sponsors were the Christian Legal Society, the American Jewish Congress, the National Association of Evangelicals, the Islamic Society of North America, the National School Boards Association, and the National Education Association.

The guidelines endorse study about religious holidays in schools as part of the academic program throughout the school year. This would include the use of religious symbols as teaching aids during the lessons on the holidays of the world's religions and the use of art, music, drama, or literature with religious themes as part of educating students about the meaning of the holidays.

On the question of what to do in December, the guidelines recommend creating holiday programs that have an educational purpose and do not make students feel excluded or identified with a religion not their own. This would mean, for example, holiday concerts with a balanced program that included both sacred and secular music from a variety of traditions and cultures. The document cautions against reenactments of sacred events such as Nativity pageants or plays portraying the Hanukkah miracle.

The guidelines also address other issues related to religious holidays in school. Schools are advised to adopt policies that allow students to be excused from holiday-related activities or discussions as long as the request is limited and may be reasonably accommodated. Such excusals, however, do not license the school to sponsor unconstitutional religious celebrations. The guidelines also recommend policies that give students a reasonable number of excused absences, without penalties, to observe their religious holidays. A growing number of schools have developed policies and practices that reflect a commitment to accommodate religious requirements of a diverse population of students.

The consensus guidelines endorsed by national organizations in 1988 together with the 1995 guidance from the U.S. Department of Education have helped many school districts avoid conflict and find common ground by integrating the study of world religions, including religious holidays, into the curriculum at various times of the year. Many other public schools, however, continue to fight over December programs. Some attempt to ban all mention of the religious meaning of Christmas and focus on the secular Christmas. Others continue to find ways to celebrate Christmas with religious overtones. And still others attempt to avoid the problem by celebrating "winter break" with little or no reference to Christmas, religious or secular. This latter approach helped trigger a national debate in 2004 and 2005 over what some conservative Christian groups have called the "war on Christmas."

Public schools that have successfully gone beyond this conflict plan educational programs in December that include religious and nonreligious elements of the holiday season. They tend to move away from Santa Claus and Christmas trees throughout the school (recognizing that many non-Christians see these as religious, not secular) and move toward decorating the school with student artwork and other material related to the curriculum. Most importantly, these schools invite representatives of diverse constituencies in the local community to help develop policies and practices that teach about religious holidays without school promotion of religion. *See also:* Common Ground Documents; U.S. Department of Education Guidelines on Religion and Public Education.

Further Reading: *Engel v. Vitale,* 370 U.S. 421 (1962); *Florey v. Sioux Falls School District 49-5,* 619 F.2d 1311 (8th Cir.), *cert. denied,* 449 U.S. 987 (1980); John Gibson, *The War on Christmas* (New York: Sentinel, 2005); Charles C. Haynes and Oliver Thomas, *Finding Common Ground: A First Amendment Guide to Religion and Public Schools* (Nashville: First Amendment Center, 2007); Warren A. Nord and Charles C. Haynes, *Taking Religion Seriously Across the Curriculum* (Alexandria, VA: ASCD, 1998).

Charles C. Haynes

Religious Orders

Religious orders or communities are free associations of adult men and women who choose to live a life founded on religious values or charisms, shared in common with others who hold similar beliefs. The men and women committed to such a lifestyle often take vows or promises, solemn and public declarations of commitment to this freely chosen way of life. Often known as vowed religious or religious men and women, these individuals constitute the membership of religious communities or orders. "Orders" in this sense refers to the organizing principle of the community, not to any commands or dictates. Religious orders are communities of people who have voluntarily agreed to live a common life and accept a common rule for that life.

In the Roman Catholic tradition, such religious orders comprise the major form of consecrated life in the church, a public, official, and stable way of living a Christian life, responding to the demands of the Christian Gospel and the example of Jesus Christ, and doing so in a defined and regulated way. Most religious orders are organizations of laity and clergy who work together in common ministries, share human and fiscal resources, and follow a specified rule for their common life under the direction of a religious superior. Each order typically has its own standards and procedures for the general organization of a daily common life, but nearly all orders require promises or vows of chastity, poverty, and obedience. These three vows, commonly known as the evangelical counsels, are considered to be Gospel-inspired and form the basis of a radical and often difficult embrace of the example of Jesus in living a life directed to the love of God and neighbor.

Religious orders are governed by the universal law of the Roman Catholic Church, known as the *Code of Canon Law* (Canon Law Society of America, 1983), in addition to the specific requirements of each particular community or order. Canons 573–746 discuss religious institutes, the proper canonical term for such communities. In general, the law recognizes two types of orders: congregations, whose members take simple vows; and orders proper, whose members take solemn vows. The difference between such vows is usually related to how the individual lives the vow of poverty. In simple vows, an individual may continue to own and possess personal, material goods, but typically yields their care and administration to the religious superior. In solemn vows, the individual formally renounces personal ownership of any material goods, ceding all to the religious community.

Some confusion is often evident in the names and governance structures of individual orders. Because how a sister or nun possesses material goods is not always publicly evident, the difference between those in simple and solemn vows is not widely known. A common, colloquial expression is the simple equation of religious sisters and nuns. Most texts and people, even those in such communities, often use the term "sister" and "nun" interchangeably. Technically, nuns are religious women who profess solemn rather than simple vows.

The Official Catholic Directory (2006) lists over 250 religious orders or communities, including their date of foundation, current membership, and postnominal initials or acronym commonly used to identify members. It is standard practice across religious communities to use such abbreviations to indicate religious community of membership. Sisters of Saint Joseph, for example, might be abbreviated as S.S.J. and members of that community even called "SSJs." Religious Sisters of the Sacred Heart are abbreviated R.S.S.H. In many orders, the official name of the congregation or community is often rendered in Latin, the ancient language of the Roman Catholic Church, and the abbreviating initials then correspond to the official Latin name of the community, not the English translations. The Congregation of Missionaries of the Most Precious Blood is officially the *Congregatio Missionariorum Preziosissimi Sanguinis,* abbreviated C.P.P.S. The Congregation of Holy Cross is officially the *Congregatio Sanctae Crucis* and is rendered C.S.C.

Religious Orders of Women

Research is unanimous in affirming the contribution of religious orders of women to the establishment, growth, and success of Catholic schools in the United States (Hunt, Joseph, and Nuzzi, 2004). Tens of thousands of vowed women religious, from hundreds of different congregations and communities, staffed Catholic schools, served as administrators and teaching faculty, and supplied a steady stream of human resources to enable Catholic schools to grow quickly, without the need for raising money to cover operating expenses. Religious orders of women, vowed to poverty, required little more than basic human sustenance, a place to stay, and a few meals, and provided valuable educational services in the schools and parishes.

Many of these orders were founded and based in Europe, so many of the sisters and nuns who came to the United States entered as missionaries, seeking to help evangelize the new world, avoid religious persecution, or simply find a better life. They were often drawn to service with the immigrant poor, establishing schools for the waves of ethnic immigrants from Europe. Others responded to needs they found in the United States, opting to serve Native American children or African American students. The first religious community for women established in the United States was the Sisters of Charity. Founded by Elizabeth Ann Seton in Baltimore in 1808, the community quickly opened a boarding school with the explicit purpose of using it to raise funds for a free school to educate the poor. Religious women, however, were already involved in Catholic education. Ursuline nuns, arriving from France, established a Catholic school in New Orleans as early as 1727, and progressively added an academy for girls, a free school for Native Americans, an orphanage, and a hospital.

Religious Orders of Men

Though not nearly as numerous as the religious orders of women, many religious communities of men worked alongside the sisters and nuns in Catholic educational settings, contributing to the birth, growth, and success of Catholic schools. Unlike the communities of women, nearly all of the men's communities were of European origin, sending members to the United States as a normal part of their missionary activity, in response to an invitation from an American bishop, or simply to flee religious persecution. Among the earliest arrivers were Spanish Franciscan Friars in 1493, Dominican Friars in 1526, and French Jesuits in 1632. Augustinian Friars came to the United States in 1796. The first group of religious brothers to come to the United States was the Brothers of Holy Cross in 1841. Around the same time Edward Sorin led a small group of Holy Cross religious to Indiana, where they established the University of Notre Dame. Christian Brothers, a French community founded by John Baptist De La Salle, came in 1846. Priests and brothers from the Society of Marianists came to Cincinnati in 1849 and eventually established the University of Dayton.

The Society of Jesus (Jesuits) played an instrumental role in establishing many universities and high schools, or in staffing already existing institutions. Among institutions with Jesuit roots are universities such as Georgetown, Saint Louis, Xavier, Fordham, and Marquette.

In providing a living witness of faith and a lifestyle that publicly affirms biblical and Gospel values, religious orders of men and women made a unique and indispensable contribution to the growth of Catholicism and Catholic education in the United States. Although recent trends have shown significant declines in the numbers of members and the general aging of the population of vowed religious, thousands of men and women still embrace this lifestyle freely as a way to respond to a personal, inner call to serve God by serving others. Most communities have designed programs for affiliates or associate members who, although they may not take the vows or live in the community, wish to help perpetuate the charisms of a community in a particular school or parish. *See also:* Catholic Schools.

Further Reading: Harold A. Buetow, *Of Singular Benefit: The Story of U.S. Catholic Education* (New York: Macmillan, 1970); Canon Law Society of America, *The Code of Canon Law* (Washington, DC: Canon Law Society of America, 1983); Carol K. Coburn and Martha Smith, *Spirited Lives: How Nuns Shaped Catholic Culture and American Life, 1836–1920* (Chapel Hill, NC: University of North Carolina Press, 1999); Silvia Evangelisti, *Nuns: A History of Convent Life* (New York: Oxford University Press, 2007); Thomas C. Hunt, Ellis A. Joseph, and Ronald J. Nuzzi, eds., *Catholic Schools in the United States: An Encyclopedia* (Westport, CT: Greenwood Press, 2004); *The Official Catholic Directory 2006* (New Providence, NJ: P.J. Kenedy & Sons, 2006); David Snowdon, *Aging With Grace: What the Nun Study Teaches Us About Leading Longer, Healthier, & More Meaningful Live* (New York: Bantam Books, 2001).

Ronald J. Nuzzi

Religious Studies in Secondary Schools

Religious Studies in Secondary Schools (RSiSS) is a loose-knit coalition of secondary school teachers of religions who, as is stated on the association's Web site (Religious Studies in the Secondary Schools, at www.rsiss.net), are committed to the idea that education is not complete without the academic study of the world's religious traditions and the ethical values, literatures, and cultures so inextricably linked to them.

The organization came into being in the late 1990s under the leadership of Tom Collins, who at the time was a religion teacher in Louisville, Kentucky, and David Streight, a religion teacher in Portland, Oregon. For two or three years prior to formal organization, Collins had been organizing seminars for his colleagues from across the nation, to study important religious texts with nationally recognized scholars. RSiSS came into being in part because the founders were independent schoolteachers at a time when the only national organization to address issues of teaching about other religious traditions with independent schools, the Council for Spiritual and Ethical Education (CSEE), was not paying sufficient attention to the teaching of "world religions." One of the RSiSS founders later became executive director of that organization.

RSiSS formed an early coalition with the Forum on Religion and Ecology (FORE), and, in addition to recommending religious studies resources for both classroom use and general teacher growth, the Web site focused on resources relating to the FORE mission, primarily nature writing and environmental concerns. Since its beginning, RSiSS existed solely through volunteer help. For a few early years, RSiSS published an online journal of "exemplary student writing" and worked to build up a bank of syllabi for use by other teachers. The student journal fell by the wayside when a volunteer editor could not be found to continue oversight of the publication. The syllabus project has continued to grow only slowly, as have other parts of the association.

In 2005, all RSiSS conferences began to be organized by CSEE (the Web site continued to be maintained by an RSiSS volunteer), through the assistance of paid CSEE staff that greatly facilitated the organization of conferences. The two associations work closely together in all areas where their missions overlap, although there are no plans for a complete merger because of the fundamental differences in their natures—one being a coalition of individuals, including public schoolteachers, and one being a school membership organization. *See also:* Council for Spiritual and Ethical Education.

Further Reading: Religious Studies in Secondary Schools, at www.rsiss.net; David Streight, "Secondary School Teacher Training in Religious Studies: Their Key Role in Interreligious Youth Education, in *Building the Interfaith Youth Movement,* ed. Eboo Patel and Patrice Brodeur (Lanham, MD: Rowman & Littlefield, 2006).

David Streight

Ruffner, William Henry

William Henry Ruffner (1824–1908) was selected as the first superintendent of public education in the Commonwealth of Virginia by the state legislature in 1870. He was an advocate of public, free schooling for all people and was tasked with creating a plan for public schooling in Virginia, which he did with the help of several influential politicians and educators of the day, including William McGuffey. Ruffner worked tirelessly, traveling throughout the Commonwealth for 12 years before resigning in 1882 over the issue of public school funding.

Ruffner's tenure as superintendent served as the culmination of several previous efforts to establish a public school system in Virginia. Thomas Jefferson (also founder of the University of Virginia) advocated for more local control of public schools in the late 1700s and early 1800s, while Charles Mercer wanted the state more directly involved in the control of schools. Ruffner's father himself in the 1840s also worked to establish public schools in Virginia, though the issue was soon eclipsed by the mounting tensions that resulted in the Civil War.

In July 1870, the governor of the Commonwealth, Gilbert C. Walker, signed a bill to establish public schools in Virginia. This bill met with strong contention from those who feared the law would put schools *in loco parentis;* parents were deemed to be the chief educators of their children by the will of God, and by replacing the parents with the governments, God was in essence being replaced by the state. Parental liberty was also feared lost at the invocation of public schools.

Ruffner, himself an ordained Presbyterian minister and former geologist, clashed with the Reverend Robert Lewis Dabney, who was also a critic of the public school system. Dabney desired Christian teachers in the classroom, as well as for the parents to assume the principal responsibility for educating their children. He felt that the church and the state should take more muted roles in education, the state protecting the influence of parents as primary educators as opposed to replacing the parents as primary educator. Most public school critics, in fact, asserted that true education should be Christian in nature and that the state, which was secular, was unable to educate accordingly. Ruffner shared the Jeffersonian view of education in that in order for democracy to be preserved, all people must be educated equally—and the church and family alone were not equipped to achieve that. Ruffner asserted that the public school system was moral, and Christian, but not sectarian in nature—in fact, a common school.

A common school accompanied the notion of common religion. According to Ruffner, a common religion that recognized God without offense and service to any one faith would be present in all public schools, and would serve to teach all children ethics, good citizenship, and good behavior and would elevate the schools—and all children in them—to a higher moral standard. Further, public schools, by promoting universal literacy, were instrumental in all people being able to read the Bible.

The support of public schools and their morality were sources of constant debate during Ruffner's tenure as superintendent. These dialogues centered not just around the questionably just nature of taxing for the education of both blacks and whites (albeit in separate schools), but also that public schools must be secular—and hence, immoral by their very nature. Ruffner's response was that in a democracy, all members should be educated and to deny this would be immoral in and of itself.

While holding to the belief that blacks and whites needed to be in segregated environments (because he believed that southern whites would not accept black freedmen), Ruffner rejected the idea that blacks were somehow intellectually inferior to whites. He asserted, however, that to educate blacks would increase the efficiency of labor, reduce crime, and reduce poverty among them. To educate its citizens would certainly lead to the advancement of the Commonwealth of Virginia, and time would ultimately erase the notion that blacks were intellectually, morally, and culturally inferior to whites.

What ultimately led to Ruffner's resignation was the financial struggle of the state following the Civil War. A substantial war debt of $45 million remained, while Ruffner continued to press the legislature for funding, though wishing to keep education free of politics. As those who maintained that the war debt should be readjusted as opposed to being paid in full came to dominate the legislature, Ruffner and many local superintendents resigned in 1882. From that point on, state politics and public education were interwoven.

After an eventful tenure as superintendent, Ruffner returned to farming and geological surveying. He then served as president of the State Female Seminary, now Longwood College, for three years, prior to retiring in 1887. He later died in 1908. *See also:* Common School; Dabney, Robert L.

Further Reading: Charles W. Dabney, *Universal Education in the South* (Chapel Hill: University of North Carolina Press, 1936); Walter J. Fraser, Jr., "William Henry Ruffner and the

Establishment of Virginia's Public School System, 1870–1874," *Virginia Magazine of History and Biography* 79 (July 1971): 259–279; Thomas C. Hunt and Jennings L. Wagoner, Jr., "Race, Religion, and Redemption: William Henry Ruffner and the Moral Foundations of Education in Virginia," *American Presbyterians: Journal of Presbyterian History* 66 (Spring 1987): 1–9.

Staci L. H. Ramsey

Rutherford Institute

The Rutherford Institute is a nonprofit legal advocacy organization that was founded in 1982 by attorney John W. Whitehead (b. 1946), a graduate of the University of Arkansas (B.A., 1969; J.D., 1974). It takes its name from the Scottish Presbyterian theologian, Samuel Rutherford (1600–1661), who authored *Lex, Rex* (1644), in which he argued that law is king and that therefore no king is above the law.

The purpose of the Rutherford Institute (RI) is to offer pro bonum legal services to those who believe that their civil liberties have been violated. RI is one of several legal advocacy groups formed in the 1980s and 1990s associated with the Religious Right and its interest in challenging what its constituencies believe was a growing hostility to religious speech and practice in public institutions, especially public schools and colleges.

Whitehead's 1978 article (coauthored with John B. Conlan) in the *Texas Tech Law Review*—"The Establishment of the Religion of Secular Humanism and Its First Amendment Implications"—suggested an innovative legal strategy for religious conservatives: because practitioners of nontheistic worldviews, such as secular humanism, have been afforded by the federal courts the protections of the First Amendment's free exercise clause, should not government policies that seem to advance the cause of secular humanism be held to the same establishment clause scrutiny as those policies that seem formed by traditional theistic understandings? That is, would not the Supreme Court's commitment to a religiously neutral reading of the First Amendment require that it treat secular humanism as it would traditional religious alternatives?

Although the establishment clause application of this 1978 article has made little headway in the courts, Whitehead's reasoning has significantly shaped free exercise jurisprudence. Culturally, it has had a tremendous influence on religious conservatives and how they perceive the public square. For example, in the abortion debate, virtually no religious conservatives find the pro-choice case remotely persuasive, that permitting women to choose abortion is a liberty that takes the government out of the picture. Rather, religious conservatives see the abortion liberty as a way for the government to force on all its citizens a secular understanding of human persons, that prenatal human beings are not full members of the moral community and ought to be protected by our laws.

Although RI's most well-known cases have involved religious liberty, it gained international notoriety in 1997 when it agreed to assist Paula Jones in her lawsuit against U.S. President William Jefferson Clinton. Jones had charged the president with sexual harassment, an incident she alleged occurred in 1991 while he was governor of Arkansas.

In addition to the Jones case, RI has been involved in many other important cases, mostly dealing with religion and public institutions (including educational ones). Among the most notable cases in which RI has participated is the U.S. Supreme Court case, *Good News Club v. Milford School District* (2001). In this case, RI represented the Good News

Club, a Christian youth group that had unsuccessfully applied to use public school facilities in Milford, New York. The group had planned to hold after-hours meetings on the school premises in which its members would, among other things, sing religious songs, read Scripture, and listen to religious lessons. Because the school building was used as a limited public forum for other organizations, the Supreme Court ruled that the district's decision was viewpoint discrimination and thus a violation of the group's free speech rights. In addition to Good News Club, RI has been involved in varying capacities in many state and federal court cases regarding public education.

The notion of "viewpoint discrimination," which is now a firm principle of religion clause jurisprudence, is the result of a strategy developed by RI and others that asks the courts to think of religious speech and practice as just another type of viewpoint—like "secular," "political," or "ideological"—that should not be marginalized just because it is religious. In this sense, a free exercise application of Whitehead's 1978 article has borne much fruit: if secular ideas and practices can be considered on par with religious ideas and practices for free exercise purposes, why can religious ideas and practices not be considered on par with secular ideas and practices for free speech and expression purposes?

Although it has aligned itself with causes associated with conservative Republicans (e.g., pro-life on abortion, establishment clause accommodationism), RI has not hesitated to criticize their policies on other issues. For example, Whitehead (with RI chief litigant counsel, Steven A. Alden) published an article critical of the U.S. Patriot Act, at the end of which they conclude, "If the American people accept a form of police statism in the name of a promise of personal security, that would be the greatest defeat imaginable." *See also: Good News Club v. Milford Central School;* Humanism and the Humanist Manifestos; Secularism.

Further Reading: Hans J. Hacker, *The Culture of Conservative Christian Litigation* (Lanham, MD: Rowman & Littlefield, 2005); The Rutherford Institute, at www.rutherford.org; John W. Whitehead, *The Rights of Religious Persons in Public Education,* rev. ed. (Wheaton, IL: Crossway Books, 1994); John W. Whitehead, *Slaying Dragons: The Truth Behind the Man Who Defended Paula Jones* (Nashville, TN: Thomas Nelson, 1999); John W. Whitehead and Steven H. Alden, "Forfeiting 'Enduring Freedom' for 'Homeland Security': A Constitutional Analysis of the U.S. Patriot Act and the Justice Department's Anti-Terrorism Initiatives," *American University Law Review* 51 (August 2002): 1083–1133; John W. Whitehead and John B. Conlan, "The Establishment of the Religion of Secular Humanism and Its First Amendment Implications," *Texas Tech Law Review* 10 (Winter 1978): 17–65.

Francis J. Beckwith

S

Santa Fe Independent School District v. Doe

This action was litigated over a period of time, due to the fact that the school board changed its policies each time its policy on prayer was challenged in court. The board would make a policy that was contingent upon the outcome of the case regarding previous policies. An example of this is the following: "The policy has chosen to permit students to deliver a brief invocation during the pre-game ceremonies or have varsity football games to solemnize the event, to promote good sportsmanship and student safety, and to establish the appropriate environment for completion." This policy provided the students would vote on whether to have an invocation, and if the vote is positive they vote again on who will deliver the invocation. The board policy then provided the following proviso: "If the District is enjoined by a court order from the enforcement of this policy, then and only then will the following policy automatically become the applicable policy of the school district." The second policy and the first were exactly the same except for the following provision that: "Any message and/or invocation delivered by a student must be nonsectarian and nonproselytizing." The addition of this last statement was apparently due to an earlier case involving another Santa Fe (Texas) School Board prayer policy saying that a graduation prayer was permissible provided "as long as the general thrust of the prayer is [student-initiated and] non-proselytizing."

Suit was filed by Mormon and Catholic students, alumni, and parents, over the various school policies that authorized school prayer in one form or another. The specific action was against the authorization of two student elections, the first [election] to determine if a prayer was to be given at football games and the second to select the student to deliver the prayer. The plaintiffs alleged the policy violated the Establishment Clause of the First Amendment.

In 2000, a divided U.S. Supreme Court ruled the policy violated the Constitution. The Court determined that the *Sante Fe* case was controlled by its previous school prayer decision *Lee v. Weisman* (1992). The Court stated: "In *Lee v. Weisman . . .*, we held that a prayer delivered by a rabbi at a middle school graduation ceremony violated [the Establishment] Clause.

Although this case [*Sante Fe*] involves student prayer at a different type of school function, our analysis is properly guided by the principles that we endorsed in *Lee*."

The Supreme Court quoted from *Weisman* and said,

> The principle that government may accommodate the free exercise of religion does not supersede the fundamental limitations imposed by the Establishment Clause. It is beyond dispute that, at a minimum, the Constitution guarantees that government may not coerce anyone to support or participate in religion or its exercise, or otherwise act in a way which "establishes a [state] religion or religious faith, or tends to do so."

The school district argued that this was student-led, therefore student-initiated, private speech. The Court maintained that the policy had the "imprint of the State" and therefore was unconstitutional. The school board policy mandated a statement invocation. The student election was to be held "upon [the] advice and direction of the high school principal." Since the invocation has the imprint of the school and appeared to be school sponsored, then all nonadherents in the audience feel that "they are outsiders, not full members of the political community, and an accompanying message to adherents that they are insiders, favored members of the political community."

The district also argued that the Court's *Lee* ruling regarding graduation prayer dealt with a practice in a setting that was more mandatory than a football game where students attended voluntarily. The board also said it was the students' choice and that football was an extracurricular activity. The Court said that the prayer was coercive whether at a football game or a graduation exercise. Some individuals were required to attend, such as cheerleaders, band members, and the football players. In some situations such as for band members, class credit was received and their attendance mandated. Also high school students feel social pressure to be involved and "adolescents are often susceptible to pressure from peers towards conformity, and that the influence is strongest in matters of social convention." The Court continued: "The Constitution moreover, demands that the school may not force this difficult choice upon these students for [i]t is a tenet of the First Amendment that the State cannot require one of its citizens to forfeit his or her rights and benefits as the price of resisting conformance to state-sponsored religious practice." In sum, the Court ruled that the district's policy violated the no establishment standard of the First Amendment. *See also: Lee v. Weisman.*

Further Reading: *Lee v. Weisman*, 505 U.S. 577 (1992); *Lynch v. Donnelly*, 465 U.S. 668 (1984); *Sante Fe Independent School District v. Doe*, 530 U.S. 290 (2000).

M. David Alexander

School Choice

Most parents in the United States engage in some form of choice of the schools that their children attend, typically by decisions about the community where they will live or by paying tuition for their children to attend private schools. Others find ways to manipulate the systems of school attendance zones and feeder patterns by which pupils are assigned to schools. In recent decades, however, public officials in the United States have begun to recognize that such parent choices should function within policies that promote equal opportunity.

The desirability of such a policy has been stated repeatedly in the various conventions protecting human rights. For example, the Universal Declaration of Human Rights (1948) states that "parents have a prior right to choose the kind of education that shall be given to their children" (Article 26, 3). According to the International Covenant on Economic, Social and Cultural Rights (1966):

> the States Parties to the present Covenant undertake to have respect for the liberty of parents ...to choose for their children schools, other than those established by public authorities, which conform to such minimum educational standards as may be laid down or approved by the State and to ensure the religious and moral education of their children in conformity with their own convictions. (Article 13, 3)

As this Covenant—ratified by the United States—recognizes, religious and moral concerns are the most frequent motivation for establishing and supporting (often sacrificially) nonpublic schools. These sacrifices are made not only by the parents, who pay tuition, but commonly by the staff who accept lower salaries, and by the religious organizations that subsidize schools. In the 2001–2002 school year, according to the National Center for Education Statistics, 83.1 percent of the pupils attending nonpublic schools in the United States were in schools with a religious character. Nearly half (47.1 percent) were in Catholic schools and more than one-quarter (28.5 percent) in schools of a generally evangelical Protestant character. The balance of the pupils were in liberal Protestant, Jewish, Islamic, and Greek Orthodox schools, with only one in six (16.9 percent) in schools with no religious identity.

Since the 1925 U.S. Supreme Court decision *Pierce v. Society of Sisters*, American law has protected the right to operate and to choose schools that are not part of the public system. Unlike in most other Western democracies, however, public funds have not generally been provided to support those parental choices. Parents in Australia, New Zealand, Canada, England, France, Sweden, Germany, and many other countries can send their children to faith-based schools at public expense, but this has not been the case in the United States, as a result of the restrictive interpretation of the First Amendment to the Constitution, which long prevailed, as well as of the lingering effects, in state laws and constitutions, of the prejudice against Catholic schools in the nineteenth century. In effect, local school systems have long enjoyed a monopoly of publicly funded (and thus free) schooling, resulting in a strong competitive advantage in comparison with nonpublic rivals, the great majority of which have a religious character, and permitting them to assign children to particular public schools on the basis of administrative convenience without concern for the preferences of parents.

This began to change in the 1960s. First, there was a flourishing of public alternative schools, responding to the demands of countercultural parents, or more commonly to serve youth who were not functioning well in the regular public schools. These were followed by public magnet schools, developed to promote racial integration through attracting racially mixed student populations on a voluntary basis. This was usually seen as a way to meet the requirements of court-ordered desegregation without the accompanying controversy of mandatory reassignments. In order to attract white parents to enroll their children in schools with a substantial proportion of black pupils, magnet schools were often given extra funding and were allowed to develop themes, like the arts or language immersion or career exploration, that were intended to be attractive. Though still lodged within public school systems, with all sorts of restrictions on personnel and curriculum, magnet schools frequently developed a distinctive character that showed that public schooling did not have to be monotonously uniform. They also began to develop the habit and expectation that parents could choose schools without changing residence or paying tuition. In some communities, beginning in Cambridge, Massachusetts, and spreading to several dozen cities nationwide, "controlled choice" policies were put in place abolishing all attendance zones and in effect making every school a magnet school.

By 1990, however, it had become apparent that magnet schools and controlled choice did not allow enough scope for real diversity and school-level autonomy. Beginning in Minnesota and soon spreading to 40 states, public charter schools became the most fundamental structural change in American education in more than a century. Although state laws differ, the fundamental pattern is that anyone may propose a charter school, spelling out in detail whom it will serve, how it will operate, and how its results will be assessed. If a charter—more than 4,000 so far—is granted by whatever body is authorized by the state legislation, the school operates as a publicly funded school under its own board or sponsoring organization. It may not discriminate in admissions, it must meet state educational standards, but otherwise it may function largely autonomously, subject only to producing the promised results. If it fails to do so after several years, the charter will usually be withdrawn, forcing it to close. Thus, with the freedom comes accountability for results of a sort not characteristic of regular public schools.

Charter schools have proved extremely popular with teachers (despite the opposition of the teacher unions) and with parents, to such extent, in fact, that they have proved a serious threat to faith-based schools. Most state charter school laws explicitly forbid charter schools to have a religious character, but the strong demand from parents for schooling consistent with their own deep convictions has begun to lead to a variety of accommodations. Lawrence Weinberg has explored in some detail the likely response of courts to various of these attempts to satisfy the desire of parents for schooling that reflects one or another faith tradition, concluding that:

> charter schools shift the balance of power in education away from the state and closer to parents.... One of the significant aspects of this shift is that it allows parents to create public schools that accommodate their religious beliefs. The Constitution, however, prevents parents from creating schools that endorse their religious beliefs. (Weinberg, 2007, p. 149)

That distinction between "accommodation" and "endorsement" is likely to remain central in decisions about the extent to which government can provide funding and other support to schools with any sort of religious character.

The forms of government policy best adapted to satisfying the demand of many parents for schooling with an explicitly religious character—as in most Western democracies—are vouchers and tax credits. Vouchers are certificates for a fixed tuition amount, issued to parents and used by them to "purchase" enrollment of their children at schools of their choice, public or nonpublic, faith-based or not. Since the decision about where the voucher will be spent is made by the parent, the U.S. Supreme Court held, in *Zelman v. Simmons-Harris* (2002), that:

> the program challenged here is a program of true private choice...and thus constitutional ...the Ohio program is neutral in all respects toward religion. It is part of a general and

multifaceted undertaking by the state of Ohio to provide educational opportunities to the children of a failed school district. It confers educational assistance directly to a broad class of individuals defined without reference to religion, i.e., any parent of a school-age child who resides in the Cleveland City School District. The program permits the participation of all schools within the district, religious or nonreligious. Adjacent public schools also may participate and have a financial incentive to do so. Program benefits are available to participating families on neutral terms, with no reference to religion. The only preference stated anywhere in the program is a preference for low-income families, who receive greater assistance and are given priority for admission at participating schools.

It is important to note that the Court did not find that parents have a *right* to public funding for their school choices, as in the case in the constitutions of a number of countries, so that it remains entirely up to state legislatures whether to adopt such programs; in addition, their consistency with state constitutional prohibitions of aid to religious schools has not been resolved, though various cases are moving forward on this point.

There are also dangers that a state could attach requirements to use of vouchers that would significantly reduce the autonomy of nonpublic schools accepting them. While this has not happened yet, it has led to support for the alternative of tuition tax credits, which would allow parents simply to deduct from their tax obligations all or part of the tuition paid for their children. The argument has been that this would leave less scope for government interference, though this may be overly optimistic given the history of the relationship of the Internal Revenue Service with religious organizations of all types.

Whatever the exact arrangements, it is evident that there is a steady trend in the United States toward recognizing that the right of parents to choose the schools that their children attend should, as in other free societies, be supported by public policies and funding. The pressing question now is whether, as has often occurred elsewhere, increased government support for the choices of parents will come with conditions that limit the real distinctiveness and distort the mission of the schools they choose.

As noted above, almost all Western democracies provide public funding for pupils to attend nonpublic schools selected by their parents. Unlike in the United States, where the religious character of most such schools has been a major legal barrier to such funding, it has been the primary reason for funding in most other countries. Typically, constitutions and laws provide guarantees for the consciences of parents in the form of school choice, without any reference to the arguments based on the merits of competition often advanced in the United States. The compromises that led to the creation of Canada in the 1850s, for example, included guarantees of schools for the Protestant minority in Quebec and the Catholic minority in Ontario, where there continues to be a publicly funded Catholic system of schools.

In the Netherlands and Flemish Belgium, two-thirds of the pupils attend nongovernment schools, mostly, though not exclusively, with a religious character, which are fully funded by government. By contrast, in England about a third of the local government schools have a religious character. In France, Spain, and Portugal, nongovernment schools, most of them Roman Catholic, operate under contracts with the government, which pays for the "secular" instruction while leaving the schools free to add religious instruction at the expense of parents. In Sweden, Chile, and parts of Italy, vouchers provide for part or most of the cost of tuition in nongovernment schools. Other variations on public support for schools chosen by parents exist in other countries (Glenn and

De Groof, 2004). *See also:* Government Aid to Religious Schools; *Mueller v. Allen;* Tuition Tax Credits; Vouchers; *Zelman v. Simmons-Harris.*

Further Reading: William Lowe Boyd and Herbert J. Walberg, eds., *Choice in Education: Potential and Problems* (Berkeley, CA: McCutchan, 1990); John E. Coons, "Intellectual Liberty and the Schools," *Journal of Law, Ethics and Public Policy* 1 (Spring 1985): 493–535; Alfred Fernandez and Siegfried Jenkner, eds., *International Declarations and Conventions on the Right to Education and the Freedom of Education* (Frankfurt am Main, Germany: Info3-Verlag, 1995); Milton Friedman, "The Role of Government in Education," in *Economics and the Public Interest,* ed. Robert A. Solow (New Brunswick, NJ: Rutgers University Press, 1955); Milton Friedman, *Capitalism and Freedom* (Chicago: University of Chicago Press, 1962); Varun Gauri, *School Choice in Chile: Two Decades of Educational Reform* (Pittsburgh: University of Pittsburgh Press, 1998); Charles L. Glenn, *Educational Freedom in Eastern Europe* (Washington, DC: Cato Institute, 1995); Charles L. Glenn, *The Ambiguous Embrace: Government and Faith-based Schools and Social Agencies* (Princeton, NJ: Princeton University Press, 2000); Charles L. Glenn and Jan De Groof, *Balancing Freedom, Autonomy, and Accountability in Education,* 3 vols. (Tilburg, The Netherlands: Wolf Legal Publishers, 2004); Frank-Ruediger Jach, *Schulverfassung und Bürgergesellschaft in Europa* (Berlin: Duncker & Humblot, 1999); Terry M. Moe, *Schools, Vouchers, and the American Public* (Washington, DC: The Brookings Institution, 2000); Paul E. Peterson and Bryan C. Hassel, eds., *Learning from School Choice* (Washington, DC: The Brookings Institution, 1998); Luisa Ribolzi, *Il sistema ingessato: autonomia, scelta e qualità nella scuola italiana* (Brescia, Italy: Editrice La Scuola, 1997); Stephen D. Sugarman and Frank R. Kemerer, eds., *School Choice and Social Controversy* (Washington, DC: The Brookings Institution, 1999); David Salisbury and James Tooley, *What Americans Can Learn from School Choice in Other Countries* (Washington, DC: Cato Institute, 2005); Lawrence D. Weinberg, *Religious Charter Schools: Legalities and Practicalities* (Charlotte, NC: Information Age, 2007); Alan Wolfe, ed., *School Choice: The Moral Debate* (Princeton, NJ: Princeton University Press, 2003).

Charles L. Glenn, Jr.

Science and Religion

The once commonplace notion that religion and science have been locked in mortal combat in an ongoing culture war has fallen into disrepute among most scholars. After all, most of the towering figures of the Scientific Revolution—Newton, Descartes, Galileo, Kepler, Copernicus, Harvey, Boyle—were deeply religious, and, at least until the latter part of the nineteenth century, the view was widespread that science and religion complemented each other. God had revealed himself in two texts: the Bible, of course; but also in the "text" of nature, which, as Galileo put it, God wrote in the language of mathematics.

This is not to say that there have not been occasional conflicts, the two nastiest of which have been over whether the Earth revolves around the Sun (a conflict that we have gotten past) and evolution (a conflict that is still very much with us). There is also, however, a continuing philosophical tension between science and religion, one that can be seen in debates regarding evolution. Many religious conservatives reject the macroevolution of species because it conflicts with the book of Genesis, read literally (though they may accept microevolution within a species). Because religious liberals do not insist on reading the Bible literally, they have accepted evolution as God's ways of creating persons. But many liberals have their own problem with the neo-Darwinian *mechanism* of evolutionary theory. If evolution is the result of natural selection acting on the random mutation and recombination of genes (neo-Darwinism is the synthesis of genetics with Darwin's theory of natural selection), that appears to make evolution a *purposeless* process, one that has no goal. Indeed, far from being the goal of evolution, human beings are, as the paleontologist Stephen Jay Gould once put it, only a minor species in the Age of Bacteria. Darwin himself was convinced that evolution has no goal or design.

Consequently, many scholars argue that the primary scientific challenge to religion is not so much particular scientific discoveries or theories (heliocentrism or evolution), but the replacement of *teleological* by *naturalistic* categories for understanding nature. Traditionally, nature was understood as the handiwork of God; it embodied God's *purposes;* it had a *telos,* a goal, a design, a purpose. But scientific method (what is often called *methodological naturalism*) prohibits any appeal to supernatural causes or to design or purpose or value (to what *ought-to-be*) in scientific explanations.

The Relationship of Science and Religion. There are four positions that are now commonly taken on the relationship of science and religion. First, there are those scientists and philosophers who, impressed with the success of science, believe that science will ultimately prove capable of providing a complete account of reality. When there are conflicts between science and religion, science trumps religion. We might call them *scientific naturalists,* and they are typically atheists.

Second, there are those theologians and believers who, because of their faith, hold that when they conflict, Scripture trumps science. So, for example, we can know evolution to be false because it conflicts with Genesis 1 (read literally). We may call them *fundamentalists* or *biblical creationists.* Advocates of the first two views tend to think of religion and science as caught up in a culture war.

There is a third view that has been common among scientists and more liberal theologians through much of the twentieth century. Science and religion cannot conflict because they make radically different kinds of claims. Science is about mechanics; religion is about meaning. Science asks: How? Religion asks: Why? Science is about nature; religion is about history and our relationship with God. On this view, science and religion are logically *incommensurable;* they are conceptual apples and oranges. Neither has any implications for the other; each is true in its own realm and can proceed independently of the other. (Clearly, theologians who take this view have not been biblical literalists.) This view, which has been called the *independence* or *two-worlds* view, was endorsed by the National Academy of Sciences in 1981. Stephen Jay Gould popularized it with the acronym NOMA or *nonoverlapping magisteria.*

There is an increasingly common fourth view, which we might call the *integrationist* view. Science and religion make claims about the *same* world—nature, the universe. Each has its own sources of knowledge, but each has only a *partial* understanding of reality so that it is essential to engage in interdisciplinary dialogue in order to develop a complete account of nature. Perhaps the fundamental problem is reconciling the religious idea of purpose and design in nature with the (purposeless) naturalism of modern science.

Over the past several decades a new *science/religion dialogue* has led to a great deal of interdisciplinary discussion of areas in which science and religion make overlapping claims, their respective limitations, and ways in which they might be integrated. This massive new wave of interest and research into the relationship of science and religion has led to hundreds of books, major interdisciplinary conferences, and new academic courses. This is an area of lively scholarly debate that goes well beyond the old conflicts over evolution. A short list of topics in the science/religion dialogue would include the following:

Before the Big Bang. There is a good deal of highly theoretical speculation among cosmologists about what, if anything, came before the "big bang." One possibility is an infinite series of big bangs each followed by a "big crunch." Could God have created the universe through the big bang? Many theologians argue that God's creation is not in time; rather God sustains the universe through all time and continues to create (perhaps through evolution). Still, there is a fascinating question here with religious significance. Is the existence of the universe just a brute fact or is some kind of religious explanation required?

Cosmological Fine-Tuning. Over the past several decades cosmologists have become aware of a variety of ways in which the physical constants and laws of nature appear to be *fine-tuned* to be *exactly* what they must be if there is to be life in the universe. Some cosmologists, philosophers, and theologians find in these remarkable coincidences an argument for God's existence, for fine-tuning would seem to require a *fine-tuner*. Perhaps the most common response is that if our universe is only one of perhaps an infinite number of universes (a *multiverse*), then it would not be surprising for a universe to come along, once every infinite number of years or so, that generates life *quite by accident*. Which is the more reasonable explanation: a fine-tuner or an infinite number of universes? Scholars disagree.

Mathematics. It is widely agreed that mathematics has provided a key to unlocking the "deep order" of the universe. But why should the structure of the universe be transparent to human minds? Some scientists and theologians argue that the intelligibility and beauty of the universe revealed mathematically gives us reason to believe that both the human mind and the universe have a common origin in the mind of God.

The Origins of Life. There is still no adequate scientific theory for how life came to be out of nonliving matter. Most scientists expect a good naturalistic theory (one that does not appeal to design or supernatural explanations) to be found, but at least a few scientists believe that the complexity of life and the information-bearing character of DNA are so extraordinary that they can only be explained in terms of some kind of design.

Biological Evolution. There are *many* religious positions on evolution other than fundamentalist creationism. Some theologians argue that God initially gave the universe its own freedom to work through chance. Others believe that neo-Darwinism provides only a partial explanation of origins; there is purpose in evolution, but scientific method is too restrictive to allow scientists to consider all the relevant evidence. Catholic theology discerns a providential God behind the "secondary" causes of evolution and claims that science cannot account for the development of animals into persons with souls. Process theologians argue for an *immanent* God embodied in the workings of nature, who guides evolution from within. And there are a few scientists who accept "Intelligent Design Theory," arguing that a *designer* is the best explanation for what they believe to be the irreducibly complex characteristics of DNA and cell biology.

Consciousness and the Soul. It is often claimed by scientists and philosophers that consciousness will eventually be explained in terms of the physical structures of nervous systems, though this continues to be very controversial. (Just what could possibly be the causal relationship between a thought and a neuron?) Of course, traditional religion has held that we have *immortal souls*. Needless to say, immortality is something of a problem if we must understand the mind or soul in terms of brains that decompose on death.

Free Will and Rationality. Modern science has been widely thought to require *determinism:* the causal laws of science (including those that explain how the brain works) leave no room for free will or rationality (believing and acting as we do because we *ought* to, not because we *have* to). But if we have no *choice* about how to act, what sense does it make to say that we are *responsible* for our actions? Many theologians and philosophers have rejected the *reductionism* of such science, arguing that the mind has its own structure, one that cannot be reduced to the naturalistic laws of science. Some scientists have argued that subatomic *indeterminacy* (as understood in quantum mechanics) provides an opening for free will. It has also been argued that indeterminacy together with chaos theory (in which major events can be explained by minuscule causes) allows room in the *causal joints* of the universe for God to act.

Morality. It is often claimed that *altruism and social behavior* can be given a Darwinian explanation in terms of group, kin, or reciprocal selection mechanisms that make social behavior and altruism a by-product of genetic selfishness. But many philosophers and theologians argue that we cannot move from what *is* the case to what *ought to be* the case: we cannot move from any scientific theory to morality; this is to commit the *naturalistic fallacy.* Moreover, most philosophers and theologians believe that morality requires a measure of self-conscious, deliberative thought that cannot be programmed into our genetic constitution; ethics depends on other kinds of abilities and knowledge than those provided by science.

The Environment. Over the past several decades theologians have begun to take the environmental crisis seriously, drawing on Biblical texts that emphasize the goodness of God's creation and the need for our stewardship of nature. Some more liberal theologians have reshaped traditional interpretations of God and nature, arguing for an immanent God who is embodied in and works through nature. Some theologians draw on Native American and Eastern religious traditions with their more spiritual understanding of nature and the need to live in harmony with it. All of these theologies are critical of the way in which *value-free* scientific (and economic) ways of thinking about nature allow for its exploitation.

Other Issues. Discussions of the role of prayer, meditation, and spirituality in *health and healing* have called purely naturalistic conceptions of illness into question and contributed to more holistic conceptions of medicine. Stem-cell research, cloning, germ-line genetic engineering, robotics, and nanotechnology raise urgent moral and religious questions about technology and what it means to be human (especially with the possibility of trans-species engineering). As the *technological ethos* of modernity becomes more influential, we reconceive the world and people as objects to be manipulated and our sense of the sacred withers. Not only is there no moral compass built into technology or the science that shapes it, but the omnipresent *technological imperative* demands that we think and act technologically, nurturing a *faith* in technological solutions to what may be moral and spiritual problems.

Several themes run through all of these controversies. Does science (or methodological naturalism) have limits? Are there aspects of nature (physical or human) that science cannot explain, perhaps even in principle? Are there moral or spiritual dangers that accompany scientific naturalism? Is it possible to have philosophical or theological knowledge of nature? Can we achieve a deeper understanding of reality through integrating religious, philosophical, and scientific claims and perspectives? Can we make sense of the idea of *purpose* in nature?

Educational Implications

The current science/religion discussion among scholars extends well beyond the old cultural controversy over evolution. Moreover, there are more than just two sides (fundamentalist creationists and evolutionists) to consider: there are a variety of religious positions on a variety of issues. In fact, the science/religion relationship is considerably more interesting, more complicated, and more important than is often realized.

At least two kinds of arguments can be made for addressing these issues in public schools. First, on almost anyone's account, the science/religion discussion addresses issues of great, perhaps even *momentous,* moral, social, and religious importance. Because these issues are so important, students should learn something about them as part of a liberal education. Second, it can be argued that constitutional neutrality between religion and nonreligion requires that students be taught about religious as well as scientific interpretations of controversial issues.

If students should learn something about the science/religion discussion, where should this take place? Representatives of the science and educational establishments usually argue for history or social studies classes, leaving science classes for science. Unfortunately, history texts say little, if anything, about these issues. Could they be discussed in science texts and courses? While courts have made it clear that religious interpretations of nature cannot be taught *as true* or *as science,* it is most likely constitutional to teach about the science/religion discussion *neutrally* in providing historical and cultural context in science texts and courses. No doubt any proposal to do so will be deeply controversial.

There is no discussion of religion in the *National Science Education Standards,* though the *Standards* do require that science courses address social and personal issues (the seventh content standard) and that science be taught in historical perspective (the eighth content standard). Arguably, it is hard to do either apart from some consideration of religion. Neither the *Standards* nor the textbooks mention the new science/religion dialogue. A few science textbooks devote one or several paragraphs to the relationship of science and religion in their chapters on scientific method, but always to claim that science and religion have nothing to do with each other—and most texts say nothing about their relationship. Nor do the texts address any of the particular issues mentioned above with the occasional exception of the controversy over evolution (which is always treated briefly and simplistically). It is true that neither the *Standards* nor the texts attack religion; indeed, they often appear to pull their punches, perhaps to avoid controversy. But they betray no doubt that science will solve all yet-unsolved problems without appeal to God or the idea of design or purpose in the universe. *See also:* Creationism; Evolution; Intelligent Design.

Further Reading: Ian Barbour, *Religion and Science: Historical and Contemporary Issues* (San Francisco: HarperSanFrancisco, 1997); John Campbell and Stephen Meyer, eds., *Darwin, Design, and Public Education* (East Lansing: Michigan State University Press, 2003); William Dembski and Michael Ruse, eds., *Debating Design: From Darwin to DNA* (New York: Cambridge University Press, 2004); Kent Greenawalt, *Does God Belong in Public Schools?* (Princeton, NJ: Princeton University Press, 2005); Neil Manson, ed., *God and Design: The Teleological Argument and Modern Science* (New York: Routledge, 2003); Warren A. Nord and Charles C. Haynes, *Taking Religion Seriously Across the Curriculum* (Alexandria, VA: ASCD, 1998); Huston Smith, *Why Religion Matters: The Fate of the Human Spirit in an Age of Disbelief* (San Francisco: HarperSanFrancisco, 2001); Richard Tarnas, *The Passion of the Western Mind* (New York: Harmony Books, 1991); Fraser Watts and Kevin Dutton, eds., *Why the Science and Religion Dialogue Matters* (Philadelphia: Templeton Foundation Press, 2006).

Warren A. Nord

Scopes Trial

John T. Scopes went on trial in Dayton, Tennessee, in 1925 for violating Tennessee's recently enacted legislation prohibiting the teaching of evolution in the state's high schools. In one of the most publicized trials in the nation's history, a team supported by the American Civil Liberties Union that included the most famous trial attorney of the era, Clarence Darrow, defended Scopes. William Jennings Bryan, three-time nominee for president of the United States, appeared as counsel for the prosecution. For all of the attention that the trial received, the outcome was never in doubt. Scopes had broken the state law banning the teaching of evolution in the public schools of Tennessee and admitted that he had done so. He was found guilty and fined $100. While Scopes went on with his life, the trial had a lasting impact on American religion, textbook publishing, and the teaching of high school science for decades to come.

Charles Darwin's *On the Origin of Species* was published in 1859, 66 years before the trial. In the first decades after Darwin published, many in the United States played down any conflict between the book's conclusions and the beliefs of Christianity. While in England some quickly began to draw a line between Darwin and Christianity, in the United States, for most of the nineteenth century, those who sought to accommodate evolutionary biology and Christian faith were in the majority. For example, University of California geologist Joseph LeConte who published one of the earliest high school science textbooks saw no conflict between the two. And the leading late nineteenth-century evangelist Dwight L. Moody dismissed a clash between religion and science, as did Bryan himself in earlier years.

By the 1920s, however, the mood among many of the next generation of conservative religious leaders was hardening towards evolution. A new generation of evangelicals directly attacked Darwinian evolutionary theory, at least as it involved humans, as a direct assault on Christianity. And as a result of their efforts between 1922 and 1925, 20 states considered legislation to outlaw the teaching of evolution in their high schools. By the 1920s it was also true that more and more high school biology textbooks were including much more detailed accounts of evolutionary theory in general and Darwin's work in specific. Perhaps equally significant in understanding the Scopes Trial was the fact that Dayton, Tennessee, opened its high school in 1906. Prior to that event, and similar events in many cities and towns across the United States in the early years of the twentieth century, no one much worried about the high school science curriculum since outside of a few major cities there were not any high schools to offer the curriculum. In 1890, 200,000 students attended high schools in the United States. By 1920 that number had risen to 2 million. No wonder the high school curriculum had become a much more significant focus of attention in the 1920s.

In 1925 all of these forces—a growing antievolutionary stance among many Protestants, a willingness to use state legislation to reinforce their beliefs, a growing commitment to evolution within the scientific community, and especially the authors of biology textbooks and the growth of high schools using the textbooks—came together in Dayton's Court. The recent advent of radio, and the presence of not only two of the nation's best-known lawyers but also H. L. Mencken, perhaps the best-known journalist in the country, guaranteed national attention to the conflict.

The Scopes case was not an accidental development. In fact Scopes had been recruited for what everyone knew would be a highly publicized trial. In the spring of 1925 leaders of the then newly formed American Civil Liberties Union decided to broaden their focus from defending political dissidents to other free speech issues. The New York ACLU staff placed an advertisement in the Chattanooga, Tennessee, *Times* seeking a Tennessee teacher who would be willing to participate in a test case of the increasing number of state laws banning evolution. Local attorneys in Dayton, primarily interested in bringing more attention to their small town, called the 24-year-old high school teacher and invited him to offer himself. He did.

In teaching high school biology, Scopes, like every other biology teacher in Tennessee was caught in a dilemma. On the one hand, the recently passed state law clearly prohibited teaching about evolution. On the other hand, the state-approved biology textbook, George William Hunter's *A Civic Biology,* was quite specific in its discussion of evolution. Not only did *A Civic Biology* discuss evolution and cite Darwin but, more troublesome to those who saw Darwinian evolution as anti-Christian, it focused on the randomness of natural selection as described by Darwin and left little room for Intelligent Design by a higher power. But Hunter's book was the authorized textbook in the state and Scopes would also have been breaking the law if he had used a substitute.

In fact, the conflict that took place in Dayton was much broader than specific issues of Scopes's guilt or innocence. For Bryan and many who supported him the trial was about the right of the majority to decide what should and should not be taught in the public schools. In a democratic society, Bryan argued, the majority rule included the rules of the appropriate public school curriculum. At the same time, for Bryan in particular, social Darwinism was a far greater concern than biological Darwinism. Throughout the late nineteenth century American capitalism had expanded in ways unimaginable to previous generations. The newly rich (obscenely rich, some said) industrial leaders lived lives of extraordinary luxury. At the same time, the ranks of the desperately poor—some of whom worked in the factories of the new industrialists—grew exponentially. And the squalor of the poor was to be seen in every city and many a rural mining camp or farm town. These new and great disparities were justified by some Darwinian economists as an extension of Darwinian biology—a new social Darwinism that included a belief held by many in the 1920s that "survival of the fittest" also meant that any social safety net to protect the nation's poor was against the rules of nature. For Bryan and many other veterans of turn-of-the-century populist movements, social Darwinism was a much greater danger than any debate about the ancient origins of the human race. On the other hand, for Darrow, Mencken, and many who followed their words before and during the trial, the prosecution of John Scopes was also about many things—free speech, the need to respect the findings of scientists, but also a perhaps larger conflict between urban and urbane America and the small town and rural values that they saw coming together in Bryan's words and Tennessee's team of prosecutors.

In the end the impact of the trial and Scopes's conviction was multifaceted. Many conservative Christians felt battered and scorned by the trial and the media discussions of it—and they had been. It would be a generation before some of them would again venture into the public arena while they focused instead on building up their own communities before reemerging in more public arenas in the 1970s. At the same time, textbook publishers, ever sensitive to the public mood, quickly reduced the discussion of evolution in their texts. The 1927 edition of *A Civic Biology* moved Darwin from a central role to a note that he was one among many important biologists. And the discussion of evolution became simply an "interpretation of the way in which all life changes." Other publishers followed a similar course.

It would be the 1950s, with the growth of high school science during the Cold War between the United States and the Soviet Union, before the discussion of evolution would be as robust in high school textbooks as it had been in the early 1920s. On the legal front, Scopes's appeal was dismissed on a technicality, and it would not be until 1968 in *Epperson v. Arkansas* that the U.S. Supreme Court would rule on the issues involved in the Scopes case. When the Supreme Court finally did rule, some 40 years after the original case, the decision was written by Justice Abraham Fortas who had grown up as a young Jewish boy in Memphis, Tennessee, during the years of the Scopes Trial. Fortas's decision, while it made clear the unconstitutionality of any law prohibiting a teacher from teaching about evolution, also opened the door, perhaps inadvertently, to a new set of issues around equal time for the teaching of intelligent design along with evolution. But that is another story. In 1925 William Jennings Bryan and most of his supporters simply wanted the public schools to keep silent on the issue of evolution while Darrow and his supporters wanted the subject taught. If one looks at the biology textbooks published for at least the first 30 years after the trial, Bryan won. *See also:* Creationism; *Edwards v. Aguillard; Epperson v. Arkansas;* Evolution; *Kitzmiller v. Dover Area School District.*

Further Reading: Edward J. Larson, *Summer for the Gods: The Scopes Trial and America's Continuing Debate Over Science and Religion* (New York: Basic Books, 1997).

James W. Fraser

Secularism

The word *secular* means "of the world" or "of this age" (as opposed to "of the church," "of the spiritual world," or "of eternity"). In medieval Catholicism, the secular clergy were those who lived in the world rather than in monastic communities. During the Reformation, the state *secularized* church property by taking it for its own nonreligious purposes.

The term *secularism* was coined by the English freethinker George Jacob Holyoake in the 1840s. For him, secularism was the view that morality and public affairs could and should be discussed apart from religion; secularism did not deny the existence of God, it just ignored God and religion. Though he was himself an atheist, Holyoake believed that secularism was a somewhat safer and more respectable position in Victorian England.

Since Holyoake's day, scholars and secularists use the term *secularism* in a variety of ways. The most important distinction to draw is between what can be called *philosophical* or *ideological secularism* (a secular worldview, one that involves skepticism about, or rejection of, belief in God) and *institutional* or *constitutional secularism* (the view that public institutions, particularly law and the constitution, should be secular, and religion should be a private matter). In each case, a *secularist* is an advocate of secularism.

Secularization is the multifaceted process by which people and institutions become secular. It has many causes, including the arguments and influence of secularists. But secularization may also be the unintended consequence of social, cultural, and religious movements.

Philosophical or Ideological Secularism

Some secularists have argued that secularism should be distinguished from atheism. Atheism is simply the belief that there is no God. Secularism is something more like a worldview, a philosophical or ideological system within which it is unreasonable to believe in God. Still, our first type of secularism implies atheism or agnosticism. (In ordinary usage an atheist is one who believes that God does not exist; an agnostic is one who does not know—or perhaps does not think one *can* know—if God exists.)

There have always been freethinkers, skeptics, and atheists who have rejected belief in God or the gods. Atheism was not uncommon among the *philosophes* of the French Enlightenment, but atheism and agnosticism became relatively common among intellectuals in the nineteenth century as secularist ideologies and worldviews developed (such as Marxism and scientific naturalism). In America, atheists and secularists enjoyed modest publicity and success for several decades at the end of the nineteenth century. Robert Ingersoll, perhaps the most famous orator of the time, was an avowed agnostic, though comparatively few Americans then or now have identified themselves as atheists or agnostics.

Surveys do not generally ask people if they are secularists, but about 90 percent of Americans claim to believe in God and, depending on the poll, somewhere between 1 and 5 percent acknowledge being an atheist or agnostic. The percentage of people in Europe who identify themselves as atheists, or claim not to believe in God, is considerably higher, perhaps even a majority of people in some countries. Of course, there are also the *merely secular*—those who are indifferent to *both* religion and atheism (or secularism); they have become a substantial percentage of people in Western countries.

Some scholars have argued that atheism is parasitic on what the conventional religion is. For example, in the Roman world, Christians were called atheists because they did not believe in the Roman gods or practice a conventional religion. Many people (perhaps a third of Americans) say that they are spiritual but not religious; such people typically reject the personal or *theist* God of traditional Western religion, but retain some idea of a spiritual force or dimension to reality. Are they atheists? Many atheists and secularists simply deny *any* conception of the supernatural.

There are a variety of recurring arguments against the traditional Western conception of God that have influenced the development of philosophical secularism. Among these are the following:

1. The fact that different religious traditions have made different claims about God has often created a general skepticism that has undermined belief. As cultures have become more pluralistic (so that our friends and neighbors hold different religious beliefs from our own) such skepticism has become more common.
2. Skeptics have long claimed to find inconsistencies and historical inaccuracies in Scripture, and modern historical and textual criticism has raised a variety of new questions about traditional assumptions regarding authorship, historical accuracy, and the meaning of Scripture.
3. The existence of suffering and evil has been notoriously hard to reconcile with the good and all-powerful God of the Western religious traditions (as many biblical writers themselves recognized).
4. Much atheism is grounded in moral objections to the God of Scripture and institutional religion. Some Scripture portrays God as cruel and vengeful, and many skeptics have found the idea of hell and eternal punishment to be sadistic. They have also charged the institutional church with a long history of oppression and violence.
5. As modern science and social science developed, particularly in the nineteenth and twentieth centuries, they rejected traditional supernaturalism and provided an alternative *naturalistic* way of making sense of both physical and human nature.
6. Philosophers and social scientists have developed a variety of *scientific* explanations of religion and religious experience, ranging from the "classical" theories of Feuerbach, Marx, and Freud, to more contemporary explanations that draw on evolutionary biology, genetics, and neuroscience.

7. Underlying all of these arguments is our Enlightenment heritage emphasizing the power of reason to understand the world. According to Kant, the motto of the Enlightenment was the following: *Think for yourself.* The Enlightenment emphases on autonomy, individualism, and progress have often been taken to undermine inherited beliefs and traditions. At the same time, secular philosophers have developed a variety of ways of thinking about morality that free it from religion and the commands of God.

Needless to say, there are many ways in which theologians and philosophers have responded to these criticisms. Among these are the following:

1. Many religious conservatives believe that God is known through faith or personal religious experience and are suspicious of *reason* (a symptom of pride, the original sin).
2. Many liberals acknowledge problems with Scripture, with traditional conceptions of God, and with the oppressive and violent record of historical religions, but respond that religion (like science) can be *progressive;* religions reform themselves in the light of what can be learned from science, history, and continuing spiritual encounters with God. Of course, those who call themselves *spiritual* rather than religious, reject even more of traditional religion.
3. Both conservative and religious critics of secularism point to the dismal record of philosophical secularism and antireligious ideologies in the twentieth century—particularly communism and fascism, but also the moral relativism and spiritual anomie that has been characteristic of much twentieth-century intellectual and popular culture.
4. Scientific explanations of physical nature, of human nature, and of the origins and development of religion and religious experience are often speculative and controversial. Indeed, over the past several decades a new, science/religion dialogue has flourished among scholars, many of whom argue that religion and science both contribute to an adequate understanding of reality.
5. Some scholars have argued that *postmodernism* undercuts any claims that science can provide a final understanding or master narrative of reality. Instead, science simply provides one interpretation among many, including those of religious traditions.

Institutional and Constitutional Secularism

Over the past several centuries many public *institutions* (the economy, social services, and education, for example) have become secular, achieving considerable autonomy from religious authority. Our concern here will be with law and the constitutional order, where two revolutions at the end of the eighteenth century created fully secular legal systems for the first time in history.

The only reference to religion in the American Constitution is its rejection of religious tests for office in the federal government. The Preamble claims that the authority of government derives from people and not, by implication, from God. The First Amendment disestablished religion, and soon Jefferson would declare that the Founders had established a "wall of separation" between church and state. Of course, the federal constitution left state establishments in place, and not all of the Founders were strict *separationists* like Jefferson. Still, the *federal* government would be fully secular. How did this constitutional secularism come to be?

The Founders were deeply committed to liberty—religious liberty, or liberty of conscience, in particular. This commitment had roots in both the Enlightenment belief in natural rights and in Protestantism. While most of the Reformers believed in (Protestant) established churches, they emphasized the importance of the individual's direct relationship to God, unmediated by religious institutions. In time, the logic of this commitment to *soul-liberty* (as Roger Williams called it) was taken to require religious toleration and eventually a more expansive conception of religious liberty and disestablishment. Williams and William Penn made this case forcefully in colonial America, but by the time of the Revolution it was the common position of those we would now call evangelicals.

Moreover, in a religiously pluralistic culture liberty is necessary for social peace. The Founders were very much aware of the religious wars, persecution, and oppression that had devastated Europe. While particular denominations were dominant in some colonies (Congregationalism in much of New England, Anglicanism in the Southern colonies), there was no dominant denomination for the whole of the new United States. Religious liberty was a practical prerequisite of any widely accepted constitutional arrangement.

It is widely accepted that disestablishment did not stem from any hostility to religion (that is, from philosophical secularism); its purpose was to protect religious liberty and religious minorities from religious majorities. In this respect, American constitutional secularism was quite different from the secularism that followed in the wake of the French Revolution, which was directed against France's religious as well as the political establishment, both of which were perceived as corrupt defenders of privilege and injustice. Consequently, France developed a form of constitutional secularism that was markedly hostile to religion.

In fact, we need to recognize a spectrum of positions regarding constitutional secularism, from the *hard institutional secularism* of the U.S.S.R., in which the state constitution (and state-sponsored education) were designed to *eliminate* religion, through French secularism or *laicite* (which, while hostile to religion, allows considerable religious liberty), through the religious neutrality and institutionalized pluralism of the United States, to the *soft institutional secularism* of some European countries that, though largely secular, have established churches (along with religious liberty). At the far end of this spectrum are a variety of constitutional arrangements that are not secular at all, ending in the kind of theocracy we find in Iran.

Institutional secularism has often been supported by religious people as well as atheists. Most of the American Founders were religious, and evangelicals were among the most fervent supporters of religious liberty and disestablishment in the colonies. While there have been many atheists who have favored *hard* institutional secularism (many Marxists, for example), most atheists (at least now, in the West) favor a somewhat softer variety of institutional secularism with guarantees of religious liberty and pluralism.

Not surprisingly, American constitutional secularism has proven controversial. Some religious conservatives argue that the Founders intended for America to be a Christian, not a secular, country. Others argue that the First Amendment was meant only to prohibit a national church, but not nondiscriminatory support for religion more generally. Some critics of the Supreme Court claim that some of its more recent decisions (such as those prohibiting official school prayer and devotional Bible reading) have violated the Free Exercise Clause's guarantee of religious liberty.

Secularism and Public Education

Many conservative religious critics have charged that public schools promote secular humanism. (Historically, *humanism* has come in religious as well as secular varieties; insofar as it advocates a secular worldview, *secular* humanism may be considered a type of philosophical secularism.) For these critics, secular humanism is objectionable both because it is secular (God is irrelevant, it makes sense of the world in exclusively secular categories) and because it is humanistic (it has an unduly favorable understanding of human beings and the power of reason to discern what is true and good; it fails to appreciate the sinfulness of persons, the necessity of faith, and the danger of human pride). Believing that schools teach secular humanism—or at least are hostile to religion—some religious parents have turned to religious schools or homeschooling since the 1970s.

A number of arguments have been given by religious (and occasionally by secular critics) to support the charge that education promotes some kind of philosophical secularism. Textbooks and the curriculum typically ignore God and religion except in historical contexts, and even there religion has often been downplayed, as a series of textbook studies have shown. Schools teach literature, science, and moral values that at least sometimes conflict with religious beliefs and values. The interpretive frameworks that students acquire in their various courses are exclusively secular, so that students are taught to make sense of their various subjects in secular rather than religious categories (indeed, they are typically not taught that there are religious alternatives). Public schools sometimes do not respect the right of students to express their own religious beliefs and values. Schools have become (largely) "religion-free" zones.

While some religious critics have charged that there is a *conspiracy* of secular humanists to take over public schools, most acknowledge that it is not the *purpose* of (most) teachers, textbook authors, or administrators to promote philosophical secularism (or secular humanism). Moreover, most of what students are taught is consistent with most religion. (Religious conservatives no doubt find more to object to than do religious liberals.) The question is whether the absence of any serious study of religion and the cumulative effect of teaching secular frameworks of interpretation in all course work has *the effect* of promoting something like a *worldview* or a *secular mentality* that marginalizes or discredits religion and is conducive to secular humanism or philosophical secularism.

American *constitutional secularism* charts a middle course, among secular states, regarding religion and public education. Clearly public education cannot promote or encourage philosophical secularism or atheism (as did the U.S.S.R.); nor can it promote or encourage religion as if we had an established religion (as do some European countries). Rather, given our constitutional framework and Supreme Court rulings, public education (as a governmental institution) must be *neutral* regarding religion, an implication of the Establishment Clause, *and* it must protect religious liberty and religious pluralism, an implication of the Free Exercise Clause.

The Supreme Court has made it clear that public schools cannot conduct religious exercises such as official school prayers or devotional Bible reading (though students are free to pray or read the Bible on their own time). But the Court also made it clear, in *Abington v. Schempp* (1963), that academic study of the Bible and religion is constitutional so long as it is conducted "objectively as part of a secular program of education." While public education must be secular, it is permissible to teach about religion in public schools. This is uncontroversial; no Supreme Court justice has ever held otherwise.

But what does it mean to *teach about religion?* As Justice Tom Clark said in *Schempp* (and as the Court has repeated any number of times), government, and therefore public schools, must "maintain strict neutrality, neither aiding nor opposing religion." As agents of the state, teachers (and schools) are not to take sides in matters of religion. Of course, neutrality is a two-edged sword: teachers cannot conduct religious exercises, proselytize, or promote religion; nor can they denigrate or oppose religion. What this means in practice may be controversial. Is it a violation of neutrality, for example, to leave religion out of textbooks or the curriculum?

Justice Clark also argued in *Schempp* that "the State may not establish a '*religion of secularism*' in the sense of affirmatively opposing or showing hostility to religion, thus 'preferring those who believe in no religion over those who do believe.'" Of course, the idea of a *religion of secularism* (or of secular humanism, a "religion" that the Court also once acknowledged) is controversial. Scholars have long noted that some of the world's traditional religions do not teach the existence of God, and they have also written about *functional* religions (like Marxism and nationalism), which have many of the characteristics of more traditional religions. A "secular religion" need not be a contradiction in terms. Still, given what Justice Clark wrote, it is hard to make a case that public schools *affirmatively oppose* religion. It might more plausibly be argued that they do prefer those who believe in no religion over those who do believe. In his concurring opinion in *Schempp* Justice Arthur Goldberg agreed with the majority opinion that "the attitude of government toward religion must be one of neutrality." But, he went on to argue, an "untutored devotion to the concept of neutrality can lead to a brooding and pervasive devotion to the secular and a passive, or even active, hostility to the religious." Arguably, an unreflective devotion to secular education, one that is insensitive to religion, that ignores it, or that fails to take it seriously, shows hostility to religion and may violate neutrality. There is at least a danger that without some care and critical reflection, institutional secularism can (perhaps unwittingly) promote philosophical secularism. *See also:* Humanism and the Humanist Manifestos; Secularization; Separation of Church and State/Wall of Separation between Church and State.

Further Reading: *Abington School District v. Schempp,* 374 U.S. 203 (1963); Noah Feldman, *Divided by God* (New York: Farrar, Straus and Giroux, 2005); Jennifer Michael Hecht, *Doubt: A History* (San Francisco: HarperSanFrancisco, 2003); Susan Jacoby, *Freethinkers: A History of American Secularism* (New York: A Metropolitan/Owl Book, 2004); Michael Martin, ed., *The Cambridge Companion to Atheism* (New York: Cambridge University Press, 2007); Alister McGrath, *The Twilight of Atheism* (New York: Galilee Doubleday, 2006); Keith Ward, *Is Religion Dangerous?* (Grand Rapids, MI: Eerdmans, 2006); Richard Tarnas, *The Passion of the Western Mind* (New York: Harmony Books, 1991); Warren A. Nord and Charles C. Haynes, *Taking Religion Seriously Across the Curriculum* (Alexandria, VA: ASCD, 1998).

Warren A. Nord

Secularization

Historically, most people have believed in God (or the gods, or the transcendent by whatever name); they have made sense of the world and organized their lives in religious categories. Over the course of the nineteenth century some intellectuals (e.g., Auguste Comte, Ludwig Feuerbach, Karl Marx, Friedrich Nietzsche, Sigmund Freud, Max Weber, and Emile Durkheim) came to believe that with science, enlightenment, and social progress, religion would wither away. During the twentieth century many scholars have held what has come to be called *The Secularization Thesis:* secularization inevitably follows in the wake of modernity. And yet, at the beginning of the twenty-first century, religion has not disappeared; far from it.

We need to begin by distinguishing among several types of secularization. Just *what* is becoming more secular? At least three possibilities exist: what people believe; their commitment to religious institutions; or public life and institutions. We might start with the first two types of secularization.

Although the numbers differ depending on the poll, about 90–95 percent of Americans claim to believe in God. Some of these believers have occasional doubts, but according to a 2006 Gallup Poll, 73 percent of Americans claim to have no doubt that God exists, and 57 percent say that religion is *very important* in their lives. About 45 percent of Americans say that they attend religious services every week or almost every week (though many scholars are skeptical of this number).

The percentage of *Europeans* who believe in God is, on average, significantly lower though percentages vary considerably among European countries (ranging from about 95 percent in Ireland and Poland, to several countries—Sweden, Germany, Estonia, and the Czech Republic—where, depending on the survey, only a minority of people believe in God). Moreover, church attendance is considerably lower than in America: in some countries fewer than 10 percent of people attend church regularly.

Worldwide, about 85 percent of people identify with a religious tradition. This is down from 1900, but up from mid-century (during communist rule). Over the past several decades there has been a remarkable *growth* of religion in the Third World, fueled in large part by converts to Islam and to evangelical and Pentecostal Protestantism.

For advocates of the Secularization Thesis, Europe is the wave of the future. As societies modernize and become postindustrial, people become less religious—as in Europe. On this view America is something of an aberration. Critics of the Secularization Thesis believe that Europe is the aberration in a world that has always been, and continues to be, highly religious. One thing about which there is agreement: because religious societies have much higher birth rates than the more secular societies of Europe (some of which are failing to reproduce themselves) the world is becoming more religious. Whether the rest of the world will eventually become more secular as it modernizes is a matter of controversy.

Of course, even in Europe, the majority of people (in most countries) continue to believe in God. But belief in God can be uncoupled from commitment to religious institutions or traditions so that belief and church attendance (a favorite sociological measure of secularization) need not go together. There are reasons for this that may be peculiar to Europe. Unlike America, Europe has a long history of anticlericalism that stems from the traditional hostility of established religions to social progress, which alienated in various ways intellectuals, the working class, and the middle class. It has also often been argued that religious establishments in Europe undermined the individual initiative that has kept religion vital in America. On this "market" analysis countries with free enterprise in religion—like America—are much more religious than countries with state-supported religious establishments (though there are European exceptions to this rule like Ireland and Poland).

There is another factor to consider. Individualism, which cuts across all modern societies, resists traditional institutions that define what one should believe and how one should live. Finding churches oppressive, more and more people say *they are spiritual but not religious.* This is an increasing trend in the United States (where about a third of Americans say that they are spiritual rather than religious) as well as in Europe. Consequently, people may continue to believe in God (of some kind), but in their own way, apart from churches, dogma, and tradition.

But we also need to remember our third type of secularization—the *institutional differentiation* that takes place when social institutions and practices (law, government, welfare, education, art, science) achieve a significant measure of autonomy from religious authority. In this case, religion need not disappear, but it is *privatized*. America is a very religious country in terms of belief in God, and it is comparatively religious in terms of commitment to religious institutions, but it is fairly secular in terms of its public institutions—in part a consequence of our historic decision to separate church and state. In fact, in *this* regard, America is *more* secular than many European countries with their established churches. With regard to public education, America is also more secular (many European countries provide tax support for religious schools). At the same time, American politics has a strong religious dimension, unlike most European countries.

What is clear, if anything, is that the extent of secularization depends on where one lives and on the kind of secularization at issue. If the United States and Europe continue to be religious in some ways, they have also become considerably more secular in others.

The Causes of Secularism

So what causes secularization? It is important, first, to distinguish between *secularization* and *secularism* (which may be, but is not always, the cause of secularization). Secularism is a philosophical or ideological position held by *secularists* who favor some type of secularization. We might distinguish between two important types of secularism—*philosophical* and *institutional* secularism. A philosophical (or ideological) secularist is an atheist. (Secular humanists are typically philosophical secularists.) An institutional secularist, by contrast, believes that *public institutions* (particularly government) should be secular, and that religion should be private, but makes no claim about God's existence. Deeply religious people (in American history Roger Williams is an influential example) have often been institutional secularists.

Secularization may be due, in part, to the influence of either kind of secularism, but it may also be the *unintended* effect of large-scale social and cultural processes. Scholars have proposed a number of causes of secularization, several of which are premodern. Six can be readily identified:

1. The Protestant Reformation removed (in varying degrees in different countries) many social practices, laws, and institutions from control of the Catholic Church, *secularizing* them. It eliminated various religious vocations and emphasized secular callings. It drew a sharp line between the sacred and the secular, disenchanting the spirit-filled world of medieval Catholicism. Its opposition to icons and images (in favor of the Bible and preaching) constricted the imaginative and spiritual dimension of religion. Its theological commitment to freedom of conscience contributed, in time, to the rise of individualism, the commitment to liberty, and the legal disestablishment of religion, all considerations of importance to the American Founders. (Individuals in this tradition were often *institutional,* but never *philosophical,* secularists.)

2. Religious wars and persecution generated a secular backlash. The increasing religious pluralism of societies in the wake of the Reformation, together with democracy and individualism necessitated religious tolerance and religious disestablishment for the sake of social peace (also matters of great importance to our Founders).

3. Capitalism undermined traditional communities and their moral, social, and religious values (particularly as industrialization forced shifts in population from the countryside to cities). Its success in creating material wealth converted people into consumers with their hearts in

the material goods of this world rather than the spiritual goods of a world to come. Insofar as insecurity fosters religion—a position taken by many advocates of the Secularization Thesis—economic well-being makes God and religion less important.

4. Exploration and travel, books and newspapers, urbanization and growing religious pluralism, all exposed people to alternative ways of making sense of the world and their lives, undermining traditional religious certainties. The Internet and contemporary media have, arguably, exacerbated this tendency.

5. The scientific revolution completed the task begun by the Reformers of disenchanting the world, providing fully *naturalistic* ways of making sense of nature. The new social sciences provided analogous scientific ways of making sense of persons and society. Both acquired considerable cultural authority (not least through education), providing an alternative framework for making sense of the world to those of traditional religions. (It is in this tradition that we are most likely to find philosophical secularists.) Technology (whether in the form of fertilizer or medicines) made prayer and religious comfort seem less important.

6. The Enlightenment encouraged people to think for themselves. It made virtues of autonomy and liberty. It emphasized progress, undercutting faith in the timeless truths of the past. Many of the major figures of the Enlightenment were keenly sensitive to moral corruption and suffering caused by religious establishments.

There can be little doubt that secularization (of different types, at different times, in different places) is taking place, but there are a variety of reasons why critics have been skeptical of the Secularization Thesis as an overarching global theory. The most important is simply that religion has not disappeared; indeed, in many places in the world—including the postindustrial United States—it is thriving. Some critics argue that secularization is influenced more by relatively local social and cultural developments (e.g., anticlericalism in Europe) than by the "universal" influence of modernity. Others have argued that Europe was never so religious, at least in terms of belief, as is commonly assumed, and that while religious belief no doubt waxes and wanes there is no *long term* decline that correlates with modernity. Some note that there has been a religious reaction against the evils of the secular ideologies of the twentieth century, particularly against communism in Eastern Europe, but also against the perceived amorality and relativism of modern liberal society. Other critics argue that people are by nature religious (a few scientists have even argued that we are hardwired to be religious) and that because religion satisfies a deep need for meaning in our lives it is unlikely to disappear. And, finally, while it may be that some forms of religion are in decline (traditional Christianity in Europe) other forms (such as spirituality) replace them.

Religious Responses to Secularization

It is customary to distinguish two different religious ways of addressing modernity and secularization. The first is the *conservative* response of drawing a bright line between religious tradition and modernity, and forcefully rejecting the ideas and ideals of modernity (at least in so far as they have implications for religious doctrine). On the right wing of this first response are those *fundamentalisms,* in a variety of cultures and religious traditions, which have militantly rejected modernity and secularization. The alternative response is that of religious *liberals* who have reformed their beliefs and traditions to take into account modern ideas (such as modern science, and various liberal social ideals such as pluralism and feminism). On the left wing of this second response is *spirituality*—that highly eclectic and individualistic movement of people who reject the doctrines of institutionalized religions while retaining something of their experiential or spiritual cores. (Some aspects of this amorphous spirituality coalesced under the banner of New Age religion.)

Each of these responses to modernity has shown some success, albeit in somewhat different cultures and subcultures. Needless to say, many people and religious movements do not fit these categories neatly.

Secularization of Public Education

Through much of the nineteenth century the Bible and religion played an important role in textbooks and the public school curriculum. The Bible was taken as essential to moral education—a major task of public schools. America's history was often viewed through a religious lens, and biblical stories were commonplace in readers and literature anthologies. Science texts and courses taught that nature was the handiwork of God and provided evidence of his existence.

From the beginning of public education in the middle decades of the nineteenth century, however, the logic of secularization was at work. Just as the Framers of our Constitution believed that in the pluralistic culture of the new United States, government must be built on common ground (rather than on the holy ground of a divisive religious establishment) so it was the task of the early public—or *common*—schools to unite an increasingly individualistic and pluralistic culture. The founders of the new public schools recognized that schooling must be *nonsectarian,* but they failed to recognize that what to them was nonsectarian was to others distinctively Protestant, and this proved divisive, especially to Roman Catholics, who began a parochial school system as a response to Protestant public schools. By the end of the nineteenth century there was broad (if not quite complete) agreement that public schools must eliminate the Bible and religion from the curriculum. "Americanism," by contrast, would unite us, and in an immigrant nation educators assigned it many of the tasks given to Protestantism in earlier times and in more homogeneous subcultures.

Our educational institutions grew more secular in tandem with our culture as the goals of life shifted from salvation in the world to come to material wealth and happiness in this world. By the end of the nineteenth century the purposes of schooling (and of higher education) had become largely economic: to acquire that practical knowledge that would enable individuals and the nation to thrive economically. *Social efficiency,* tracking, and vocational education replaced elitist "bookish" curricula, the classics, and the Bible. Moral education grounded in the Bible gave way to secular character education by the end of that century.

Science increased its cultural authority over the course of the nineteenth century and gradually shed its commitment to *natural theology* (which provided evidence of God's providence in nature) to embrace, in the wake of Darwin, a more purely *naturalistic* science that found any mention of God unnecessary. Scholars in the new social sciences found God irrelevant in explaining history, society, or the economy—and many of them believed that religion inhibited social progress. By the end of the century, textbooks were being written by scientists and secular university professors rather than by clergymen. Scientific testing, educational psychology, classroom management, and scientific administration became integral parts of education, and as public education was professionalized it was reconceived in scientific categories. For the educational *progressives* science replaced religion as the source of authority, and traditional evils became problems susceptible to solutions provided by scientific experts.

As a result of all these developments, religion had largely disappeared from *textbooks and the curriculum* by the end of the nineteenth century, and public education had become a secular, rather than a religious, enterprise. It is true, of course, that a *ceremonial husk of religion*—school prayers, devotionals, and Bible reading—survived in some places, even after the Supreme Court's rulings on official school prayers and devotional Bible readings in 1962 and 1963.

Some conservative religious critics have blamed either the Supreme Court or a conspiracy of secular humanists for secularizing public education. But the Supreme Court did not rule on the role of religion in public schools until 1948, when it banned in-school religious release time. While there were *philosophical* secularists who argued for secularizing public schools, secularization was much more due to the very open influence of *institutional* secularists, most of whom were personally religious, and the long term effect of that cluster of social forces—pluralism, individualism, Americanism, capitalism, science, and technology—that shaped public education just as it did so many social institutions.

Whether public education contributes to the secularization of society is difficult to determine. Surveys show that the more education people have, the less likely they are *to believe* in God or consider themselves religious, though the differences are not great. It is true that *intellectuals* tend not to be religious, but a number of recent surveys show that university faculty members are not dramatically less likely to believe in God, or consider themselves religious or spiritual, than the population more generally. (Biologists and psychologists are the least likely to believe in God.)

It can also be asked whether education contributes to *institutional secularization* and the privatization of religion. There are no relevant surveys here, but it has been argued that even though schooling does not diminish belief in God (much) it does nurture a secular mentality in which religion is irrelevant to students' understanding of public life and institutions (including morality, economics, the arts, and the sciences). *See also:* Religion and the Public School Curriculum; Secularism; Separation of Church and State/Wall of Separation between Church and State.

Further Reading: Peter Berger, ed., *The Desecularization of the World* (Grand Rapids, MI: Eerdmans, 1999); Steve Bruce, *God is Dead: Secularization in the West* (Malden, MA: Blackwell Publishers, 2002); Joan DelFattore, *The Fourth R: Conflicts Over Religion in America's Public Schools* (New Haven, CT: Yale University Press, 2004); James Fraser, *Between Church and State: Religion and Public Education in a Multicultural America* (New York: St. Martin's, 1999); Charles Glenn, Jr., *The Myth of the Common School* (Amherst: University of Massachusetts Press, 1987); Robert Michaelsen, *Piety in the Public School* (London: Macmillan, 1970); Warren A. Nord, *Religion and American Education: Rethinking a National Dilemma* (Chapel Hill: University of North Carolina Press, 1995); Pippa Norris and Ronald Inglehart, *Sacred and Secular: Religion and Politics Worldwide* (New York: Cambridge University Press, 2004); Christian Smith, *The Secular Revolution* (Berkeley: University of California Press, 2003); Rodney Stark and Roger Finke, *Acts of Faith* (Berkeley: University of California Press, 2000).

Warren A. Nord

Separation of Church and State/Wall of Separation between Church and State

"Separation of church and state" and "wall of separation between church and state" are two phrases that convey equivalent ideas and are ubiquitous in American church-state discussions. Although Thomas Jefferson is often credited with coining this figurative language, it has been a part of western theological and political discourse for at least a half millennium. The "wall of separation" was used most famously in an 1802 letter to a Baptist Association in Danbury, Connecticut, in which President Thomas Jefferson opined that the First Amendment to the U.S. Constitution had built "a wall of separation between church and state."

This metaphoric language is accepted by many Americans as a concise description of the constitutionally prescribed church-state arrangement. Furthermore, influential jurists have invoked it as the organizing theme of much church-state jurisprudence, even though this language is not found in the Constitution or elsewhere in the organic laws of the United States. In *Everson v. Board of Education* (1947), the U.S. Supreme Court was asked to interpret the First Amendment's prohibition on laws "respecting an establishment of religion." "In the words of Jefferson," the justices declared, the First Amendment has erected "'a wall of separation between church and State.'...That wall must be kept high and impregnable. We could not approve the slightest breach."

The concept and accompanying rhetoric of church-state separation have been a source of controversy in American law and policy. The terms "separation of church and state" and "wall of separation" express an alternative vision to the model of an exclusive ecclesiastical establishment. Proponents of these phrases argue that they promote private, voluntary religion and liberty of conscience in a secular polity. A "wall of separation" prevents ecclesiastical establishments and avoids conflict among religious denominations competing for the civil government's favor and aid. A restrictive barrier prohibits not only the formal recognition of, and legal preference for, one particular church (or sect) but also all other forms of government assistance or encouragement for religious objectives. A policy of strict separation, defenders contend, is the best, if not the only, way to promote religious liberty, especially the rights of religious minorities.

Critics counter that this figurative language evades clear definition and predictable application in actual church-state conflicts. They also question whether this rhetoric accurately or adequately encapsulates American traditions and constitutional principles governing church-state relationships. What is meant by the words "church" and "state"? Is "church" limited to ecclesiastical institutions, or does it encompass, more broadly, any expression or manifestation of religion in public life? Does the "wall" disallow all governmental acknowledgments of God and all public roles for religion? Is "state" limited to official actions of civil government, or does it encompass both the public and private actions of public officials, and does it include all activities in the public square that are authorized or tolerated by civil government, including activities of private actors? Ambiguity in the meaning of these key terms invites uncertainty and, eventually, disputes.

The concept of "separation" and the instrument of a "wall" can serve diverse objectives and interests. There are those who view a wall as a symbol of protection and freedom; for others it is a restrictive structure that imposes undue restraints on the legitimate roles of church and state in civil society. Some believe a wall of separation shields individual conscience from unwarranted intrusion by civil or clerical authorities. Religious dissenters, in particular, hope that placing a wall between church and state will provide a measure of autonomy from religious establishments in the exercise of religion. There are those who believe a wall safeguards the purity of religious truth and ecclesiastical institutions from corrupting external entities, especially the civil state. Still others think a wall of separation protects the civil polity from ecclesiastical interference or domination. A high barrier between church and civil state also promises to avoid conflict among religious sects competing for government favor or assistance. All these functions of walls have figured in the diverse applications and interpretations of the wall of separation.

In *Of the Laws of Ecclesiastical Polity*, the sixteenth-century Anglican apologist for England's ecclesiastical establishment under the governorship of the monarch, Richard Hooker (1554–1600), decried "walls of separation between...the *Church* and the *Commonwealth*" that denied the crown its divine prerogative to rule over both the church and the commonwealth. Roger Williams (1603?–1683), the seventeenth-century colonial advocate for religious liberty and founder of Rhode Island, wrote in a 1644 tract that a "hedge or wall of separation between the garden of the church and the wilderness of the world" was peculiarly appropriate to safeguard the religious purity of Christ's church from worldly corruptions. In his work *Crito* (1766, 1767), the eighteenth-century dissenting Scottish reformer James Burgh (1714–1775), who distrusted ecclesiastical establishments, proposed building "an impenetrable wall of *separation* between things *sacred* and *civil*" in order to prevent the church from "getting too much power into her hands, and turning religion into a mere state-engine."

In *Separation of Church and State* (2002), Philip Hamburger argued that the rhetoric and attendant doctrine of church-state separation emerged in American political and legal thought much later than is often presumed. He traced the evolution of this rhetoric in America, starting as a political principle of separation between religion and politics, which began to gain currency in disestablishment debates of the late eighteenth century and in the presidential contest of 1800. Jeffersonian partisans adopted the rhetoric to silence the Congregationalist–Federalist clergymen who had denounced candidate Jefferson as an infidel or atheist. In a celebrated 1802 missive to the Danbury Baptist Association, with its metaphoric "wall of separation," President Jefferson deftly transformed the political principle into a constitutional principle by equating the language of separation with the text of the First Amendment. Not until well into the nineteenth century did separation of church and state come to be viewed widely as a constitutional principle. The constitutional principle was eventually elevated to constitutional law by the U.S. Supreme Court in a series of influential mid-twentieth-century rulings, starting with *Everson v. Board of Education*. Jefferson's wall, pursuant to the original construction of the First Amendment, separated church and national government only, whereas the wall described in *Everson* imposed restriction on both national and state governments.

In the American context, the phrases "separation of church and state" and "wall of separation" are typically used as figurative expressions for the First Amendment. Therefore, an important legal and political consideration is the question whether these terms accurately represent the constitutional principles governing church-state relations. In *Everson,* the justices described a "high and impregnable" wall erected by the First Amendment. This First Amendment wall ensured that

> Neither a state nor the Federal Government can set up a church. Neither can pass laws which aid one religion, aid all religions, or prefer one religion over another. Neither can force nor influence a person to go to or to remain away from church against his will or force him to profess a belief or disbelief in any religion. No person can be punished for entertaining or professing religious beliefs or disbeliefs, for church attendance or non-attendance. No tax in any amount, large or small, can be levied to support any religious activities or institutions, whatever they may be called, or whatever form they may adopt to teach or practice religion.

> Neither a state nor the Federal Government can, openly or secretly, participate in the affairs of any religious organizations or groups and *vice versa*.

Critics contend that the metaphoric rhetoric of church-state separation misrepresents First Amendment principles. Although "separation of church and state" and the First Amendment concept of "nonestablishment" are often used interchangeably today, in the lexicon of the late eighteenth and early nineteenth centuries, the expansive notion of "separation" was distinct from the narrow institutional concepts of "nonestablishment" and "disestablishment." Advocates of disestablishment or nonestablishment, such as evangelical dissenters, did not necessarily embrace the concept of separation because they feared it could divorce religion's beneficent influences from public life and policy.

Furthermore, "separation of church and state" indicates an equivalent restriction on both the church and the state. Similarly, a wall is a bilateral barrier that inhibits the activities of both the civil government and religion—unlike the First Amendment, which imposes restrictions on civil government only. The various First Amendment guarantees were entirely a check or restraint on civil government, specifically on Congress. As a bilateral barrier, however, the wall unavoidably restricts religion's ability to influence the conduct of civil government, and, thus, it necessarily exceeds the limitations imposed by the Constitution. A product of this separationist rhetoric, critics say, is that the First Amendment, which was written to limit civil government, has been reinterpreted to restrict religion in the public square and to secularize public life.

The wall of separation has figured prominently in leading U.S. Supreme Court rulings on religion and education. In *Everson,* the Court considered the constitutionality of state reimbursements to parents for money expended in the transportation of their children to and from parochial schools. Invoking Jefferson's metaphor, the Court opined: "Neither a state nor the Federal Government...can pass laws which aid one religion, aid all religions, or prefer one religion over another....No tax in any amount, large or small, can be levied to support any religious activities or institutions." The phrase was frequently referenced in *McCollum v. Board of Education* (1948), which held that an Illinois released-time program that permitted religious instruction at private expense in public school facilities during regular school hours violated the First Amendment nonestablishment provision. In *Engel v. Vitale* (1962), the first of the major school prayer decisions, the Court agreed with the petitioners that "the State's use of the [New York State Board of] Regents' prayer in its public school system breaches the constitutional wall of separation between Church and State." This set the stage for rulings the following term holding that state-sponsored prayer and Bible reading in public schools are unconstitutional.

Judicial uses of the "wall" have not been without criticism and controversy. In *McCollum,* Justice Stanley F. Reed protested that "A rule of law should not be drawn from a figure of speech." Justice Potter Stewart similarly cautioned his fellow justices in *Engel v. Vitale* that the Court's task in resolving complex constitutional controversies "is not responsibly aided by the uncritical invocation of metaphors like the 'wall of separation,' a phrase nowhere to be found in the Constitution." In *Wallace v. Jaffree* (1985), then Justice William H. Rehnquist renounced the "wall," declaring that the "'wall of separation between church and State' is a metaphor based on bad history, a metaphor which has proved useless as a guide to judging. It should be frankly and explicitly abandoned."

A separationist construction of the First Amendment was ascendant in Supreme Court jurisprudence for nearly 40 years following *Everson.* Since the mid-1980s, this construction has been increasingly contested, and separationist rhetoric has lost influence on the Court. Nonetheless, "separation of church and state" and "wall of separation" remain ubiquitous and influential phrases in legal, political, and popular discourse. *See also: Everson v. Board of Education of the Township of Ewing;* First Amendment Religious Clauses and the Supreme Court; Jefferson, Thomas; Religious Accommodation.

Further Reading: Daniel L. Dreisbach, *Thomas Jefferson and the Wall of Separation between Church and State* (New York: New York University Press, 2002); *Engel v. Vitale,* 370 U.S. 421 (1962); *Everson v. Board of Education,* 330 U.S. 1 (1947); Forum, *William and Mary Quarterly,* 56 (October 1999): 775–824; Philip Hamburger, *Separation of Church and State* (Cambridge, MA: Harvard University Press, 2002); *McCollum v. Board of Education,* 333 U.S. 203 (1948); *Wallace v. Jaffree,* 472 U.S. 38 (1985).

Daniel L. Dreisbach

Seton, Elizabeth

Elizabeth Bayley Seton (1774–1821) was the founder and first Mother Superior of the Sisters of Charity in the United States. She is often credited with establishing the first Catholic parochial school in the United States, but the claim is dubious. Without question, however, Seton should be credited with spreading and systemizing Catholic education in the first quarter of the nineteenth century. Seton was born in New York on August 28, 1774, the daughter of a surgeon, Richard Bayley, and Catherine Charleston. As a student, Seton showed real aptitude and was described as personable but introspective. She wed William Seton, Jr. in 1794 and was responsible for raising five children.

In 1798, Elizabeth and William inherited responsibility for both the family company and the welfare of his three young sisters. Elizabeth managed the care of both families in the Seton household and homeschooled her own children and her sisters-in-law. The family fortunes took a turn for the worse in 1801 when the company went bankrupt and William showed signs of tuberculosis. In 1803 Elizabeth, William, and their oldest daughter traveled to Italy in an effort to restore his health. He died shortly after arrival and left Elizabeth a widow with five young children.

A family friend, Antonio Filicchi, and his wife provided gracious hospitality until the Setons could return to the United States the next spring. In fact, it was the Filicchis who introduced Elizabeth to Catholicism. Seton returned to the United States in 1804 and became a Catholic on March 14, 1805. Her initial years in the Church were marked by a community hostility that prevented her from beginning a school in New York.

The Sulpicians, an order of French priests, invited Seton to Baltimore in 1808 to establish a small school in the city for the education of Catholic children. Within a year, Elizabeth took religious vows and established the Daughters (later Sisters) of Charity of St. Joseph and was given the title "Mother Seton" by Archbishop John Carroll. A wealthy seminarian and fellow convert gave Seton land for the establishment of a motherhouse near Emmitsburg, and Elizabeth and her group arrived in the small community in June 1809. The Reverend John Dubois, founder of Mount Saint Mary's College and Seminary in Emmitsburg, offered his cabin on Saint Mary's Mountain for the women to use until they were able to move to their property. Elected by the members of the community to be the first Mother Superior of the Sisters of Charity in 1812, Seton was reelected successively and remained as superior until her death.

In February 1810, Elizabeth opened Saint Joseph's Free School for the education of "needy girls"; it was the first free Catholic school for girls in the country staffed by sisters. Saint Joseph's Academy began in May of that year. By boarding pupils who paid tuition, the Sisters of Charity subsidized their charitable free school operations. The order grew in numbers during the first decade of its existence. Numerous women joined the Sisters of Charity. Of the 98 candidates who arrived at the convent in Elizabeth's lifetime, 86 candidates actually joined the order and 70 percent remained Sisters of Charity for life. Illness and early death were a constant in Elizabeth's life. In addition to her two daughters and her sisters-in-law, she buried 18 sisters at Emmitsburg,

The Sisters of Charity intertwined social ministry with education in the faith and religious values in all they undertook in their mission. Elizabeth dispatched sisters to Philadelphia to manage Saint Joseph's Asylum, the first Catholic orphanage in the United States in 1814. The next year she opened a mission at Mount Saint Mary's to oversee the infirmary and domestic services for the college and seminary near Emmitsburg. In 1817, sisters from Saint Joseph's Valley went to New York to begin the New York City Orphan Asylum.

Seton died January 4, 1821. Her remains repose in a basilica that bears her name in Emmitsburg, Maryland. Her work of education and charity lives on in the order that she founded. Cardinal James Gibbons of Baltimore began the process of canonization for Seton in 1882. Pope John XXIII declared Seton "venerable" in December 1959, and also beatified her in March 1963. Pope Paul VI canonized Saint Elizabeth Ann Seton in September 1975. *See also:* Catholic Schools; Religious Orders.

Further Reading: Joseph I. Dirvin, *Mrs. Seton: Foundress of the American Sisters of Charity* (New York: Farrar, Straus, and Giroux, 1962); Ellen M. Kelly and Annabelle M. Melville, eds., *Elizabeth Seton: Selected Writings* (Mahwah, NJ: Paulist Press, 1987); Annabelle M. Melville, *Elizabeth Bayley Seton, 1774–1821* (New York: Scribner's, 1951).

Timothy Walch

Seventh-day Adventist Schools

The Seventh-day Adventist elementary and secondary schools in the United States are part of a worldwide educational system operated by that denomination. The church had its beginnings in the religious awakening of the mid-nineteenth century, especially in the northeastern states. Many of the followers of William Miller, who had predicted the literal return of Jesus to this earth in 1844, continued in fellowship after the great disappointment of that year when Christ did not come. In further Bible study they determined that Christ would indeed come in a literal manner; however, the exact date was not to be predicted. Other distinctive doctrines held by the small group of Adventists included worship on the seventh day, as introduced in the creation story of Genesis and required by the Fourth Commandment given at Mount Sinai, and a unique belief in the ministry of Christ in the heavenly sanctuary following his ascension from earth.

The denomination was formally organized in 1863 and today has a worldwide membership of over 15 million with 1 million adherents in the United States. Throughout its history, the Adventist church has been marked by three major institutions: health care, publishing, and education. Its doctrines are essentially consistent with evangelical

Protestantism while it attempts to spread the gospel with evangelistic fervor. It was this commitment to evangelism that provided a catalyst for the development of a school system as part of the mission of the Church. The growing church needed pastors and other workers to provide a solid basis for leadership. Because of its unique doctrines, it was felt that church workers could not be best trained by other institutions. So Battle Creek College was founded in 1874 in the city of that name. This college was later moved to the little village of Berrien Springs in southwest Michigan and renamed Emmanuel Missionary College. It later became Andrews University in honor of the first official missionary sponsored by the denomination.

As the church's early adherents developed a lifestyle counter to the dominant culture, they found that their children were subject to a degree of cognitive dissonance as they attended public schools. Church members soon discovered the need to have their own elementary and secondary schools to inculcate their children with their religious beliefs in preparation for membership in the faith community. The first official elementary school (1872) was nothing more than a homeschool, but soon other small schools began to operate on a more formal basis. Like many rural public schools in America at the time, early Adventist schools were small one-room schools taught by teachers with little formal pedagogical preparation. The Adventist church today still operates many small schools, though with teachers who are fully certified to teach.

The operation of secondary schools posed unique problems for the church because of the scattered nature of the membership. In response, the denomination developed coeducational boarding high schools with a large enough student body to offer a full range of high school subjects. Since most of the members were from the working-class, they could not afford the tuition charged by the school. Facing this problem, most of the boarding schools developed a program where students could earn at least a portion of their tuition by working part time. Most early Adventist high schools operated a farm that not only provided income for the school but also provided employment for students. Other industries were developed over the years that allowed students to earn a wage and pay for a major portion of their school expenses. Eventually the concept of work-study became embedded within the Adventist philosophy of education.

The boarding schools were coeducational and were characterized by strict rules, especially in controlling the relationship between boys and girls who lived in dormitories on the campus. To accommodate the work program, the academic schedule was split so that students would attend classes half the day and work the other half. Good health was an essential part of the Adventist teaching, and early on, vegetarianism became a dominant lifestyle within the church. At Adventist schools no meat or caffeinated drinks are served in the cafeteria.

A regimented lifestyle, rather rigid rules of behavior, and emphasis on good work habits provided a foundation to the strong academic requirements of the school. In addition, students were required to take one class in religious studies each year. Further, morning and evening devotions were required, along with a full round of religious services on the weekend. Thus, students attending Adventist schools were fully immersed in the life of the church and surrounded by spiritual influences. An early Adventist leader, Ellen White, wrote extensively on education as well as other subjects vital to the developing denomination. Her writings continue to provide a philosophical foundation for Adventist schools.

To maintain the emphasis on spiritual values and the teachings of the church, all faculty and staff at Adventist schools are required to be members of the church in good standing.

In the early years it became a challenge to find enough adherents to the denomination to staff a growing number of schools. To meet this need, Adventist colleges developed teacher training programs specifically preparing teachers for their unique role in Adventist schools. Today most teachers in Adventist schools have been prepared by the denomination's colleges in North America.

As the denomination in North America grew in membership, so too did the schools. Since the church is organized around hierarchical lines, so is the system of schools. Schools are operated through a dual governance system with a local congregation electing members to an operating board that deals with day-to-day matters while the central church authority is responsible for overall educational policy and employment matters. Larger congregations are able to operate their own secondary school programs and the need for boarding schools has diminished, resulting in several closures in recent years. Along with the development of the day schools has been a decline in the work-study program which, in essence, is no longer a part of the Adventist philosophy.

Early Adventist educators became concerned regarding the textbooks that were used in their schools. In response, the church published as many books as possible to maintain a consistency with the central beliefs of the church. First came the publication of textbooks for Bible classes followed by reading textbooks that inculcated spiritual values as well as the teaching of reading. Eventually, the denomination found it necessary to publish books for science classes because of concern about the teaching of evolution in popular textbooks.

Adventists have developed some unique configurations for their elementary and secondary schools. Among these is the Junior Academy, which includes grades kindergarten through nine or ten. This enabled parents to keep their children at home during the early adolescent years rather than sending them away to boarding schools. The denomination has also developed a system of certification for teachers and administrators and accreditation of schools in which minimum standards for school operation are maintained. While many Adventist teachers and administrators have state certification, they all have denominational credentials that require courses in religious studies as well as denominational history and doctrines. As of the year 2003 the Adventist church in North America operated 679 K–8 elementary schools, 53 K–9 schools, 111 K–10 schools also known as junior academies, 68 K–12 schools, and 55 secondary schools with grades 9 to 12. It also operated 13 colleges and universities in North America.

The Seventh-day Adventist schools in the United States face some unique challenges as they continue their operation in support of the denomination's evangelistic goals. With demographic changes in recent years, many of the small rural schools have closed because of declining enrollment. There is a concentration of membership in the urban and suburban areas and an increased emphasis on developing day schools, which has accelerated the closure of boarding schools. As Adventist teachers become more highly educated, there is upward pressure on salaries, which provides financial challenges to the operation of the school. The popular culture of America provides additional challenges to maintaining the church's youths' focus on the unique lifestyle beliefs of the church without being overwhelmed by the temptations of modern life. Further, the resurgence of the public schools in improving their academic quality, fueled in part by the No Child Left Behind Act, has put renewed pressure upon Adventist schools to improve their academic performance. This is a real challenge to small underfinanced church-operated schools in competition with the better financed and larger public schools.

Denominational leaders have risen to meet the challenges before them as they provide leadership for the Seventh-day Adventist schools. While the church's pay scale is not as high as that of the public sector, it has been maintained at a level that makes teaching in an Adventist school a worthwhile career goal. Further, the availability of advanced academic degrees in Adventist universities has resulted in a highly educated teaching staff. Additionally, efforts such as *Project Affirmation* have maintained a focus on the Adventist distinctives in its educational system. Thus, the denomination's schools continue to be seen as vital to the mission of the Seventh-day Adventist church. *See also:* Council for American Private Education.

Further Reading: Roger L. Dudley, *Valuegenesis: Faith in the Balance* (Riverside, CA: La Sierra University Press, 1992); George R. Knight, *Anticipating the Advent: A Brief History of Seventh-day Adventists* (Boise, ID: Pacific Press, 1993); Richard W. Schwarz and Floyd Greenleaf, *Light Bearers: A History of the Seventh-day Adventist Church,* rev. ed. (Nampa, ID: Pacific Press, 2000); Ellen G. White, *Education* (Mountain View, CA: Pacific Press Publishing Association, 1952).

Lyndon G. Furst

Sex Education and Religion

Sex education provides information about human reproductive organs and processes, intercourse, gestation, and childbirth. It may also cover such topics as masturbation, homosexuality, gender roles, and abortion. Ordinarily taught in middle and secondary schools, sex education has long been surrounded by controversy about the age at which students should receive such information and whether they should receive it from school personnel or from parents or from religious instructors. In particular, opponents deplore what they see as the clinical presentation of human sexuality as a mere body of facts without reference to religious and moral values.

Proposals to include information about human sexuality in the public school curriculum arose as early as the 1880s, and in 1912 the National Education Association (NEA) began advocating teacher training in so-called "sex hygiene." Conflicts over sex education as it is understood today date back to the 1960s, when conservative organizations led by the Christian Crusade and the John Birch Society rose up in protest against the growth of sex education courses backed by such groups as the NEA and the American Medical Association.

At issue in most current disputes is a conflict between two approaches to sex education: abstinence-only and comprehensive. Abstinence-only programs teach that abstaining from sex outside of marriage constitutes the only socially acceptable form of behavior as well as the only means of maintaining physical and psychological health. Comprehensive programs, while they may encourage abstinence as the preferred choice, also provide information about contraception and safe sex.

The struggle over these two approaches to sex education depends heavily on nonprofit agencies that engage in grassroots organizing, legislative lobbying, and litigation. Supporting comprehensive sex education are such groups as the Sexuality Information and Education Council of the United States, Advocates for Youth, and Planned Parenthood. They maintain that abstinence-only programs privilege religious values over effective instruction, fail to reduce teen pregnancy and sexually transmitted diseases (STDs), and use scare tactics based on inaccurate medical information (e.g., about the risk of cancer, the transmission of HIV, the failure rate of contraceptives, and the cognitive capacity of fetuses).

On the other side of the debate are such organizations as the Heritage Foundation, Focus on the Family, and Concerned Women for America. In their view, comprehensive sex education encourages extramarital and homosexual sex, minimizes the social and personal costs of extramarital sex and childbearing, and misleads students into believing that contraception is 100 percent effective in preventing pregnancy and disease.

Congress joined the fray on the abstinence-only side in 1981, when it passed the Adolescent Family Life Act (AFLA) as Title XX of the Public Health Service Act. It provides federal funding for abstinence-only sex education in schools, community-based programs, religious institutions, and homes, with emphasis on parental involvement. The U.S. Supreme Court upheld AFLA in *Bowen v. Kendrick,* ruling that the promotion of abstinence outside of marriage merely coincides with certain religious beliefs but does not advance religion as such. The Court also upheld the awarding of sex education grants to religious institutions, although it permitted review of specific grants alleged to be used for religious advocacy.

In 1996, Congress authorized further funds for abstinence-only sex education by adding it to the activities funded under Title V of the Social Security Act. Since then, Title V has provided millions of dollars for programs whose sole purpose is to promote abstinence from sex outside of marriage. Programs thus funded must emphasize the dangers of extramarital sex and may not recommend such measures as contraception and the use of condoms for disease prevention. They must also teach that "a mutually faithful monogamous relationship in the context of marriage is the expected standard of human sexual activity" (42 U.S.C. 710, 510).

States that choose to apply for Title V funds may allocate them not only to public schools but also to community-based programs, including religious groups that target young adults as well as adolescents. Accordingly, Title V, like AFLA, generates controversy about the alleged use of federal funds by religious groups for sex education based as much on religious dogma as on scientific fact. Some states, such as California, Connecticut, Rhode Island, New Jersey, and New York, have opted to forgo Title V support and use their own funds to pay for public school sex education that includes information on contraception, safe sex, and homosexuality. As a result, community-based and religious organizations in those states have no access to Title V funds.

A third federal funding stream for abstinence-only sex education was created in 2000, when Congress authorized the Community-Based Abstinence Education Program (CBAE). Bypassing the states, CBAE allows nonprofit, community, and religious organizations to apply for funds directly. The guidelines for defining abstinence-only sex education are the same as those for Title V.

In addition to disagreeing about the presentation of heterosexual intercourse and its results, participants in the sex-education debate clash over the treatment of homosexuality. Particularly since the AIDS epidemic unfolded in the 1980s, advocates of comprehensive sex education have been calling for the inclusion of accurate, nonjudgmental information about same-sex relations and the avoidance of HIV and other STDs. This position is supported by such groups as the Lambda Legal Defense Fund and the Human Rights Campaign, which seek equal treatment for homosexuals in American society. Abstinence-only supporters protest that such instruction might recruit naïve teenagers to a homosexual lifestyle. Moreover, such organizations as the Catholic Church and the Christian Coalition oppose supposedly value-neutral education about homosexuality on the ground that it undercuts religious teachings by suggesting that homosexuality is a normal and natural human condition and that homosexual relationships deserve the same respect accorded to the traditional nuclear family.

Debates about the portrayal of homosexuality extend beyond formal sex education to affect any area of the curriculum in which lifestyles and values are discussed. Conflicts frequently arise, for instance, over the inclusion of gay-themed children's stories in the elementary-school reading curriculum: among others, *Heather Has Two Mommies,* by Leslea Newman and Diana Souza; *Daddy's Roommate,* by Michael Willhoite; *King and King,* by Linda de Haan; and *And Tango Makes Three,* by Peter Parnell and Justin Richardson. Supporters and opponents generally agree that the use of such material would tend to validate homosexual relationships and influence the children to regard them as normal. The point at issue is whether those results represent long-overdue justice for a traditionally disfavored population or age-inappropriate propaganda aimed at undercutting traditional social and religious values.

At the secondary-school level, homosexual students and their supporters have generated similar controversies by establishing gay-themed clubs, such as the Gay/Straight Alliance, over the objections of school authorities. Their right to establish such clubs is based on the Equal Access Act (EAA), signed into law in 1984 by President Ronald Reagan. Intended primarily to allow students to establish religious clubs within the schools' extracurricular programs, EAA stipulates that students as individuals are entitled to engage in the speech of their choice even if the school could not or would not endorse it. Despite the efforts of some school officials to exclude gay-friendly clubs on the grounds that they are potentially disruptive and detrimental to the students' welfare, several federal courts have upheld the students' right to advocate not only social acceptance of homosexuality, but also changes in the law, such as the legal recognition of homosexual partnerships. *See also:* Christian Coalition; Focus on the Family.

Further Reading: *Bowen v. Kendrick,* 487 U.S. 589 (1988); *Coleman v. Caddo Parish School Board,* 635 So. 2d 1238 (1994); *East High Gay/Straight Alliance v. Board of Education of Salt Lake City School District,* 81 F. Supp. 2d 1166 (1999); *Gay-Straight Alliance of Okeechobee High School v. School Board of Okeechobee County,* 483 F. Supp. 2d 1224 (2007); Janice M. Irvine, *Talk About Sex: The Battles Over Sex Education in the United States* (Berkeley, CA: University of California Press, 2002); Steven P. Ridini, *Health and Sexuality Education in Schools: The Process of Social Change* (Westport, CT: Bergin & Garvey, 1998); James T. Sears, ed., *Sexuality and the Curriculum: The Politics and Practices of Sexuality Education* (New York, NY: Teachers College Press, 1992).

Joan DelFattore

Smith v. Board of Commissioners of Mobile County

The Smith case was a continuation of the Alabama prayer case, *Wallace v. Jaffree* (1985). The U.S. Supreme Court ruled in *Jaffree* that a state statute authorizing a period for meditation or voluntary prayer violated the Establishment Clause. A federal district court had upheld the statute allowing prayer in Alabama schools. In the decision upholding the prayer at the district court level, a footnote stated that the teaching of secular humanism was occurring in the public schools. The rationale was that if there was no religion taught then what was taught must be secular humanism. The district court also implied that if this question were raised at a later date then the court would rule in favor of the plaintiffs.

In the remand of the *Jaffree* case to the district court from the U.S. Supreme Court, the issue of secular humanism in the curriculum was raised. If Christianity is not permissible, then other religions, such as secular humanism, would also be prohibited. The plaintiffs asserted that the Mobile County School District unconstitutionally advanced the religion of humanism. They argued that since the textbooks in the areas of history, social studies, and home economics were devoid of Christianity they therefore established the religion of secular humanism. The federal district court ruled that the textbooks promoted the religion of secular humanism. It also found that 44 of the textbooks violated the Establishment Clause and enjoined the Alabama public schools from using these books.

The Eleventh Circuit Court of Appeals ruled that the textbooks did not advance secular humanism or inhibit theistic religion in violation of the Establishment Clause and therefore reversed the lower court's decision. The appellate court made this ruling, assuming that there might be something called a religious or secular humanism.

The circuit court applied the *Lemon* test: "First the statute must have a secular Legislative purpose; second its principal or primary effect must be one that neither advances nor inhibits religion; . . . [third] the statute must not foster an excessive government entanglement with religion." The parties agreed that there was no question about two of the *Lemon* test prongs, these being religious purpose and excessive government entanglement. Therefore the court addressed only whether the "challenged textbook had the primary effect of either advancing or inhibiting religion."

The appellate court examined all the textbooks and closely reviewed those that the district court had noted as establishing secular humanism. Was there evidence that the textbooks were antagonistic to theistic beliefs? The court stated:

> [The] contents of these textbooks, including the passages pointed out by [Plaintiffs] as particularly offensive, in the context of the books as a whole and the undisputedly nonreligious purpose sought to be achieved by their use, reveals that the message conveyed is not one of endorsement of secular humanism or any religion. Rather, the message conveyed is one of a governmental attempt to instill in Alabama public school children such values as independent thought, tolerance of diverse views, self-respect, maturity, self-reliance and logical decision-making. This is an entirely appropriate secular effect. Indeed, one of the major objectives of public education is the inclusion of fundamental values necessary to the maintenance of a democratic political system. It is true that the textbooks contain ideas that are consistent with secular humanism; the textbooks also contain ideas consistent with theistic religion.

The court noted, however, that "mere consistency with religious tenets is insufficient to constitute unconstitutional advancement of religion." The U.S. Supreme Court declined to review the appellate court's decision. *See also:* Humanism and the Humanist Manifestos; Secularism; *Wallace v. Jaffree.*

Further Reading: *Bethel School District No. 403 v. Fraser,* 478 U.S. 675 (1986); *Smith v. Board of Commissioners of Mobile County,* 827 F. 2d 684 (11th Cir. 1987); *Wallace v. Jaffree,* 472 U.S. 38 (1985).

M. David Alexander

Southern Baptists and Education

The Southern Baptist Convention (SBC) was organized in 1845 in Augusta, Georgia, when it split with the Baptist General Convention over structural, economic, and political issues, including slavery. It claims over 16 million members who worship in over 42,000 churches, and it is the largest Protestant denomination in the United States. Southern Baptists meet annually for a convention to debate resolutions and elect their leadership. Its congregational polity allows members to submit resolutions, interpret doctrine, and shape institutional priorities and direction.

The SBC has a long and inconsistent history of engagement with issues related to religion and education. Prior to the mid-1980s, it was a strong advocate of the separation of church and state as evidenced by its support for the controversial Supreme Court prayer decisions in the 1960s (*Engel v. Vitale*, 1962, and *Abington v. Schempp*, 1963) and its strong opposition to voucher and related initiatives that authorize the use of public funds to support private (including religious) schools. An ideological shift in the organization occurred in the mid-1980s, however, when the SBC took stances that were in direct opposition to these earlier positions. A brief overview of this history will help explain this seemingly abrupt change.

Through a series of resolutions, commentaries, and expressions of legal advocacy, the SBC was quite vocal in its pre-1980 support of a strict separationist stance between religion and government as exemplified in the following: It opposed *Everson v. Board of Education* (1947) where the court ruled that the use of public funds to pay transportation costs for parochial students attending Catholic schools was constitutional, and it supported *McCollum v. Board of Education* (1948) where the Court banned religious groups from providing religious instruction in schools during school hours. SBC support for both resolutions is often interpreted in the context of anti-Catholic sentiment that was widespread in the United States and especially pronounced among Southern Baptists. Other representations of this influence include a 1972 resolution that opposed tax support for parochial schools, including voucher plans; a resolution passed in 1981 entitled "Affirming Religious Liberty and Separation of Church and State" where the SBC protested against "tax proposals which would finance education and other activities of churches or religious groups" (Jones, 2004, p. 14); and a similar resolution passed in 1982 that again opposed tax credits for parochial school tuition and expressed concern regarding perceived threats to the First Amendment separation between church and state.

Though anti-Catholic sentiment was certainly a contributing factor in the examples cited above, it does not account for the SBC's support of both *Engel v. Vitale* (1962) where school-sponsored prayer was banned and *Abington v. Schempp* (1963) where school-sponsored recitation of the Lord's Prayer and devotional Bible reading were also declared unconstitutional. Whereas other conservative Protestants (including the National Association of Evangelicals) vigorously condemned these rulings, the SBC supported them. Furthermore, while other conservative Protestants were rallying behind the Becker Amendment proposed in 1963 to clarify that "Nothing in this Constitution shall be deemed to prohibit the offering, reading from, or listening to prayers or biblical scriptures, if participation therein is on a voluntary basis" (DelFattore, 2004, p. 111), the Baptist Joint Committee on Public Affairs (BJCPA) joined an anti-Becker coalition that included the American Civil Liberties Union, the Anti-Defamation League, and the National Council of Churches of Christ. The BJCPA, the public policy arm of the SBC, asserted that the Becker Amendment misrepresented the 1960s Supreme Court rulings as banning free exercise as opposed to the establishment of religion. It urged Baptists to reject any religion that was offered on a "government platter" (Jones, 2004, p. 12). Finally, in debates regarding an Equal Access Bill introduced in the Senate in 1983, the

BJCPA opposed its application in elementary schools. John W. Baker (general counsel of the BJCPA at the time) asserted that elementary students are not mature enough to understand the distinction between student- versus parent- or teacher-initiated religious expression: "The introduction of religion at this level would be neither voluntary nor student initiated. It would be the product of parents who want their own religious beliefs given voice to all the students in a class, or it would be a reflection of the religious beliefs of the teacher" (DelFattore, 2004, p. 203).

The notion that strict separation was the best protection for religious expression guided SBC policy until the early to mid-1980s when those who promoted an emphasis on free exercise rose in political prominence. Tensions within the organization became apparent when the SBC supported the 1982 Reagan Amendment (another legislative attempt to pass an amendment to the Constitution supporting school prayer) while the BJCPA opposed it by citing the long history of SBC support for the 1960s Supreme Court decisions. In 1991, the SBC defunded the BJCPA and transferred its responsibilities to the Christian Life Committee.

The SBC shift in focus from establishment to free exercise foundations for its policy stances on religion in the schools was also exemplified in several other resolutions and statements, including the following: a 1982 resolution in support of "scientific creationism"; its agreement with Justice Antonin Scalia's dissent in *Edwards v. Aguillard* (1987) where the court declared that the "balanced treatment" of creation science with evolution in biology classrooms was unconstitutional; and its support of numerous resolutions opposing issues related to positive depictions of gay, lesbian, and bisexual identified people in school programs and curricula. One of the most dramatic expressions of the change in SBC policy, however, is a 1991 resolution entitled "Parental Choice in Education," where it reversed its long-standing opposition to vouchers. One key to understanding this larger shift in strategy and focus is embedded in the resolution itself when it claims that "More and more Southern Baptist parents are concerned that their public school systems are increasingly hostile to Christian convictions" (Jones, 2004, p. 15). The experience of the schools as increasingly hostile to Christianity and (by extension) Christians is central to the SBC promotion of free exercise from its newly perceived status as marginalized.

The SBC remains heavily involved in public policy issues related to religion in the schools. Though tensions still remain regarding differing strategies, ideologies, and priorities, the emphasis on free exercise remains the prominent strategy employed. *See also:* Baptist Joint Committee on Religious Liberty; The Bible in the Public Schools; Prayer in the Public Schools; Vouchers.

Further Reading: Abington School District v. Schempp, 374 U.S. 203 (1963); Joan DelFattore, *The Fourth R* (New Haven, CT: Yale University Press, 2004); *Edwards v. Aguillard,* 482 U.S. 578 (1987); *Engel v. Vitale,* 370 U.S. 421 (1962); *Everson v. Board of Education,* 330 U.S. 1 (1947); Michael B. Jones, "Southern Baptist Convention: A Case Study in Religious Fundamentalism and Church/State Separation," in *Conference Papers—Western Political Science Association,* 2004 Annual Meeting, Portland, OR, 1–39; *McCollum v. Board of Education,* 333 U.S. 203 (1948); Diane L. Moore, *Overcoming Religious Illiteracy* (New York: Palgrave Macmillan, 2007); Jay Alan Sekulow, *Witnessing Their Faith* (New York: Rowman and Littlefield, 2005); Southern Baptist Convention, at www.sbc.net.

Diane L. Moore

Spirituality

"Spirit" may be defined as the "animating or vital principle held to give life." The root words, "spirits" (Latin) for breath and "enthusiasms" (Greek) for "the God within," combine to stand for "the breath of God within." Spirituality includes emphasis upon self-exploration or consciousness, reliance on self for problem solving, holistic and nonrational thinking, flexibility, connectedness with others, especially a source greater than self, transcendence, reluctance to harm others, tendency to ask why and what if questions, and ability to work against conventional thought. One source said simply, "it is heart knowledge," while others believe it has kinetic energy levels.

Do spirituality and religion overlap? Religion is often described as worship of God in formally articulated theological systems practiced in socialized settings, a structured attempt to facilitate and interpret the search for meaning in life. Some conclude a person can be both religious and spiritual, with spirituality the goal to find self and a higher power; religion is the road to that goal. Others, however, argue that processes and purposes are significantly dissimilar, so a person can be spiritual but not religious, or vice versa.

Before turning to spirituality in the context of schooling, consider the shifting forms of religion and spirituality in the United States. Native Americans have had a rich tradition of spirituality. Roman Catholic priests and missionaries of the 1600s and 1700s either incorporated spiritual traditions into their religious rituals or suppressed them. As Eck (2002) notes, white settlers of New England and later the Midwest established formal religious practices located in houses of worship, increasingly linked to specific doctrines and dogma. Wuthnow (2000) identifies this cluster of practices, which lasted until the 1950s, as "a spirituality of dwellings."

A "spirituality of seeking" emerged during the 1960s, fueled by criticisms of the Vietnam War. A flood of new ways to ask questions of ultimate meaning and personal enlightenment emerged, as businesses, government, religion, and educational systems were found wanting. *American Spiritualities* (Albanese, 2001) provides a helpful summary of movements; *Contemporary Spiritualities* (Erricker and Erricker, 2001) is organized under the rubric of influential thinkers.

The United States presents an excellent microcosm of spiritual opportunities available globally. The *American Religious Identification Survey* offers quantitative data on the scope of America's spiritual diversity (Kosmin, Mayer, and Keysar, 2001). In part, it is the result of the separation of church and state policy, which allows "religious" groups to flourish. Another factor is the generous immigration policy following the Vietnam War. Los Angeles, California, for example, is now considered to have the largest variety of Buddhist "schools of thought" in the world (Eck, 2002).

Robert Coles's *The Spiritual Lives of Children* (1990) provides a helpful overview of this age group. The values education movement (1960s and 1970s) nurtured some spiritual qualities, but focused more on the secondary school level. In the past 20 years (1990 to present), elementary school children are more likely to have seen curriculum activities associated with character education—developing traits such as honesty, respect, commitment, and not spirituality instruction per se (*Education Leadership* special issue, December 1998/January 1999). Zohar and Marshall (2000) posit that brain research has identified not only cognitive and emotional centers, but also a spiritual intelligence center. In *The Spirit of the Child,* David Hay (2006) asserts brain research supports the need for spirituality in the curriculum.

A 1950s National Education Association publication, *Moral and Spiritual Values in the Public Schools,* listed ten "common" values that were to be emphasized in secondary schools. Today, there are many supporters of spirituality curriculum in secondary schools. Some voice deep concern about expecting too much from schools. Chief among them is Parker Palmer. At a "Spirituality in Education Conference" (1997) sponsored by the Holistic Education Network, Parker and others contended formal schooling retards rather than enriches the spiritual life for both students and teachers.

Spiritual concerns were typical of the church-related and liberal arts colleges of the seventeenth through nineteenth centuries, capped by a moral philosophy course taught by the president. Spirituality has been a vigorous part of religious groups such as Roman Catholicism; it is not antithetical to faith traditions. Since the late 1800s, the scientific mode of learning (focus on naturalism) has downplayed the spiritual. But newer science models resist a dualist perspective (science vs. religion) and are more open to holistic learning. There is clearly a trend in higher education to have faculty and staff incorporate spiritual dimensions in their courses and programs (Tisdell, 2006).

The most extensive past and ongoing data on student spirituality can be found at the Higher Education Research Institute of the University of California Los Angeles. A cooperative research program is the Collaborative on Spirituality in Higher Education consisting of Education as Transformation, the Community for Integrative Learning and Action, and the Initiative for Authenticity and Spirituality in Higher Education.

Faith traditions have never abandoned spirituality education for adults. An estimated 40 percent of American adults participate in support groups, a number of them focused on spirituality (Wuthnow, 1994). There are also a wide variety of institutes, workshops, and resources in such areas as spirituality and health and spirituality in the workplace.

In this treatment of spirituality, limited to educational settings, Americans seem to be going full circle. Both within formal education and in informal and new ways, the trend is away from a secular outlook and an interpretation of science as using only objective measurement to a more holistic approach to life that recognizes the power of the individual and his/her connectedness to sources of meaning beyond self. *See also:* Council for Spiritual and Ethical Education.

Further Reading: Catherine Albanese, ed., *American Spiritualities: A Reader* (Bloomington, IN: Indiana University Press, 2001); Arthur Chickering, John Dalton, and Liesa Stamm, *Encouraging Authenticity and Spirituality in Higher Education* (San Francisco: Jossey Bass, 2006); Robert Coles, *The Spiritual Lives of Children* (Boston: Houghton Mifflin, 1990); Diana Eck, *A New Religious America: How a "Christian Country" Has Become the World's Most Religiously Diverse Nation* (New York: HarperCollins, 2002); *Educational Leadership* 54 (December 1998/January 1999), special issue on Spirituality; Clive Erricker and Jane Erricker, eds., *Contemporary Spiritualities: Social and Religious Contexts* (London: Continuum: 2001); David Hay, with Rebecca Nye, *In the Spirit of the Child* (New York: Jessica Kingsley Publishers, 2006); Barry A. Kosmin, Egon Mayer, and Ariela Keysar, *The American Religious Identification Survey* (New York: Graduate Center of the City University of New York, 2001).National Education Association (Education Policies Commission), *Moral and Spiritual Values in Public Schools* (Washington, DC: National Education Association, 1951); Elizabeth Tisdell, "Diversity and Spirituality in Secular Higher Education: The Teaching Paradox," *Religion & Education* 33 (Winter 2006): 49–68; Robert Wuthnow, *After Heaven: Spirituality in America Since the 1950s* (Berkeley: University of California Press, 2000); Robert Wuthnow, *Sharing the Journey: Support Groups and America's New Quest for Community* (New York: Free Press, 1994); Danah Zohar and Ian Marshall, *Spiritual Intelligence* (London: Bloomsbury, 2000).

Charles R. Kniker

State Regulation of Religious Schools

The United States has 28,384 private elementary and secondary schools with 5,122,772 students enrolled. These private schools comprise about 23 percent of U.S. elementary and secondary schools, and enroll about 10 percent of U.S. elementary and secondary school students. While only 76 percent of private schools are categorized as sectarian, 82 percent of private school students are identified as attending faith-based schools (National Center for Education Statistics, 2006).

The right of states to regulate religious schools is part of the same broad authority implied in the Tenth Amendment for states to control education. Such control, however, is not without limitations. Three U.S. Supreme Court decisions have framed the limits on a state's control over religious schools. In *Meyer v. Nebraska* (1923), the Supreme Court overturned the criminalization of teaching course instruction in a religious school in a language other than English, reasoning that what is taught in religious schools is an extension of the Fourteenth Amendment liberty clause that recognizes the parents' right to direct the education of their children. Two years later, the Court, in *Pierce v. Society of Sisters* (1925), invalidated a state statute requiring all students to attend public schools, again reasoning that the parents' right to direct the education of their children included the choice of the educational venue in which that instruction would take place. Finally, 47 years after *Pierce,* the Supreme Court, in *Wisconsin v. Yoder* (1972), prohibited the state from applying a compulsory attendance requirement to Amish children where the effect would be the destruction of the Amish religious community. In the process, the *Yoder* Court devised a test whereby a state would have to demonstrate that it had a compelling interest before being permitted to burden the religious beliefs of parents.

None of these three cases invalidated the authority of states to regulate education pursuant to the implied power under the U.S. Constitution's Tenth Amendment. In *Pierce,* the Supreme Court had observed:

> No question is raised concerning the power of the state reasonably to regulate all schools, to inspect, supervise and examine them, their teachers and pupils; to require that all children of proper age attend some school, that teachers shall be of good moral character and patriotic disposition, that certain studies plainly essential to good citizenship must be taught, and that nothing be taught which is manifestly inimical to the public welfare.

Yoder involved not only the Fourteenth Amendment's parents' right to direct the education of their children, but the First Amendment's Free Exercise Clause as well. The Supreme Court's decision in *Yoder* energized many religious schools in the 1970s and 1980s to challenge the efforts of state departments of education and local school districts to impose upon them the same state statutes and regulations applied to public school districts. Generally, the success of these challenges varied among the states and frequently devolved into a discussion of the reasonableness of the statutes or regulations, or into an analysis of whether the *Yoder* compelling interest test needed to be applied at all to parents of children in religious schools where the parents' lives demonstrated none of the simplicity of style and separation from the world that had characterized the Amish in *Yoder.* In effect, many courts limited *Yoder* to the Amish and reduced the *Yoder* compelling interest test to one of reasonableness.

The end result was that the *Yoder* test was interpreted and applied with varying degrees of consistency. State and lower federal court decisions failed to agree regarding compliance of religious schools with state approval, curriculum, and teacher certification requirements.

In *State v. Olin* (1980), a state compulsory attendance requirement that students attend a school with a certified teacher was unreasonable as applied to a non-Amish child in an Amish school, whereas in *Fellowship Baptist Church v. Benton* (1987), a state statute exempting Amish schools from teacher certification requirements did not apply to a Baptist school. In *Bangor Baptist Church v. State of Maine* (1983), the state's department of education did not have express statutory authority under the compulsory attendance statute to impose direct sanctions against unapproved private schools, whereas in *State v. Faith Baptist Church of Louisville* (1981), the enforcement of compulsory attendance laws included authority to enjoin operation of the school and to incarcerate the pastor.

Case law regarding compliance with state curricular requirements presented the same differing results. In *State of Ohio v. Whisner* (1976), state curriculum requirements regulating not only the courses to be offered but also the amount of instructional time to be allocated to the subjects offered in a religious school were held unreasonable, whereas in *State v. Shaver* (1980), a state's department of education regulations specifying the courses to be offered were held to be reasonable. In *Kentucky State Board v. Rudasill* (1979), a Kentucky constitutional provision prohibiting any person being compelled to send his child to any school to which he may be conscientiously opposed was interpreted as prohibiting the Kentucky State Board of Education from requiring that any teacher in a nonpublic (including religious) school be certificated and prohibited the state's determination of basic texts to be used in private and religious schools. However, in *Care and Protection of Charles* (1987), a statutory provision prohibiting a Massachusetts school committee from withholding school approval to operate a nonpublic school on account of religious teaching did not exempt home instruction parents from the obligation to furnish outlined curriculum, materials to be used, and qualifications of instructors.

The confrontation between the state and religious schools diminished beginning in the late 1980s as state legislatures intervened and enacted laws freeing religious (and other nonpublic) schools from many of the more onerous of state requirements. Much of the post-*Yoder* litigation had arisen under the Free Exercise Clause and the intervention of state legislatures was propitious in light of the Supreme Court's *Employment Division v. Smith* (1990) decision that dealt a near-fatal death blow to the effective use of that clause as a defense to government regulations. In *Employment Division,* the Court held that the Free Exercise Clause would no longer be a defense to a neutral, generally applicable regulatory law. Fourteen years later, the Supreme Court gave added force to *Employment Division* in its *Locke v. Davey* (2004) decision, holding that state action protecting a religious claim is not required under the First Amendment's Free Exercise Clause simply because it is not prohibited under the Establishment Clause. The Supreme Court carved out an exception for use of the Free Exercise Clause in *Church of the Lukumi Babalu Aye, Inc. v. City of Hialeah* (1993) when government actions are hostile to particular religions but finding such hostile animus is difficult.

Litigation involving religious schools arises regarding the application of nondiscrimination laws to personnel in the schools. Implicit in the Free Exercise Clause is the right of religious schools to enforce their religious and moral codes, a right that survived *Employment Division v. Smith* and is referred to as a ministerial exemption. Federal courts have applied this exemption to discharge of a Catholic school religion teacher who lent her name to an advertisement in support of abortion rights (*Curay-Cramer v. Ursuline Academy of Wilmington, Delaware,* 2004) but have refused to apply the exemption where charges of sexual harassment are involved (*Smith v. Raleigh District of North Carolina*

Conference of United Methodist Church, 1999). *See also:* Bennett Law; Christian Day Schools; *Farrington v. Tokushige; Meyer v. Nebraska; Pierce v. Society of Sisters.*

Further Reading: *Bangor Baptist Church v. State of Maine,* 576 F.Supp. 1299 (D. Me. 1983); *Care and Protection of Charles,* 504 N.E.2d 592 (Mass. 1987); *Church of the Lukumi Babalu Aye, Inc. v. City of Hialeah,* 508 U.S. 520 (1993); *Curay-Cramer v. Ursuline Academy of Wilmington, Delaware,* 344 F.Supp.2d 923 (D. Del. 2004); *Employment Division v. Smith,* 494 U.S. 872 (1990); *Fellowship Baptist Church v. Benton,* 815 F.2d 485 (8th Cir. 1987); *Kentucky State Board v. Rudasill,* 589 S.W.2d 877 (Ky. 1979); *Locke v. Davey,* 540 U.S. 712 (2004); *Meyer v. Nebraska,* 262 U.S. 390 (1923); National Center for Education Statistics (NCES), *Characteristics of Private Schools in the United States: Results from the 2003–2004 Private School Universe Survey* (Washington, DC: U.S. Department of Education, 2006); *Pierce v. Society of Sisters,* 268 U.S. 510 (1925); *Smith v. Raleigh District of North Carolina Conference of United Methodist Church,* 63 F.Supp.2d 694 (E.D.N.C. 1999); *State v. Faith Baptist Church of Louisville,* 301 N.W.2d 571 (Neb. 1981); *State v. Olin,* 415 N.E.2d 279 (Ohio 1980); *State v. Shaver,* 294 N.W.2d 883 (N.D. 1980); *State of Ohio v. Whisner,* 351 N.E.2d 750 (Ohio 1976); *Wisconsin v. Yoder,* 406 U.S. 205 (1972).

Ralph D. Mawdsley

Stone v. Graham

The Kentucky State Legislature passed a statute requiring the posting of a copy of the Ten Commandments to be hung in all public school classrooms. The plaques were mandated to be 16 inches wide by 20 inches high. Each copy was required to have a notation that stated, "The secular application of the Ten Commandments is clearly seen in its adoption as the fundamental legal code of Western Civilization and the Common Law of the United States." The copies were to be purchased with funds from voluntary contributions to the state treasurer. The plaintiffs filed suit alleging the statute violated the Establishment and Free Exercise Clauses of the First Amendment.

In 1980, the U.S. Supreme Court used the *Lemon* test (*Lemon v. Kurtzman,* 1971) to review the alleged Establishment Clause violation in *Stone.* The tripartite test used in this case: "First, the statute must have a secular legislative purpose; second, its principal or primary effect must be one that neither advances nor inhibits religion...; finally the statute must not foster 'an excessive government entanglement with religion.'"

To be constitutional any statute must pass muster under all three prongs of the *Lemon* test. If any one prong is not met, then the act is unconstitutional under the Establishment Clause. A divided Court (5-4) concluded that "Kentucky's statutes requiring the posting of the Ten Commandments in public schoolrooms had no secular legislative purpose, and is therefore unconstitutional."

The Ten Commandments are without question sacred to the Christian and Jewish faiths. The Kentucky Legislature could not make them secular by placing a notation at the bottom saying they were secular. It did not matter that the plaques were financed by voluntary contributions, and placing them in the classroom still involved an official state action. *See also:* Civil Religion and Education; Ten Commandments.

Further Reading: *Lemon v. Kurtzman,* 403 U.S. 602 (1971); *Stone v. Graham,* 101 S. Ct. 192 (1980); *Van Orden v. Perry,* 125 S. Ct. 2854, 545 U.S. 677, 162 L. Ed. 2d 607 (2005).

M. David Alexander

T

Teaching about Religion

"Teaching about Religion: Worldview Education" is a Web site produced by Objectivity, Accuracy, and Balance in Teaching about Religion (OABITAR). Based in San Mateo, California, this educational nonprofit organization participates in educational networking, conferences, and school presentations, although the maintenance of the Web site constitutes its primary activity. It was founded by peace activist John B. Massen in response to a 1987 revision of the California History/Social Science Framework. Among other things, the revised curriculum encouraged instruction on world religions, particularly Judaism, Christianity, Islam, Buddhism, and Hinduism.

Although OABITAR does not oppose teaching about religion, it maintains that by failing to present ethical and moral beliefs not based on religious faith, public schools promote the idea that belief in the supernatural is the only worldview worthy of mention. Accordingly, one of the group's early projects was a book entitled *Freethought Across the Centuries: Toward a New Age of Enlightenment,* intended to provide teachers with information about the social, political, intellectual, and economic contributions nonbelievers have made to human progress. Its author, Gerald A. Larue, is an emeritus professor of biblical history and archaeology at the University of Southern California who now serves as religious consultant for the "Teaching about Religion" Web site.

"Teaching about Religion" defines itself as "a Free Thought project," with a freethinker defined as "one who refuses to submit his reason to the control of authority in matters of religious belief." Its self-defined goal is to "provide academic information and teaching materials related to teaching about religion in public schools in support of:

an educational commitment to pluralism; acknowledgment that public schools are for students of all worldviews, whether religious or nonreligious; and the professional understanding that public school teachers need to exercise a scrupulous neutrality regarding religion." (Teaching about Religion, at www.teachingaboutreligion.org)

In pursuit of this goal, "Teaching about Religion" compares different worldviews, including nonbelief, with respect to their conceptualizations of such issues as nature, the supernatural, creation, time, death, and the afterlife. It also explains the conceptual bases underlying the free thought perspective on public education. Examples include intellectual diversity, religious neutrality, religious pluralism, and civic pluralism. Consistent with its overall orientation, the Web site defines these terms in such a way as to promote the inclusion of nonreligious as well as religious concepts in public school teaching. As the site observes, "The very notion of 'teaching about religion' seems to rule out the idea of and any need for providing academic study of *non*religious worldviews. Educators need to *be aware of a 'concept trap' in the terminology* that disregards a very real portion of the spectrum of human worldviews" (www.teachingaboutreligion.org).

To help teachers operationalize the principle of religious neutrality as defined by "Teaching about Religion," the Web site provides curricular aids developed by its curriculum consultants, Paul Geisert and Mynga Futrell. Some of these materials are guidebooks or minicourses for teachers, while others take the form of lesson plans to be taught in class. Examples of the former include "Religious Neutrality: Teaching in a Pluralistic Classroom," a methods minicourse that prepares public school teachers to include nonbelief and nonbelievers in their instruction; and "Acknowledging Religious Diversity and Nonbelief: Toward Impartial Teaching about Religion," a 21-page booklet instructing teachers about the principles of free thought and encouraging them to be aware of cultural biases with respect to religion and nonreligion. The lesson plans and instructional activities presented on the Web site, designed primarily for the secondary-school level, include *Different Drummers: Nonconforming Thinkers in History,* as well as lesson plans offering a variety of perspectives on such topics as altruism, citizenship, prejudice, and cultural change.

In addition to expanding the concept of teaching about religion to include the views and contributions of nonbelievers, "Teaching about Religion" discusses current news issues involving religion, such as the controversies surrounding embryonic stem cell research and the retention of the phrase "under God" in the Pledge of Allegiance. As an example, the Web site argues at length that Intelligent Design does not belong in science classrooms because, contrary to the claims of its advocates, it is not science. The Web site also provides copious links to other sites, such as those of the Anti-Defamation League, the First Amendment Center/Freedom Forum, the American Civil Liberties Union, and the National Humanities Center. *See also:* Humanism and the Humanist Manifestos; Secularism.

Further Reading: Brant Abrahamson, "Thinking about Religion from a Global Perspective," *Teaching Anthropology Newsletter* 33 (Fall 1998): 7; Mynga Futrell and Paul Geisert, *Different Drummers: Nonconforming Thinkers in History* (Victoria, BC, Canada: Trafford Publishing, 1999); Gerald A. Larue, *Freethought Across the Centuries: Toward a New Age of Enlightenment* (Washington, DC: Humanist Press, 1996); John B. Massen, "Teaching about Religion...And Nonreligion," *Humanist* 55 (May–June 1995): 40; John B. Massen, "Thinking 'about' Religion: The Need for Freethought in the Curriculum," *Free Inquiry* 16 (Spring 1996): 23–24. Teaching about Religion, at www.teachingaboutreligion.org.

Joan DelFattore

Ten Commandments

According to the Hebrew Bible, the Ten Commandments, also known as the Decalogue, are precepts graven on stone tablets that God gave to Moses on Mount Sinai. Most displays of the Commandments are based on Exodus 20:2–17, although similar accounts may be found in Exodus 34:12–26 and in Deuteronomy 5:6–21. The Qur'an (7.145) also states that God gave tablets of law to Moses, and the imperatives embodied therein appear elsewhere in the text.

Since Exodus does not provide a clear list of ten commandments, the wording and numbering of the Decalogue differ slightly from one denomination to another within Judaism and Christianity. Of particular historical significance is the distinction between the version used by most Protestants and that accepted by Catholics and Lutherans. The first commandment, which declares "I am the Lord thy God" and forbids the worship of other gods, is common to both. At the second commandment, however, the two traditions diverge. The Protestant second commandment bans the worship of graven images, but no such reference appears in the Catholic/Lutheran version. Rather, the Catholic/Lutheran second commandment prohibits taking the Lord's name in vain, as does the Protestant third commandment. As a result of the inclusion of an additional commandment in the Protestant version, each of its subsequent commandments has a higher number than the corresponding Catholic/Lutheran mandate. For instance, "Thou shalt not kill," the Protestant sixth commandment, is the Catholic/Lutheran fifth commandment. Nevertheless, each version includes a total of ten precepts because the final Protestant commandment, an omnibus prohibition against several kinds of covetousness, is divided into two separate commandments in the Catholic/Lutheran version.

The differences between the Protestant and Catholic versions of the Commandments became relevant to American public education in the nineteenth century, when the daily program of most schools included readings from the King James Bible and the use of other Protestant texts, prayers, and hymns. Among other things, required participation in such exercises was viewed as a means of "Americanizing" the children of immigrants, many of whom were Catholic. An example of this practice as it applied to the Decalogue arose in 1859 in the Eliot School in Boston, whose directors decreed that all students were to recite the Protestant version of the Ten Commandments every Monday morning. At first, teachers led group recitations and did not reprimand Catholic students who remained silent or recited their own version. When the school directors clarified that each student was to recite the Protestant version individually, the local Catholic priest ordered his parishioners to disobey. Eleven-year-old Thomas Wall led the Catholic students in resisting the school directors' mandate, but vice principal McLaurin F. Cooke beat him on the hands with a rattan cane until he submitted. In a subsequent lawsuit filed by his parents, the Boston Police Court ruled that parents who sent their children to public schools thereby surrendered such of their authority as conflicted with what the court considered the reasonable requirements of the school. Indeed, the court scolded the priest and the parents for having incited Thomas to an act of insubordination. It also defined the caning, which took place on and off for approximately half an hour, not as a single episode but as a series of events in which the boy was punished for separate acts of defiance. As the court noted, he could have ended the beating at any time by agreeing to comply with the rule.

The practice of beating or expelling students for refusing to participate in religious exercises grew increasingly rare throughout the late nineteenth and early twentieth centuries, as the excusal of dissenters became the norm. Indeed, some states even banned such exercises altogether. Then, in the mid-1960s, the U.S. Supreme Court declared in *Engel v. Vitale* and *Abington v. Schempp* that school-sponsored Bible reading and prayer violate the Establishment Clause of the U.S. Constitution. Amid heated controversy, some school districts attempted to retain elements of religion in the public schools by means other than prayer—for instance, by displaying the Decalogue in classrooms. In a debate that remains alive and well today, proponents of such displays maintain that unlike the mandated recitation of the Commandments in earlier generations, the mere posting of the text neither advances any particular religion nor coerces any profession of faith. Moreover, they declare, such displays serve a valid secular purpose because the Commandments form the basis of American civil and criminal codes. Asserting that the Founders' moral convictions were based on the Bible, they justify the display of the Decalogue as a means of enhancing the students' appreciation of American history as well as their understanding of the foundation on which its system of government rests. Opponents retort that fewer than half of the commandments correspond to secular statutes. The first few concern the worship of God, and even such acts as dishonoring parents, committing adultery, and entertaining covetous thoughts are not necessarily illegal. They also note that those precepts found both in the Decalogue and in secular law are common to many cultures and belief systems. Accordingly, they conclude, the assumption that such moral imperatives arise uniquely from the Bible reflects a religious conviction, and posting the Commandments where students cannot help but see them daily is indeed coercive and an advancement of Bible-based religion. Finally, they distinguish between describing the Founders' faith as a matter of historical fact and defining present-day Americanism in biblical terms.

In a 1980 decision, *Stone v. Graham,* the U.S. Supreme Court rejected the argument that posting the Commandments in public schools serves a secular purpose. Nevertheless, a rash of school shootings in the late 1990s and the terrorist attack of 9/11/2001 gave rise to renewed calls for displaying the Commandments as a means of encouraging morality and patriotism. Among the numerous pieces of legislation first introduced during this period was the Ten Commandments Defense Act, sponsored by Representative Robert Aderholt (R-Alabama). The intent of this bill, which has been repeatedly reintroduced into Congress, is to allow each state to decide whether to post the Commandments in its public schools. In 1999, it was attached as an amendment to the House version of the Juvenile Justice Act, where it replaced a gun-control provision. The Juvenile Justice Act ultimately failed, as have subsequent attempts to enact federal Ten Commandments legislation. Several state legislatures, as well as local school boards, continue to experiment with various means of displaying the Commandments (e.g., by incorporating them into larger exhibits of historical materials and by placing them on the school grounds rather than indoors). No such display in public schools has yet been upheld, although lawsuits continue to arise, as do new legislative proposals.

As a matter of context, it should be noted that attempts to post the Commandments in public schools interact with similar efforts involving other government buildings. The Ten Commandments Defense Act, for instance, was inspired by the actions of Judge Roy Moore, who hung the Decalogue in his county courtroom. He was subsequently elected chief justice of the Alabama Supreme Court in 2000 and caused a four-foot granite statue of the Commandments to be placed in the rotunda of the state courthouse. A federal court order to remove it was upheld by the U.S. Court of Appeals for the Eleventh Circuit, and Moore was unseated when he refused to comply. Similarly, in 2005 the U.S. Supreme Court ordered the removal of framed copies of the Commandments from two Kentucky county courthouses despite the inclusion of other historical documents in the displays. In another decision handed down on the same day, however, the Court upheld the continued display of a Ten Commandments sculpture among other statuary on the grounds of the Texas state Capitol. As the outcome of these two cases suggests, the place of the Ten Commandments in American public life will continue to be a matter of debate and litigation for the foreseeable future. *See also:* The Bible in the Public Schools; Civil Religion and Education; *Stone v. Graham.*

Further Reading: *Abington v. Schempp,* 374 U.S. 203 (1963); Calum M. Carmichael, *The Origins of Biblical Law: The Decalogues and the Book of the Covenant* (Ithaca, NY: Cornell University Press, 1992); Joan DelFattore, *The Fourth R: Conflicts Over Religion in America's Public Schools* (New Haven, CT: Yale University Press, 2004); *Engel v. Vitale,* 370 U.S. 421 (1962); James Fraser, *Between Church and State: Religion and Public Education in a Multicultural America* (New York: Palgrave Macmillan, 2000); *McCreary County v. American Civil Liberties Union,* 545 U.S. 844 (2005); *Stone v. Graham,* 449 U.S. 39 (1980); *Van Orden v. Perry,* 545 U.S. 677 (2005).

Joan DelFattore

Thomas More Law Center

The Thomas More Law Center is a public-interest, nonprofit law firm headquartered in Ann Arbor, Michigan, with a threefold mission of upholding religious liberty for Christians, protecting family values, and defending the sanctity of human life. Founded in 1999 by Christian philanthropist Tom Monaghan and attorney Richard Thompson, the center has been highly active in litigation involving a variety of legal topics dealing with the intersection of law, education, politics, and religious faith. Richard Thompson, a former longtime Oakland County, Michigan, prosecutor, currently serves as the center's president and chief counsel. The center is assisted by an advisory board consisting of a wide spectrum of people from the business, legal, and political arenas. Alongside the board of advisors, the center also has a Board of Legal Review. The current membership of this board consists of Charles Rice, an emeritus professor at Notre Dame Law School and one of the leading Catholic legal scholars in the country, and Professor Gerald Bradley, also of the Notre Dame Law School.

The center is named for St. Thomas More (A.D. 1478–1535), the Lord Chancellor of England during the reign of Henry VIII. A brilliant lawyer, judge, and Christian humanist scholar, More was the first layman to serve as the Lord Chancellor of England. In that role he was drawn into Henry's dispute with the Catholic Church regarding the status of his marriage to Katherine of Aragon. Henry eventually decided to divorce his wife despite papal disapproval and formed the Church of England. More could not in good conscience follow Henry in the matter of the divorce, and he refused to take the Oath of Supremacy acknowledging Henry as head of the Church in England. After incarceration in the Tower of London, he was martyred by beheading. His reported last words were that he was "the King's good servant, but God's first."

Unlike similar public interest organizations that seek to protect the rights of religious believers in general, the Thomas More Law Center's work is focused on defending the rights of Christians to practice their faith and to be active in the public square on a variety of pressing social and moral issues. Motivated by a conviction that there is a culture war ongoing against those who hold to traditional Christian values, the center provides *pro bono* legal representation in cases where the rights of Christians to be active in the public square are at issue. The Thomas More Law Center seeks "to be the sword and shield for people of faith," working through litigation in the courts, to advance and defend the rights of believers (Thomas More Law Center, at www.thomasmore.org).

The center is one of the most active public interest law firms in the country, seeking to shape the national culture through its legal work. To effectuate this goal, the center actively seeks out clients with cases consistent with its mission. The Thomas More Law Center's strong focus on litigation arises out of recognition that many, if not most, of the pressing social and moral issues of the day are being decided by the courts rather than legislatures. This approach to the need for litigation has led the center to have a significant profile on the national legal stage, with active cases in over 40 states. Along with its commitment to nationwide outreach, the Thomas More Law Center has a stated policy of seeking high moral and ethical conduct by its attorneys, in light of the requirements of both legal professionalism and the Christian faith.

The center's work deals with several issues that impact public education. The center strongly supports equal access for students who seek to form Christian clubs in public schools, as well as free speech rights for students to discuss religious matters, and the right of students to pray in public schools. On a related note, the center also supports the concept of school vouchers and defends the practice of homeschooling. Alongside these positions, the Thomas More Law Center supports public religious displays, the recognition of Christmas through various activities, including the display of nativity scenes, the recognition of the national motto "In God We Trust," the Pledge of Allegiance, and public displays of the Ten Commandments.

The center's commitment to defending the freedom of religion in the public square also expresses itself in two other areas of activity: its work to defend human life and its efforts to defend the unique legal status of the traditional family. The center is committed to building a culture of life predicated on the intrinsic value of each and every human life. The center uses its resources to fight both abortion and the movements to legalize assisted suicide and euthanasia. It also works to defend partial-birth abortion bans. Its lawyers work to protect the rights of pro-life demonstrators, as well as the free speech rights for pro-life advocates; the center also supports crisis pregnancy centers, opposes cloning, and defends the conscience rights of professionals and others who are opposed to abortion and other threats to human life. In the area of family law, the center believes in the sacred nature of the traditional family, and that the traditional family is currently under assault from a variety of recent legal developments. Because the family stands at the foundation of society, the center seeks to defend the traditional family against a variety of threats, including pornography and same-sex marriage.

The center's most high profile case to date has been *Kitzmiller v. Dover Area School District*. That case arose out of a decision by the Dover, Pennsylvania, school board to incorporate discussion of Intelligent Design theory into the public school science curriculum. The Thomas More Law Center defended the school board after a lawsuit was filed by the ACLU and Americans United for Separation of Church and State challenging the board's action on behalf of several of the students' parents. The case was taken to trial in the fall of 2005, and Federal District Judge John E. Jones III ruled against the school district. *See also: Kitzmiller v. Dover Area School District*.

Further Reading: Thomas More Law Center, at www.thomasmore.org.

Mark DeForrest

Torah Umesorah (National Society for Hebrew Day Schools)

Torah Umesorah—National Society for Hebrew Day Schools—is an independent association supporting a loose affiliation of about 700 Orthodox Jewish day schools, serving more than 140,000 children in North America. The Hebrew name, Torah Umesorah, refers to the Five Books of Moses, the *Torah,* and the laws; and "Masorah" means to pass on the traditions and practices of Judaism: literally Torah Umesorah means "Laws and Tradition." Led currently by Rabbi Joshua Fishman, Torah Umesorah was founded in 1944 during World War II when the Jews of Europe were facing genocide under the Nazi regime, and the Jews of North America called for a new system of private Jewish day schools to keep their religion alive and growing.

The founder of Torah Umesorah was Hungarian-born Rabbi Shraga Feivel Mendlowitz (preferring the title, "Mr. Mendlowitz"), who was leader of the Yeshiva Torah Vodaas in Brooklyn, New York. He led this movement to convince Jewish families to move their children from the conventional "common" schooling model of nonsectarian public schools during the day—and Jewish education in after-school and Sunday programs, in schools called a Cheder or Talmud Torah—to full-time Jewish day school education in an Orthodox setting. The model that emerged, and has flourished in many day schools, is a *dual-curriculum* Jewish day school program, with a half-day of intensive Jewish study of Hebrew and Torah/Talmud study coupled with a half-day of secular subjects. An ordained rabbi often leads the religious portion of the day as the school's principal; and a "general studies" educator, as the assistant principal, is in charge of the so-called "English studies" program that usually includes mathematics, English, sciences, and social studies.

Not all American Jews wanted separate Jewish schools for their children; many Conservative and Reform Jewish families, and their associations, preferred to support their local public schools and receive their Jewish education after school and on Sundays. Some critics felt that full-time private Jewish schools were a return to "ghetto-ization" and led to isolation for a large group of Jews seeking to assimilate and become Americanized. Since the 1940s, however, the growth of Jewish schools—particularly those affiliated with Torah Umesorah—has increased. The period saw a successful movement to create the State of Israel, and to build Jewish pride and knowledge of Hebrew and Jewish traditions. Thus, in the words of Torah Umesorah:

> Many American Jews now felt that they needed to provide the means for their children to learn the Hebrew language connected with the Hebrew Bible, the core of Judaism, even teach Religious Zionism that would connect the children and their families with pride in Israel, and simultaneously not neglect a secular education as citizens of the United States living in an open society, with hopes and plans for attending college in the future as well. (Torah Umesorah, at www.torah-umesorah.com)

Torah Umesorah was created at a time when Orthodox Jews were starting other parallel associations, such as the Hasidic Chabad-Lubavitch movement, started by Rabbi Joseph Yitzhak Schneersohn (1880–1950), the Chabad movement, and efforts to educate Orthodox Jewish girls in the Bais Yaacov (House of Jacob) schools and the boys in the growing number of yeshivas. Torah Umesorah, while more mainstream, was often asked to help prepare and train teachers for the Chasidic schools, although these schools were not affiliated with Torah Umesorah directly.

In 1946, Torah Umesorah appointed Dr. Joseph Kaminetsky, or "Dr. Joe," as he was called, to be their first director, based in New York City. His goal was to open a yeshiva day school in every city with 5,000 or more Jews, at a time when so few communities had Orthodox Jewish day schools. By the end of the twentieth century, over 600 such schools had opened, and in a recent study, Bruce Cooper and Marc Kramer (2002) found that any community with 3,000 or more Jews had a Jewish day school (not always Orthodox).

And recently, under an effort called Project SEED, students from yeshivas (teenage boys and girls) are recruited to six-week or more summer camp trips, to smaller Jewish communities, to teach children in a summer day-camp setting. It gives these yeshiva teenagers a chance to learn teaching and supervision skills, and for the campers to receive an intensive, rich summer Torah-oriented experience. Like the Torah Umesorah schools, these summer day camps are separated by gender, but both the teen counselors and the young children benefit from Project SEED. According to one account, "All out-of-town girls receive an all-expense paid stay at their destination, which includes air-fare, room and board, trips, transportation, and nicely wrapped gifts." In all then, Torah Umesorah has created, sponsored, and supported the major Jewish day school movement in the United States, helping to build the large segment of Jewish private schools, along with the smaller Conservative and Reform Jewish movements. *See also:* Jewish Schools.

Further Reading: Bruce S. Cooper and Marc N. Kramer, "New Jewish Community, New Jewish Schools," *Catholic Education: A Journal of Inquiry and Practice* 5 (June 2002): 488–501; Samuel C. Feuerstein, "Torah Umesorah 1944–1969: A Quarter of a Century," in *Hebrew Day School Education: An Overview,* ed. Joseph Kaminetsky (New York: Torah Umesorah, 1970); Alvin I. Schiff, *The Jewish Day School in America* (New York: Jewish Education Committee Press, 1968); Marshall Sklare and Joseph Greenblum, *Jewish Identity on the Suburban Frontier: A Study of Group Survival in the Open Society* (Chicago: University of Chicago Press, 1979); Torah Umesorah, at www.torah-umesorah.com.

Bruce S. Cooper

Traditional Values Coalition

The Traditional Values Coalition (TVC) is a nondenominational Christian lobbying organization based in Anaheim, California, and Washington, D.C., which, according to its 2007 estimate, serves over 43,000 churches in the United States. It was founded in 1980 by the Reverend Louis Sheldon to "empower people of faith through knowledge" in the defense of traditional values, which TVC defines as "a moral code and behavior based upon the Old and New Testaments" (Traditional Values Coalition, at www.traditionalvalues.org). TVC lobbies corporations, legislative bodies, schools, and other groups to support its positions regarding pornography, family tax relief, education, the right to life, religious liberties, and most prominently what it refers to as the "homosexual agenda." Sheldon's first foray into politics, and the impetus for the founding of TVC, was his unsuccessful work on a state initiative that would have required the dismissal of openly homosexual teachers in California.

TVC's involvement in public education has predictably focused on countering the "homosexual agenda" within schools. In 1991, Sheldon led a well-publicized but unsuccessful challenge to school district observance of Gay and Lesbian Pride Month. TVC works on local and national levels to protest Gay Straight Alliances (GSAs) and other support groups for gay teenagers, arguing that they promote high-risk behaviors and normalize destructive behaviors. Of particular concern to TVC is what Sheldon calls "homosexual recruiting." In "Homosexuals Recruit Public School Children," a report published on the TVC Web site, Sheldon writes that "since homosexual couples can't reproduce, they will simply go after *your* children for seduction and conversion to homosexuality." He refers to sex education about HIV and the effort by some support groups to designate safe spaces within schools for GLBTQ (Gay, Lesbian, Bisexual, Transgender, and Questioning) youth as tactics by "homosexual militants." The organization encourages its members to monitor legislative proposals that include the word "gender" (since "gender is code for cross-dressers, transvestites, and transsexuals"); to oppose GSAs on school campuses; and to distribute to educators and parents the TVC-sponsored video *SHAPE* (Stop Homosexual Advocacy in Public Education). The organization has cultivated a self-consciously oppositional stance and counters mainstream criticism of its positions by stating that the organization is "not tolerant of behaviors that destroy individuals, families, and our culture" and that it practices "'discrimination' in the good sense" (www.traditionalvalues.org).

Though concerns about homosexuality do top TVC's agenda in the schools, the organization also advocates broadly for religious liberties for Christian students, whom it sees as treated unfairly in public school settings dominated by liberal and anti-Christian interests. Instances in which Muslims receive special dietary consideration by school cafeterias, for example, have prompted Sheldon to rail against the double standard that he perceives between the treatment of Muslim students versus Christians and Jews.

The widespread estimation of TVC's rhetoric as purposely inflammatory may have kept the group from achieving the same national prominence as other similar organizations, but it has wielded discernible political sway nonetheless. Its video *Gay Rights/Special Rights,* which includes a section devoted to public schools and has been distributed to educators, features power brokers such as former Senate majority leader Trent Lott, former director of the Christian Coalition Ralph Reed, former attorney general Ed Meese, and Tim Wildmon of the American Family Association. During the first Bush administration, Sheldon extracted a commitment from Speaker of the House Newt Gingrich to fight liberal sexual-education programs in the schools. Sheldon's network and contacts brought him continued visibility and influence with the second Bush administration and Republican Party, including private meetings with then Speaker of the House Tom Delay. Sheldon's personal credibility, however, was tarnished in 2006 upon revelations by *The Washington Post* that he had received funds from disgraced lobbyist Jack Abramoff in return for his help (including the use of TVC contacts) in defeating antigambling legislation in Congress. *See also:* Sex Education and Religion.

Further Reading: David W. Dunlap, "Minister Brings Anti-Gay Message to the Spotlight," *New York Times,* December 19, 1994, sec. A, p. 16; Rene Sanchez, "Homosexuality in the Classroom," *The Record,* June 23, 1996, sec. O, p. 10; Susan Schmidt and James V. Grimaldi, "How a Lobbyist Stacked the Deck; Abramoff Used DeLay Aide, Attacks on Allies to Defeat Anti-Gambling Bill," *Washington Post,* October 16, 2005, sec. A, p. 1; J. Christopher Soper and Joel S. Fetzer, "The Christian Right in California: Dimming Fortunes in the Golden State," in *The Christian Right in America: Marching to the Millenium,* ed. John C. Green, Mark J. Rozell, and Clyde Wilcox (Washington, DC: Georgetown University Press, 2003); Traditional Values Coalition, at www.traditionalvalues.org.

Shipley Robertson Salewski

Tuition Tax Credits

During the past century, political forces in the United States have searched for ways to provide government funding for private schools. Since most private schools in the United States are religious in nature and, in fact, most of them are supported by a particular faith community, such schemes frequently run afoul of the Constitution of the United States. The First Amendment to the Constitution states in part that "Congress shall make no law respecting an establishment of religion." Direct financial aid to religious schools has been determined by the courts to be a violation of the First Amendment. In response, legislators at both the state and federal levels have searched for indirect methods of providing support for religious schools that would meet the constitutional requirement. A system of allowing parents or corporations to take a credit or deduction on their state income tax liability is one form of such aid that has been approved by the courts. While as of 2008, only nine states have such a plan, the tax credit/deduction scheme, which does not involve distributing state funds, remains an important possibility in providing assistance to parents whose choice for the education of their children includes religiously affiliated schools.

There are three basic tax credit plans that have been utilized by the states. One allows parents who make expenditures for the education of their children to take all or a portion of the total as a credit against their state income tax liability. Another plan is to allow such expenditures to be taken as a deduction to income that is considered to be taxable. Either of these plans provides some degree of financial relief to parents who enroll their children in religious schools. Not all of the plans include tuition, though Minnesota does allow such a deduction. A third plan involves a third-party payer arrangement known as a school tuition organization (STO) or scholarship granting organization (SGO). Here, tax credits are allowed for contributions by either individuals or corporations to an STO/SGO, which then makes scholarships available to families whose children attend private and/or religious schools.

The constitutionality of tuition tax credits was first tested in the U.S. Supreme Court in 1973. Its decision in *Committee for Public Education and Religious Liberty v. Nyquist* relied on its previous ruling in *Lemon v. Kurtzman* where the court laid down a three-part test to determine the constitutionality of public aid to religious schools: first, any aid must have a secular legislative purpose; second, the primary effect of the aid must not advance religion; and third, such aid must not foster excessive entanglement between government and religion. The Court in *Nyquist* found that New York's attempt to provide aid to private and religious schools failed the "primary effect" part of the *Lemon* test.

At issue in *Nyquist* were several provisions, including reimbursement to parents for tuition at religious schools and also a tax deduction to parents who did not qualify for the reimbursement because of their higher income level. The New York plan was not based on the amount of the tuition parents paid to religious schools but rather on their level of income. Parents got either a reimbursement or a tax deduction regardless of the amount of tuition they paid. The Court viewed this as an open attempt to subsidize religious schools rather than primarily a benefit to parents whose children attended such schools. Thus, the first attempt at a tuition tax credit failed to pass constitutional scrutiny.

New Jersey also enacted legislation that would give tax relief to parents whose children attended religious schools. Its plan was slightly different from New York's in that it allowed a $1,000 tax exemption for each child who attended a nonpublic school. Since most of the nonpublic schools in New Jersey were religious schools, the federal court in the case *Public Funds for Public Schools v. Byrne* found that the tax credit plan had the primary effect of advancing religion. In this decision it relied heavily on the Supreme Court's reasoning in *Nyquist*. As with the New York plan, New Jersey's benefit was restricted to parents whose children attended the nonpublic schools and was not available to parents whose children attended the public schools. It was this narrowness of the class of individuals who benefited that seemed to be controlling in the Court's decision finding the plan in violation of the Constitution.

Minnesota, in contrast to the other two states, found a permissible method of providing tax relief to parents of children attending religious schools. In this plan, the state allowed an income tax deduction for actual expenses paid by parents for tuition, textbooks, and transportation for their children who attended any school within the state including public schools. The Supreme Court in *Mueller v. Allen* (1983) found this distinction to be controlling in its decision. While in *Nyquist* the state's plan was an obvious attempt at subsidizing religious schools, the Minnesota plan was a benefit to a broad base of citizens, not just those whose children attended religious schools. Thus, it had a secular educational purpose and its primary effect did not advance religion as mandated in *Lemon*. Further, the Court found that the Minnesota plan did not foster excessive entanglement between government and religion as mandated by the third prong of the *Lemon* test.

The Minnesota plan provides a good template for other states who wish to give some financial relief to parents whose children attend religious schools. It must not be narrowly tailored to benefit only religious schools. This plan was open to parents of all children for a broad array of educational expenses they incur, both in public schools and in providing for the individualized needs of the child, as well as costs associated with religious schools. Furthermore, the Court noted that these deductions were among many different kinds of deductions allowed the citizens of the state, not all of which were aimed at education. Thus, the Minnesota plan, providing a direct benefit to a broad group of citizens, met the constitutional requirements of the First Amendment.

In addition to federal constitutional issues, many states have constitutional provisions that prohibit the government from providing any aid, direct or indirect, to any religiously affiliated school. Thus, the matter of tuition tax credits must be tested both by federal law and also at the state level before it can be considered a viable option to assisting parents who desire to send their children to religious schools.

Apart from the legal issues, tuition tax credits have a number of benefits not enjoyed by other methods of providing financial aid to religious schools such as school vouchers. First, the legality of tax credits is no longer a question, at least at the federal level. The tax credit lacks potential entanglement of government with religion that is inherent in other forms of more direct aid to religious schools. With tax credits government does not have to deal with the religious school at all, it is merely a matter for the parents who take the credits to verify their expenditures as a legitimate educational expense.

Of major concern to religious schools is the matter of government regulation, which it is feared might follow any government financial aid provided to them. It would not be beneficial for a religious school to lose its coveted independence merely to gain some limited financial benefit from the government. This specter of government control hangs heavily in the minds of many leaders of religious schools. The tax credit scheme provides enough distance between government and the school to make that fear mostly unfounded.

A further benefit of tuition tax credits is the matter of political viability. Supporters of public schools are well-organized and alert to any attempt by a state government to siphon off a portion of the funds normally available to them in support of private and religious schools. This has been seen in recent years in several states that have attempted to institute various forms of voucher plans. Vouchers tend to raise the emotional level of opposition to a high pitch. Tax credits, to date, have not met with such a volatile response in the political sphere. Thus, tuition tax credits seem to be the best hope to provide financial relief to parents who choose to educate their children in religiously affiliated schools. They pass both the legal test and the political viability test. *See also: Committee for Public Education and Religious Liberty v. Nyquist;* Government Aid to Religious Schools; *Mueller v. Allen.*

Further Reading: *Byrne v. Public Funds for Public Schools,* 442 U.S. 907 (1979); *Committee for Public Education and Religious Liberty v. Nyquist,* 413 U.S. 756 (1973); Luis A. Huerta and Chadd d'Entremont, "Education Tax Credits in a post-Zelman Era: Legal, Political, and Policy Alternatives to Vouchers?" *Educational Policy* 21 (January 2007): 73–109; *Lemon v. Kurtzman,* 403 U.S. 602 (1971); *Mueller v. Allen,* 463 U.S. 388 (1983).

Lyndon G. Furst

U

U.S. Department of Education Guidelines on Religion and Public Education

Beginning in 1995, the U.S. Department of Education (DOE) has periodically issued legal guidance on religion in public schools. The stated purpose of the guidelines has been to inform state educational agencies and local school officials about current law regarding religious expression in schools, as interpreted by the DOE in consultation with the U.S. Department of Justice.

The first DOE guidance, "Religious Expression in Public Schools: A Statement of Principles," was sent to every public school superintendent in August 1995 by U.S. Secretary of Education Richard Riley at the direction of President Bill Clinton. The document emphasizes the various ways in which students have the right to express their faith during the school day, including the right to pray, read their Scriptures, and share their religious views with others. At the same time, the guidelines caution that students do not have the right to have a captive audience listen or to compel other students to participate in their prayers or religious discussions.

The statement underscores the constitutional obligation of public school administrators and teachers to remain neutral regarding religion when acting in their official capacity. According to the guidelines, this does not mean that school officials should ignore religion: Teachers may teach *about* religion (as distinguished from religious instruction or indoctrination) as part of the study of history, literature, and other subjects.

The 1995 DOE guidelines were developed during a period of heated congressional debate over a constitutional amendment proposed by Representative Ernest Istook (R-OK) that critics charged would return state-sponsored prayer to public schools. With new Republican majorities in both houses of Congress, the Clinton administration was worried that the Istook proposal or a similar amendment might prevail. By outlining all of the ways in which student religious expression was already protected under current law, the president hoped to counter arguments for a constitutional amendment and simultaneously demonstrate support for religious freedom in public schools.

During the drafting process, Secretary Riley consulted with many advocacy and educational organizations with divergent views about religion in schools. He discovered that a coalition of 35 religious and civil liberties groups, chaired by the American Jewish Congress, was already working on a consensus statement entitled "Religion in the Public Schools: A Joint Statement of Current Law." Since the coalition included groups from across the religious and political spectrum—from the National Association of Evangelicals to the American Civil Liberties Union—the Secretary decided to use the Joint Statement as the basis for the administration's guidelines.

The Clinton guidelines were updated in 1998 to reflect the U.S. Supreme Court's decision in *Boerne v. Flores* (1997) declaring the Religious Freedom Restoration Act of 1993 (RFRA) unconstitutional as applied to state and local governments. Congress had enacted RFRA in response to the Supreme Court's 1990 decision in *Employment Division of Oregon v. Smith,* sharply curtailing the application of the "compelling interest test" in cases in which religious expression is substantially burdened by government law or regulations. With the demise of RFRA, school officials no longer had to show a compelling state interest when determining whether or not to accommodate religious requests for exemption from school policies or curriculum.

In December 1999, President Clinton announced his intention to send the guidelines to every public school principal in the nation. He expanded the scope of the guidance by including a DOE publication encouraging collaboration between public schools and religious communities. Entitled "How Faith Communities Support Children's Learning in Public Schools," the document describes successful partnerships in mentoring programs, after-school activities, and similar initiatives. Also included in the packet were three consensus statements from the First Amendment Center: "A Teacher's Guide to Religion in the Public Schools," "A Parent's Guide to Religion in the Public Schools," and "Public Schools and Religious Communities: A First Amendment Guide."

The packet of five documents was mailed by the DOE to all schools in January 2000. Although some separationist groups were critical of the Clinton administration's effort to encourage more collaboration between public schools and religious communities and some conservative Christian groups did not think support for student religious expression went far enough, the guidelines were generally well-received by a broad range of religious and educational organizations.

The Clinton-era guidance was used in some school districts to draft new policies on permissible student religious expression and teaching about religion. But many districts largely ignored the advice. Conflicts that might have been prevented continued to erupt in schools around the nation. One year after the DOE mailing, the First Amendment Center surveyed administrators and teachers to find out how familiar they were with the guidelines. Only 8 percent of administrators and 2 percent of teachers were very familiar with the guidelines, while another 34 percent and 13 percent, respectively, were somewhat familiar. But 39 percent of administrators and 69 percent of teachers were not at all familiar with the DOE guidelines (*First Amendment Survey of Teachers and Administrators,* 2001).

For many religious and political conservatives, the reluctance of many school officials to proactively protect student religious expression was another example of what they saw as public school hostility toward religion. In 2001, congressional Republicans succeeded in adding language to the No Child Left Behind Act directing the DOE to issue new guidelines on student prayer in public schools.

In response to the congressional mandate, Secretary of Education Rod Paige issued "Guidance on Constitutionally Protected Prayer in Public Elementary and Secondary Schools" on February 3, 2003. As the title suggests, the document focuses on the various ways in which students are free to pray during the school day under current law. During their free time, students may pray and read their Scriptures to the same extent that they may engage in nonreligious activities. And students may organize prayer groups or gatherings to the same extent that students are permitted to organize other noncurricular student groups or gatherings.

Although much of the 2003 document tracks the advice given in 1998 and 2000, the new guidance differs on the extent to which students may pray or express religious views at school-sponsored events. According to the guidelines, when student speakers are selected by neutral criteria and retain primary control over the content of their speech, school officials may not restrict the content because of religious or antireligious content. While conservative Christian groups have hailed this advice, some religious and educational groups have charged that it ignores conflicting lower court decisions on the constitutionality of student prayers at graduation and school assemblies. According to critics, this and other parts of the 2003 guidance reflect where the DOE wants the law to be rather than where the law actually is. Critics also argue that some lower court decisions may be in tension, if not conflict, with the DOE document.

Unlike the advisory nature of the Clinton-era guidelines, the 2003 directive requires schools to comply or risk loss of federal funding. By congressional mandate, school districts must certify annually that they have no policy that prevents, or otherwise denies, participation in constitutionally protected prayer as set forth in the guidance.

As of 2007, it was unclear how effective the guidance has been in helping local schools deal with problems regarding religion and religious liberty. Superintendents have routinely certified that they have no policy that conflicts with the guidelines. But the fact that many districts have few or no policies in this area has enabled some school officials to report compliance without addressing how well or poorly they are handling religious liberty issues in practice. *See also:* Common Ground Documents; First Amendment Center.

Further Reading: Joan DelFattore, *The Fourth R: Conflicts Over Religion in America's Public Schools* (New Haven, CT: Yale University Press, 2004); First Amendment Center, *First Amendment Survey of Teachers and Administrators* (Nashville: First Amendment Center, 2001); Charles C. Haynes and Oliver Thomas, *Finding Common Ground: A First Amendment Guide to Religion and Public Schools* (Nashville: First Amendment Center, 2007); Thomas Hutton, "Sins of Omission: Federal Prayer Guidance May Cause Headaches for Schools," *Inquiry and Analysis* (April 2003): 1–5; U.S. Department of Education, at www.ed.gov.

Charles C. Haynes

Utah 3 Rs Project: Rights, Responsibilities, Respect

The Utah 3 Rs Project is a nonprofit, nonpartisan teacher and community education initiative designed to promote religious liberty and education about religion in the state's public schools. The project is built on the conviction that the guiding principles of the First Amendment to the U.S. Constitution stand at the heart of democracy and at the foundation of citizenship in a diverse society. Foremost among these shared civic principles are the "3 Rs" of religious liberty—rights, responsibilities, and respect—as defined in the *Williamsburg Charter,* a reaffirmation of religious liberty signed by nearly 200 leaders from every sector of American life in 1988. The Utah 3 Rs project was launched in 1991 and became an official program of the Utah State Office of Education, in collaboration with the Freedom Forum First Amendment Center at Vanderbilt University, in 1997.

Local school districts in parts of Texas, Oklahoma, Pennsylvania, and New York have partnered with the First Amendment Center to promote the 3 Rs approach to finding common ground on issues of religion and values in public schools, but Utah is one of only two states, along with California, that has a statewide organization. Yet while California is one of the most religiously and ethnically diverse states in the nation, Utah is known for the pervasive influence of the Church of Jesus Christ of Latter-day Saints (aka the Mormons) in its history, culture, and politics. In spite of their very different demographic characteristics, 3 Rs Projects have succeeded in both Utah and California and have enabled these two states to become national leaders in promoting and protecting the religious liberty rights of students of all faiths and none.

The 3 Rs Projects are based upon a broad civic consensus that has emerged since the mid-1980s regarding the place of religion in American public schools. Rooted in the religion clauses of the First Amendment, this consensus is set forth in a number of documents that have been endorsed by a remarkably broad range of educational, religious, and civic organizations and distributed by the U.S. Department of Education to every public school in the nation (see Beauchamp, 2002). At the foundation of this consensus is a sharp distinction between teaching *about* religion on the one hand, and the promotion of religion or religious indoctrination on the other hand. As stated in one of these consensus documents, *A Teacher's Guide to Religion in the Public Schools:*

The school's approach to religion is *academic,* not *devotional.*
The school strives for student *awareness* of religions, but does not press for student *acceptance* of any religion.
The school sponsors study *about* religion, not the *practice* of religion.
The school may *expose* students to a diversity of religious views, but may not *impose* any particular view.
The school *educates* about all religions; it does not *promote* or *denigrate* religion.
The school *informs* students about various beliefs; it does not seek to *conform* students to any particular belief. (Haynes and Thomas, 2007, pp. 45–46)

The Utah 3 Rs Project began as a response to conflicts and misunderstandings between the Mormon majority and religious and secular minorities in Utah's public schools. In an effort to promote civil dialogue on religious diversity, Ray Briscoe, a former school board member and researcher for the Church of Jesus Christ of Latter-day Saints, enlisted the First Amendment Center's Charles C. Haynes to conduct workshops for school personnel and community members on the civic and legal principles that must govern public school policies toward religion. Follow-up workshops have prepared teachers to teach about religions and cultures in ways that are constitutionally permissible and academically sound. School superintendents and teachers in all of Utah's 40 school districts have received 3 Rs training, and teacher education programs in several of the state's universities include courses on 3 Rs principles. Direction and oversight of the Utah 3 Rs Project is provided by a governing board and a state advisory board, which consist of representatives from educational, religious, governmental, and business organizations. Since its inception, the project has been funded entirely by grants from private foundations raised by veteran teacher and Utah 3 Rs Project director, Martha Ball. *See also:* California 3 Rs Project: Rights, Responsibilities, Respect; First Amendment Center.

Further Reading: Marcia Beauchamp, "Guidelines on Religion in Public Schools: An Historic Moment," *Spotlight on Teaching—Religious Studies News, AAR Edition* 17 (March 2002): 2, 4, 10; Charles C. Haynes and Oliver Thomas, *Finding Common Ground: A First Amendment Guide to Religion and Public Schools* (Nashville, TN: First Amendment Center, 2007); John O'Neill and Kristen Loschert, "Navigating Religion in the Classroom," *NEA Today* (November 2002).

Bruce Grelle

V

Vouchers

Educational vouchers are certificates that allow students to attend a school of their choice rather than one mandated by a local public school district. The school then redeems the certificate for a specified sum to pay the tuition that would normally be charged to the student. The concept of vouchers in education was developed some 50 years ago by free-market economists, such as Milton Friedman, who suggested that competition would be good for American education. They described the public school system as monopolistic, which gives rise to poor quality. At the time most children attending public schools were assigned a specific school near where they lived. The student had no choice but to attend the neighborhood school. Parents with economic advantage could choose a better school by moving to the neighborhood near such a school, but parents on the lower end of the economic scale could not make such a choice.

The concept of educational vouchers has never really caught on in America. This is partly due to growing choice within the public school system. A number of states allow for charter schools, which are public schools that operate outside the control of a locally elected school board. They get funding directly from the state just like other public schools but have much greater freedom to focus on a unique educational program. Children who desire to attend charter schools are not restricted to the neighborhood school plan. Several states also have what is known as "public-school choice," which allows children to attend schools outside of their own neighborhood attendance area. Both of these plans have resulted in a great deal of choice for parents with school-age children within the traditional public school setting, providing the competition that some think will bring about improvement in school operation. Neither of these plans, however, allows for the choice of private and/or religious schools. Supporters of school vouchers suggest that the true benefits of competition in any school choice plan will not be achieved until religious schools are included. To date no large-scale publicly funded educational voucher plan has been instituted.

Supporters of school vouchers claim that the additional competition to public schools by including religious schools in the mix would be beneficial to the public. There is some research to show that children in religious schools have an educational advantage over those in public schools. The research to date, however, is mixed on this matter. There is no definitive proof of an educational benefit for any voucher plan. Opponents also claim that a statewide educational voucher plan would result in significant increases in educational costs or the siphoning off of the funds that are used to support public schools. While it is true that if students attending public schools would transfer to private schools under a voucher plan, there would be a possible savings of public monies. If the voucher plan included students already attending private schools, however, there would likely be a significant increase in the cost of publicly funded education to the state.

Further concerns by those opposed to vouchers relate to the matter of social cohesiveness that is purportedly fostered by the American public schools. A state-funded voucher plan, by opening up attendance possibilities at faith-based schools, might result in institutionalized divisiveness among the population. One could point to the situation in Northern Ireland with its Catholic and Protestant schools operating in opposition to each other as an example of this possibility. A basic tenet of the American public school system is that it provides a common core of social understanding among all citizens that is necessary for a successful democracy. Public school advocates and voucher opponents fear that a widely available voucher program would lead to less diversity in all schools.

It is the inclusion of religious schools in voucher plans that is most problematic. The First Amendment to the U.S. Constitution states in part, "Congress shall make no law respecting an establishment of religion." This restriction was extended to action by state government through the Fourteenth Amendment. It is well-established in the law that state funding provided directly to religious schools is a violation of the First Amendment Establishment Clause. Further, more than half of the states have their own constitutional provisions (often called "mini-Blaine amendments") prohibiting tax money from being paid in support of religion, which would include religious schools. Thus, any voucher plan would have to be fashioned in such a way as to overcome these legal barriers.

The first major voucher program to meet this challenge was developed by the State of Wisconsin for the City of Milwaukee in 1989. Known as the Milwaukee Parental Choice Program, it was targeted at students whose family income was not more than 1.75 times the federal poverty level. Religious schools were not initially included in the plan. In 1995, however, the Milwaukee voucher plan was amended to allow inclusion of religious schools. The Supreme Court of Wisconsin ruled that this plan did not violate either the First Amendment of the U.S. Constitution or the Wisconsin Constitution.

In the landmark Supreme Court decision, *Lemon v. Kurtzman,* a three-part test was formulated to determine the legality of government aid to religious institutions: first, any such aid must have a secular legislative purpose; second, the primary effect of the aid must neither advance nor inhibit religion; and third, such aid must not foster excessive entanglement between government and religion. The Wisconsin high court relied on *Lemon* in its own decision regarding the Milwaukee voucher plan in *Jackson v. Benson* (1998). It found that there was definitely a secular purpose, which was to provide low-income parents with a real choice in selecting a school, either public or private, for their children. It also found that any benefit to the religious school was a matter of private choice on the part of parents and not an action by the state. The voucher plan did not specifically favor religious schools; it was made available to both religious and nonsectarian schools on an equal basis. Thus, any aid to religion was indirect on the part of the state. The original voucher plan had included extensive supervision by government agents but, as amended, that supervision was deleted from the program. The Wisconsin court noted that a certain level of oversight was already in place for private and religious schools. Thus, the plan did not involve excessive entanglement between state government and religion.

After considering the First Amendment issues, the Wisconsin court turned its attention to the state constitution and challenges under several of its provisions. First was the benefits clause, which prohibits any public money being used for the benefit of a religious society or school. The court applied the same reasoning as used with the federal Constitution, the primary effect test. It found that the primary effect of the voucher plan was not the advancement of religion. It also noted that in Wisconsin, parents have traditionally been given the primary role in deciding where their children should attend school. Nothing in the state constitution would prohibit payments made as directed by parents for the education of their children, as long as the program was neutral between religious and nonreligious alternatives.

Another part of the Wisconsin Constitution prohibited any person from being compelled to support a place of worship. Opponents of the voucher plan charged that using public money to pay tuition at a religious school compels taxpayers to support the religion against their will. The court thought otherwise. In fact, it noted that the voucher program specifically prohibited religious schools from requiring children in the program to attend religious activities.

The Wisconsin Constitution also has a provision that requires the state to establish a system of public schools that are uniform in nature. Opponents of the voucher plan claimed that including private and religious schools violated this constitutional requirement since such schools were markedly different from the public schools. The court ruled that mere inclusion in the voucher program did not make a private school into a public school. Thus, the private schools were not part of the state system of public education. A further issue was the public purpose doctrine: that public funds may be expended only for a public purpose. The Wisconsin court ruled that private schools could certainly be employed to achieve a public purpose and that there were sufficient accountability safeguards to ensure that the program did, in fact, fulfill this constitutional mandate.

The Wisconsin educational voucher plan was narrowly tailored to include only the city of Milwaukee where the public schools were of notoriously low quality. The purpose of the plan was to provide the free-market benefits envisioned by economists who first suggested vouchers as a means of reforming the public schools by introducing competition to them. The State of Ohio followed suit by developing a similar plan for schools in the city of Cleveland. It, too, was challenged in court as being a violation of the Establishment Clause of the First Amendment.

The Cleveland plan included not only tuition aid for children attending public schools who wanted to attend a private school, but also provided funding for tutorial aid for those who chose to remain in the public schools. The financial aid was distributed to parents based on their financial need. Vouchers were just one of a number of programs undertaken by the state to improve the public schools in Cleveland. The Supreme Court of the United States in its decision in *Zelman v. Simmons-Harris* (2002) had no trouble finding that the Cleveland plan was enacted for an appropriate secular purpose: to provide educational assistance to economically disadvantaged children in a public school system that was failing to carry out its educational mission effectively. It then turned to the question of the primary effect possibly advancing religion in violation of the First Amendment.

In dealing with the issue of government aid benefiting religion, the Court cited several cases where it rejected challenges to programs providing aid to religious schools. As with these cases, it noted that the Cleveland voucher program provided assistance to a broad class of citizens who by their own private choice directed state funds to the religious schools. It was these numerous private choices that resulted in government aid going to the schools, not a specific plan by the state to do so. The Court further found that there was no specific financial incentive that benefited religious schools. In fact, religious schools received less funding than the public schools under the Ohio plan.

It is interesting to note that the Supreme Court in *Zelman* did not apply the third prong of the *Lemon* test. Rather, it touched briefly on two other tests that have been used on occasion by the Court in First Amendment cases. It found that the Cleveland plan did not function as an "endorsement" of religious schooling in general, but rather was a widespread undertaking to assist economically disadvantaged children to get a better education. Additionally, the Court applied the "coercion" test and found that Ohio was not coercing parents to send their children to religious schools. Thus, the Cleveland voucher plan passed the constitutional mandate found in the First Amendment.

From a review of these two cases, one decided by a state supreme court and the other decided by the U.S. Supreme Court, it appears that any voucher plan must be carefully crafted to meet the requirements of both state and federal constitutions. Voucher plans cannot be targeted to benefit just religious schools. They must be open to a variety of schools, both religious and secular. Further, religious schools may not impose religious requirements on students who attend under a voucher plan. Both of the voucher plans studied here were focused on economically disadvantaged students attending inner-city public schools. To date there has been no legal test of a statewide broadly based voucher plan open to all students in the state. It remains to be seen how such a plan would pass judicial scrutiny.

Many leaders in religious schools were heartened by the decisions in Wisconsin and Ohio, which opened up state funding to their schools even if on a limited basis. Other religious leaders, however, are not so excited about the possibility of state aid to their schools. They have deep concerns that such aid, while beneficial financially, might be detrimental to the freedom they currently enjoy to carry out their specifically religious mission.

It is well settled in the law that state government has a right to reasonably regulate religious schools. The state can, for example, mandate a minimal level of educational offerings and length of the school year. It also can require private schools to make regular reports to the state. There are, however, limitations on what regulations can be imposed upon such schools. Any regulation that would impede the school in carrying out its religious mission would not be upheld by the courts. If there were a broad-based voucher plan that included religious schools, however, the courts might not be so protective of these schools from the state's regulatory desires. The same concern is true of federal regulations, especially the rather draconian mandates of the No Child Left Behind Act. Many religious schools would be hard-pressed to comply with this federal law if it was applied to them.

Religious schools are dependent upon the almost absolute freedom they have in choosing the personnel who will carry out their religious mission. They are exempted from the laws forbidding discrimination on the basis of religion in employment matters. Further, they are exempt from laws regarding unionization and collective bargaining. Public employees have protections under the due process and equal protection clauses of the Fourteenth Amendment. These protections only apply to employees of organizations involved in state action. Religious schools are not considered to be so involved. Therefore, their employees do not have constitutional protections that public school employees have. It is not known how the courts will look at this if religious schools are heavily involved in accepting students under an educational voucher plan.

The same concerns apply to the selection of students who attend religious schools. Such schools have a great deal of discretion in determining who is and who is not admitted to their school. The nature of the student body is a major factor in determining success in carrying out the school's religious mission. Religious schools can discriminate on the basis of religion in admitting students. They also can impose behavioral requirements for continued enrollment. Religious schools are relatively free in imposing discipline on students who violate the rules of the school. Public schools do not have such freedom. They are bound by the Due Process and Equal Protection Clauses of the Fourteenth Amendment. Religious schools that enroll large numbers of students under an educational voucher plan may be considered as engaged in state action and thus lose their freedom regarding the selection and discipline of their students.

With the possibility of widespread educational voucher plans in the future, religious leaders have some hard decisions to make. They have much to offer the public in providing quality education. The financial benefits of a steady flow of students with guaranteed payment by the state is certainly tempting to schools located in the inner cities that have seen their enrollments decline in recent years. Such schools must consider, however, to what extent they are willing to jeopardize their freedom to function and carry out their religious mission. If accepting state money under a voucher plan means that they lose their distinctive religious culture, such a school may become just another private school that functions much like a public school. Thus, the possibility of educational vouchers being made available to religious schools, while providing some financial benefits, may not be the "silver bullet" for which they had hoped. While many of the concerns presented here are speculative, they must be considered when the decision to participate or not to participate in a state-funded educational voucher plan is being made. *See also:* First Amendment Religious Clauses and the Supreme Court; Government Aid to Religious Schools; *Mueller v. Allen;* School Choice; Tuition Tax Credits; *Zelman v. Simmons-Harris.*

Further Reading: Chad d'Entremont, and Luis A. Huerta, "Irreconcilable Differences? Education Vouchers and the Suburban Response," *Educational Policy* 21 (January 2007): 40–72; Milton Friedman, *Capitalism and Freedom* (Chicago: University of Chicago Press, 1962); *Jackson v. Benson,* 578 N.W. 2d 602 (Wis. 1998); *Lemon v. Kurtzman,* 403 U.S. 602 (1971); Henry M. Levin, "A Comprehensive Framework for Evaluating Educational Vouchers," *Educational Evaluation and Policy Analysis* 24 (Fall 2002): 159–174; Martha McCarthy, "Determining the Legality of School Vouchers: Are State Courts the New Venue?" *Journal of Education Finance* 32 (Winter 2007): 352–372; Brent Shelly, "The Impact of School Vouchers on Employment Law: State Regulatory Interference with Private Religious Schools," *Regent University Law Review* 18 (Fall 2005): 129–155; *Zelman v. Simmons-Harris,* 536 U.S. 639 (2002).

Lyndon G. Furst

W

Wallace v. Jaffree

In a 6-3 opinion, the U.S. Supreme Court in 1985 struck down as unconstitutional an Alabama statute that permitted, but did not require, a teacher-initiated moment of silence in public schools. According to the law, "the teacher in charge of the room in which each class is held may announce that a period of silence not to exceed one minute in duration shall be observed for meditation or voluntary prayer, and during any such period no other activities shall be engaged in." This portion of the code is one of three parts brought to the attention of the Court. The first, which required meditation and did not mention prayer, was not challenged by the appellees. The third—"enacted in 1982, which authorized teachers to lead 'willing students' in a prescribed prayer to 'Almighty God...the Creator and Supreme Judge of the world'"—was struck down by the Court a year earlier in *Wallace v. Jaffree* (1984).

Unlike the third portion of the code, the second portion did not specifically permit teachers to lead students in a particular prayer. The Court, nevertheless, struck down the second portion because the Court concluded that it violated the purpose prong of the *Lemon* test: "the statute must have a secular legislative purpose." (*Lemon v. Kurtzman,* 1971). Authored by Justice William Brennan, the Court's majority opinion drew this conclusion because the law's chief sponsor, State Senator Donald Holmes, was, according to the Court, motivated by a desire "to return voluntary prayer to our public schools...[I]t is a beginning and a step in the right direction." Moreover, because "Senator Holmes unequivocally testified that he had 'no other purpose in mind,'" the Court concluded that "the record not only provides us with an unambiguous affirmative answer [as to the religious purpose of the statute], but it also reveals that the enactment of [it] was not motivated by any clearly secular purpose—indeed, the statute had no secular purpose."

In her concurring opinion, Justice Sandra Day O'Connor, rather than relying on the *Lemon* test, appeals to what she called "the endorsement test": because a fully informed citizen would interpret this statute as an endorsement of religion, it violates the Establishment Clause. Like Justice Brennan, Justice O'Connor would have thought this statute constitutional if the prayer provision were omitted.

The three dissenting opinions by Justice William Rehnquist, Justice Byron White, and Chief Justice Warren Burger each make several important legal points, some of which may influence subsequent school moment-of-silence and/or prayer cases. Justice White, for example, points out that if more than half of his brethren would "approve statutes that provided for a moment of silence but did not mention prayer," then where precisely would his brethren come down in the case of a teacher who answered "yes" when asked by a student if she could silently pray during the approved moment of silence? And if the giving of that answer by a state actor, the teacher, is permissible, then why is it not permissible for the Alabama legislature to provide precisely the same answer before the question is asked?

In his dissent Chief Justice Burger argues that because earlier cases against school-sponsored prayer may have led some citizens to mistakenly believe that all prayer is prohibited in public schools, a secular purpose of this legislation is to remedy that misconception by showing that the state is not hostile to religious free exercise voluntarily engaged in by its citizens. Burger also asserts that the public comments of the bill's sponsor should not serve as the Court's lone basis for determining legislative purpose, since there are many legislative supporters with a variety of motives, some of which may be secular.

Justice Rehnquist offers an historical narrative of the Establishment Clause to counter the one offered by Justice Brennan in his majority opinion. Rehnquist argues that those who composed and passed the Establishment Clause would have had no objection to a statute that allowed a state's public school teachers to single out prayer as a permissible activity for their students during a moment of silence.

In contrast, Justice Brennan, in his own narrative, does not deny the history outlined in Justice Rehnquist's opinion. Rather, Justice Brennan maintains that there is a reason why such a moment of silence statute may have been permissible in the minds of those in early America even though it is, in fact, impermissible under today's understanding of the Constitution. According to Justice Brennan, in early America the underlying principle that justified religious disestablishment and religious free exercise was not applied to the citizenry of the sort of nation the United States had become by 1985, a country consisting of a much wider range of opinions, practices, and beliefs on matters of religion. Writes Brennan: "But when the underlying principle has been examined in the crucible of litigation, the Court has unambiguously concluded that the individual freedom of conscience protected by the First Amendment embraces the right to select any religious faith or none at all." *See also: Engel v. Vitale;* Moments of Silence; *Smith v. Board of Commissioners of Mobile County.*

Further Reading: Francis J. Beckwith, "The Court of Disbelief: The Constitution's Article VI Religious Test Prohibition and the Judiciary's Religious Motive Analysis," *Hastings Constitutional Law Quarterly* 33 (Winter/Spring 2006): 337–360; Bruce J. Dierenfield, *The Battle Over School Prayer: How* Engel v. Vitale *Changed America* (Lawrence, KS: University Press of Kansas, 2007); *Engel v. Vitale,* 370 U.S. 421 (1962); Philip Hamburger, *Separation of Church and State* (Cambridge, MA: Harvard University Press, 2002); *Lemon v. Kurtzman,* 403 U.S. 602; *Wallace v. Jaffree,* 472 U.S. 38 (1985); *Wallace v. Jaffree,* 466 U.S. 924 (1984).

Francis J. Beckwith

Warshaw, Thayer S.

An English teacher in Newton North High School, Massachusetts, Thayer Warshaw (1915–2000) is recognized as a pioneer in developing both curriculum and pedagogical techniques for teaching about religion (especially literature) in public schools. During the 1962–1963 school year, he discovered that his high school literature students reading Steinbeck's *The Pearl* were "completely ignorant of the Bible." So he inaugurated a Bible unit, later a semester course, on biblically related literature. A February 1964 article in *English Journal* brought much publicity. He was featured in *Time* magazine as the first teacher to encourage the objective teaching of religion, consistent with the guidelines of the U.S. Supreme Court's *Schempp* decision of 1963.

Working with others in the field, including James S. Ackerman at Indiana University, Warshaw developed workshops for secondary school teachers of literature. The Lilly Endowment funded summer workshops on "Bible As/In Literature" for ten years at Indiana University. Ackerman and Warshaw trained over 500 teachers from all 50 states, as well as from five foreign countries in the program, officially named "The Institute on Teaching the Bible in Secondary English." The Institute published eight books, most of them edited or written by Warshaw. A student textbook that they co-edited is still in print. Their most famous book, *The Bible as/in Literature,* was still being used in over 700 U.S. school districts in the late 1990s.

Warshaw was involved in professional organizations related to the academic study of religion. He became a member of the Professional Advisory Council that was linked to the Public Education Religion Studies Center (PERSC) at Wright State University. PERSC guidelines from 1973–1974 for the K–12 public schools are still in use today. Through workshops sponsored by PERSC and other groups, Warshaw aided in the development of quality teaching materials and academically appropriate teaching methods for religion in the K–12 curriculum.

Following retirement, he became involved in the National Council on Religion and Public Education (NCRPE). Established by mainline denominational representatives and leaders of educational and liberal legal groups, the NCRPE's mission was to present a proactive response to those groups calling for organized prayer in public schools. NCRPE's preferred alternative was the preparation of curriculum that would meet the Supreme Court's guidelines. Thayer Warshaw was a prime contributor to that organization's mission, serving as its newsletter editor until the 1980s.

In the mid-1980s, Charles Kniker, Iowa State University, proposed that NCRPE publish a refereed journal. Thayer Warshaw became manuscript editor of *Religion & Public Education,* later *Religion & Education.* In addition to editing, he read over 50 newspapers, journals, and other sources, and contributed a "news" column for each issue. Warshaw partnered with Linda L. Meixner to prepare a textbook, *The Bible in Literature Courses: Successful Lesson Plans,* which the NCRPE published in 1992.

The NCRPE leadership and editorial board honored him by establishing the Thayer S. Warshaw Prize. Its purpose was to recognize outstanding essays whose subject was on the interfacing of religion and education.

What impact did Thayer S. Warshaw have upon the field of teaching about religion(s) in public education? Charles Haynes of the First Amendment Center mentions the following:

• In 2000 the Office of the President of the United States sent packets of religious-liberty guidelines to every public school in America. In the packet were statements about the importance of the "study of religion" in the curriculum—statements that Warshaw's work had helped to develop.

- Within public school curriculum circles, the question today is no longer *Should* we teach about religion, but rather *How?*
- All existing national and state social studies standards now encourage considerable study of religions.
- Statewide teacher preparation programs in California and Utah, among other states, either mandate or strongly encourage future educators to integrate religious studies into their courses. During the 1980s especially, Warshaw provided much guidance to state groups on what realistically should be required of teachers who wished to incorporate the academic study of religion in their classrooms.

In summary, Thayer S. Warshaw was a pioneer in the field of teaching about religion(s) in public schools. More than being a model for teaching the Bible as/in literature, he helped craft standards for curriculum, guidelines for current teachers, and high standards for future educators. While he would be pleased with some progress, no doubt he would be dismayed by some of the "Bible history" curriculum now being adopted by some school districts for being either too "sectarian" or for not acknowledging past "negative" actions by faith traditions (Chancey, 2007). *See also:* National Council on Religion and Public Education.

Further Reading: James S. Ackerman and Thayer S. Warshaw, *The Bible as/in Literature* (Glenview, IL: Scott, Foresman and Company, 1976); Mark A Chancey, "Bible Bills, Bible Curricula, and Controversies of Biblical Proportions: Legislative Efforts to Promote Bible Courses in Public Schools," *Religion & Education* 34 (Winter 2007): 1–27; "Thayer S. Warshaw—A Tribute," *Religion & Education* 28 (Fall 2001): 86–98; Thayer S. Warshaw, *Handbook for Teaching the Bible in Literature Classes* (Nashville, TN: Abingdon Press, 1978); Thayer S. Warshaw, "Studying the Bible in Public School," *The English Journal* 53 (February 1964): 91–100.

Charles R. Kniker

West Virginia State Board of Education v. Barnette

This case addressed the constitutionality of a state department of education regulation requiring all students, as a condition of continuing in school, to pledge allegiance to the U.S. flag. The U.S. Supreme Court's decision in *West Virginia State Board of Education v. Barnette* (1943) must be viewed in the context of another Supreme Court decision with an almost identical set of facts, *Minersville School District v. Gobitis* (1940), a Pennsylvania case decided just three years earlier.

In *Gobitis,* the Court upheld, as not violative of due process, a local school board's requirement that pupils salute, with their right hands extended, the American flag in daily school exercises as a condition of attending free public school. Plaintiffs in *Gobitis* were Jehovah's Witness parents who alleged that requiring their children to salute the flag was contrary to their religious beliefs. Because the children refused to salute the flag, they were suspended and their parents had to enroll them in a private school. The parents sued the school district, alleging that punishing their children for an exercise of their religious beliefs violated the liberty clause of the Fourteenth Amendment. The federal district court granted the parents injunctive relief and the Third Circuit Court of Appeals affirmed. The Supreme Court granted certiorari and reversed. The Court in *Gobitis* balanced what it perceived as a conflict between religious duty and the secular interests of one's fellow men, deciding in favor of the latter and concluding that "We are dealing with an interest inferior to none in the hierarchy of legal values. National unity is the basis of national security." The Court observed that neither the First Amendment's free exercise nor free speech clauses relieves an individual from obedience to a general law not aimed at the promotion or restriction of religious beliefs. Painting with a broad brush, the Supreme Court in *Gobitis* upheld the right of school boards to use their quasi-legislative function to develop children in the area of citizenship.

Following the Court's *Gobitis* decision, the West Virginia legislature amended its statutes to require additional courses in history, pursuant to which the state board of education adopted a regulation imposing on all students in public schools a flag salute similar to the one upheld in *Gobitis*. The failure of students to participate in the flag salute constituted insubordination for which students would be expelled. The plaintiffs in *West Virginia State Board of Education v. Barnette* were Jehovah's Witnesses whose children had been expelled for refusal to salute the flag. A three-judge federal district court granted plaintiffs an injunction prohibiting enforcement of the regulation and the Supreme Court affirmed.

Contrary to the *Gobitis* majority that had emphasized the importance of the pledge from the perspective of national unity, the *Barnette* majority viewed the state's regulation from the individual's perspective as a compulsion on students to declare a belief. The Court emphasized that fundamental rights enumerated in the Bill of Rights, and in particular the rights of free exercise and speech, serve to remove these rights from the vicissitudes of political controversy and to place them beyond the reach of majorities and officials. This emphasis on constitutional rights is what moves the *Barnette* Court in a different direction from its *Gobitis* predecessor. While the Court in *Barnette* made no claim that an individual's constitutional rights are absolute, the Court emphasized that they are susceptible of restriction only when necessary to prevent grave and immediate danger to interests that the state may lawfully protect.

Although not expressly referring to the occurrence of its decision in the midst of a worldwide conflict, the *Barnette* Court responded eloquently to the *Gobitis* Court's use of national unity as the counterweight to individual rights. The *Barnette* Court reflected on the relatively recent phenomenon of nationalism and the ever-increasing severity of its methods to attain unity, with the ultimate certainty that the greater the governmental pressure to attain unity, the more bitter will be the strife as to whose unity was to be the one adopted. In the end, the *Barnette* Court reasoned that greatest division of a people in the context of education would come from finding out which doctrine and whose program would be invoked by educational officials to compel youth to unite. The test of freedom, the Court observed, is to permit challenges to that which is important, in this case the extent to which everyone must demonstrate respect for one's flag. As the Court noted in conclusion, "To believe that patriotism will not flourish if patriotic ceremonies are voluntary and spontaneous instead of a compulsory routine is to make an unflattering estimate of the appeal of our institutions to free minds." *See also: Elk Grove Unified School District v. Newdow;* First Amendment Religion Clauses and the Supreme Court; *Minersville School District v. Gobitis;* The Pledge of Allegiance.

Further Reading: *Minersville School District v. Gobitis,* 310 U.S. 586 (1940); *West Virginia State Board of Education v. Barnette,* 319 U.S. 624 (1943).

Ralph D. Mawdsley

Wisconsin v. Yoder

Wisconsin v. Yoder (1972) was the third of three significant U.S. Supreme Court cases, the other two being *Meyer v. Nebraska* (1923) and *Pierce v. Society of Sisters* (1925), that upheld the Fourteenth Amendment right of parents to direct the education of their children. Neither the *Meyer* nor *Pierce* decisions raised the First Amendment's constitutional right to free exercise of religion because that constitutional right had not been made applicable to states through the Fourteenth Amendment until the Supreme Court decision of *Cantwell v. Connecticut* (1940). Thus, *Yoder* was the first Supreme Court decision to raise both claims against government action.

Yoder involved a criminal truancy charge against two Amish fathers who refused to enroll their children in a school after they had completed the eighth grade in a one-room Amish school. The State of Wisconsin required, pursuant to its compulsory attendance law, that parents enroll their children in a school between the ages of 7 and 16 years, which meant that Amish children who had completed eighth grade at ages 13 or 14 would not have been enrolled in a school until age 16. The fathers were found guilty of truancy and each was fined $5. The Supreme Court of Wisconsin reversed the convictions, finding the application of the truancy law to the Amish to constitute a violation of the First Amendment's free exercise of religion provision.

In a thorough and carefully reasoned opinion that explicated in a comprehensive manner the religious beliefs of the Amish, the U.S. Supreme Court upheld the decision of the state supreme court. The Supreme Court referenced 300 years of Amish Christian life that de-emphasized material success, rejected the competitive spirit, and sought to insulate themselves from the modern world. As part of this separation from the world, Amish beliefs required members of the community to make their living by farming or closely related activities. In sum, the Court found that, for over three centuries, the Amish religious community had inseparably and interdependently merged their Amish religious beliefs with their practical lives.

Amish objection to formal education beyond the eighth grade was firmly grounded in their central religious beliefs. The Amish considered formal high school education beyond the eighth grade contrary to Amish beliefs, not only because it placed Amish children in an environment hostile to Amish beliefs with increasing emphasis on competition in class work and sports and with pressure to conform to the styles, manners, and ways of the peer group, but also because it took the Amish children away from their community, physically and emotionally, during the crucial and formative adolescent period of life. To expose secondary-age Amish children to worldly influences during their crucial adolescent stage of development would substantially interfere with their religious development, as well as their integration into the way of life of the Amish community. In effect, to compel Amish children to enroll in public high schools past the eighth grade would mandate that they either abandon belief and be assimilated into society at large or be forced to migrate to some other and more tolerant region.

One of the avenues of appeal to the U.S. Supreme Court is from a decision of a state supreme court. The State of Wisconsin, having lost in its state supreme court, petitioned for a writ of certiorari from the U.S. Supreme Court, which was granted. The issue for the Court was whether a state's interest in an educated citizenry, as reflected in its compulsory attendance law, should prevail against the religious beliefs of a close-knit religious community.

In balancing the interests of the State of Wisconsin and the Amish religious community, the Supreme Court fashioned a three-step shifting burden of proof. First, the Amish had to produce evidence that their religious beliefs were legitimate and sincerely held, something that they had done in most convincing fashion by referencing three centuries of integrating their religious beliefs and their practical farming lives. Second, the Amish had to present evidence that their religious beliefs had been burdened by the application of the State of Wisconsin's compulsory attendance statute, something they also accomplished with the likelihood of Amish children leaving the Amish community if exposed to the world in public high schools. Third, the burden then shifted to the State of Wisconsin to produce evidence that it had a compelling interest in Amish children attending school until age 16, something it attempted with assertions that attendance was necessary to ensure that the children could participate effectively and intelligently in our open political system and that they could be prepared to be self-reliant and self-sufficient participants in society so as not to become burdens on that society. No one seriously challenged that the religious beliefs of the Amish were not sincerely held. The conflict came down as to whether the State of Wisconsin had presented sufficiently compelling interests to warrant requiring Amish children to attend school until age 16, and then, even if such compelling interests had been presented, whether their application to the Amish would work a substantial hardship.

The Court rejected outright the State of Wisconsin's argument that its interests in its system of compulsory education were so compelling that the Amish's established religious practices had to give way. With regard to the state's interest in participation in a democratic society, the Supreme Court observed that the Amish alternative to formal secondary school education had enabled them to function effectively in their day-to-day life under self-imposed limitations on relations with the world, and to survive and prosper in contemporary society as a separate, sharply identifiable and highly self-sufficient community for more than 200 years in this country. Regarding the state's interest in Amish not becoming a burden on society, the Supreme Court noted that nothing in the record indicated that young people demonstrating the Amish qualities of reliability, self-reliance, and dedication to work would not find employment or that persons possessing such valuable vocational skills and habits would be doomed to become burdens on society.

Although the Supreme Court in *Yoder* upheld the Amish way of life against the State of Wisconsin's compulsory attendance challenge, the Court was careful to observe that this case in no way prohibited states from regulating education nor did the case determine the proper resolution of possible competing interests of parents, children, and the state. In his dissent to *Yoder*, Justice William Douglas challenged the assumption that parents speak for their children on matters of education and queried as to why the Amish children had not been asked at the trial whether they might have wanted to attend public schools until age 16.

Yoder was an immediate sensation and spawned a considerable amount of litigation involving the authority of states to regulate religious schools. Generally, though, courts limited the application of *Yoder* to its facts, finding that most of the religious claimants lacked the comprehensive historical and practical demonstration of religious beliefs that had characterized the Amish. Indeed, some states codified *Yoder* by amending their compulsory attendance statutes to exempt Amish from attendance beyond age 16, but refused, then, to apply those exemptions to non-Amish religious groups. The effect of *Yoder*, however, is best viewed in the long term, in that, within 25 years after the Supreme

Court's decision, most states had relaxed their regulatory control over religious schools so that the same result in *Yoder* had been achieved, although for different reasons.

The most interesting post-*Yoder* development, though, has been judicial flirtation with Justice Douglas's observation in dissent that, "[i]t is the student's judgment, not his parents', that is essential if we are to give full meaning to what we have said about the Bill of Rights and of the right of students to be masters of their own destiny." The constitutional right of parents to direct their children's education as enshrined in *Meyer* and *Pierce* has dominated the discussion thus far regarding children's rights, but the emergence of students' rights pursuant to *Tinker v. Des Moines Independent School District* (1969) has somewhat eroded the notion that a student's legal claims must necessarily be coterminous with those of their parents. Thus, a few tantalizing cases, such as *Circle Schools v. Pappert* (2004), are emerging. In *Circle Schools,* a court upheld a student's constitutional claim to not pledge allegiance to the flag and to prevent the school from notifying his parents of his nonparticipation, while denying to the parents a constitutional claim grounded in their right to direct the education of their child. *See also: Farrington v. Tokushige; Meyer v. Nebraska; Pierce v. Society of Sisters.*

Further Reading: *Cantwell v. Connecticut,* 310 U.S. 296 (1940); *Circle Schools v. Pappert,* 381 F.3d 172 (3d Cir. 2004); *Meyer v. Nebraska,* 262 U.S. 390 (1923); *Pierce v. Society of Sisters,* 268 U.S. 510 (1925); *Tinker v. Des Moines Independent School District,* 393 U.S. 503 (1969); *Wisconsin v. Yoder,* 406 U.S. 205 (1972).

Ralph D. Mawdsley

Wolman v. Walter

Wolman v. Walter (1977) involved a far-reaching statute from Ohio that provided a wide range of aid to religiously affiliated nonpublic schools and their students. The law offered loans of textbooks for secular subjects, reimbursements for testing and record keeping, diagnostic and therapeutic auxiliary services, loans of instructional materials, and the use of buses for transportation to field trips. After a federal trial court rejected a challenge to the statute's constitutionality, a divided U.S. Supreme Court, in a majority decision by Justice Harry Blackmun that generated a total of seven different opinions in which various justices concurred and dissented, upheld parts of the law while vitiating others. Blackmun largely based his judgment on the Court's precedent in the tripartite *Lemon v. Kurtzman* (1971) test, the standard for reviewing Establishment Clause controversies. According to this test: "First, the statute must have a secular legislative purpose; second, its principal or primary effect must be one that neither advances nor inhibits religion; finally, the statute must not foster "an excessive government entanglement with religion."

Justice Blackmun began his analysis with the statute's textbook loan provision. Consistent with the Court's own precedent in *Board of Education v. Allen* (1968) and *Meek v. Pittenger* (1977), both of which upheld similar provisions, he was satisfied that the law was constitutional.

Turning to the part of the law that reimbursed religiously affiliated nonpublic schools for testing and scoring of standardized tests and scoring services that were similar to those used in public schools, Justice Blackmun agreed that it was constitutional. In so doing, he distinguished the statute at issue from the New York law that the Court struck down four years earlier in *Levitt v. Committee for Public Education and Religious Liberty* (1973), because the tests here were not created or scored by educators from the religious schools and none of the payments were for costs associated with their being administered. Instead, since the schools were simply reimbursed for costs associated with complying with state law, Blackmun held that there were adequate safeguards in place to ensure that public funds were not used for religious purposes.

As to diagnostic and therapeutic services, Justice Blackmun upheld the former, but not the latter. In treating the two differently, he noted that it was acceptable to allow public school employees to go on-site in religious schools to perform diagnostic tests to evaluate whether students needed speech, hearing, and psychological services because insofar as they were neutral, secular, and nonideological, there was no risk of creating excessive entanglement between the religious schools and public school officials. Blackmun maintained, however, that if students were to receive the actual therapeutic services, they had to be provided off-site in order to avoid the risk of entanglement between religions and public officials.

In examining the provision of instructional materials, consistent with the Court's opinion in *Meek v. Pittenger* two years earlier, Blackmun invalidated the provision that would have allowed the loans of such equipment as projectors, tape recorders, record players, maps and globes, and science kits. He was of the opinion that this arrangement was unacceptable because insofar as it would be impossible to separate the secular and religious functions for which these items were being used, this part of the law violated the *Lemon* test because it provided support for the religious roles of the schools.

As to the statute's final aspect, which allowed religiously affiliated nonpublic schools to use school buses to take their students on field trips, Justice Blackmun struck it down as unconstitutional. In his rationale, he asserted that the situation at hand was very different than in *Everson v. Board of Education* (1947), wherein the Supreme Court upheld a statute from New Jersey that allowed parents to be reimbursed for the cost of transporting their children to their religiously affiliated nonpublic schools. Blackmun determined that this provision was unconstitutional because insofar as field trips were oriented to the curriculum, they were in the category of instruction rather than that of nonideological secular services such as transportation to and from school.

Interestingly, in a plurality opinion in *Mitchell v. Helms* (2000), a dispute from Louisiana, the Supreme Court upheld the constitutionality of a federal law that permits the loans of instructional materials including library books, computers, television sets, tape recorders, and maps to religiously affiliated nonpublic schools. While the plurality explicitly reversed those parts of *Wolman* that were inconsistent with its judgment in this regard, insofar as less than the required five justice majority signed on to the same opinion, the status of such loans remains uncertain. *See also: Mitchell v. Helms.*

Further Reading: *Board of Education v. Allen,* 392 U.S. 236 (1968); *Everson v. Board of Education,* 330 U.S. 1 (1947), *rehearing denied,* 330 U.S. 855 (1947); *Lemon v. Kurtzman,* 403 U.S. 602 (1971); *Levitt v. Committee for Public Education and Religious Liberty,* 413 U.S. 472 (1973); *Meek v. Pittenger,* 421 U.S. 349 (1975); *Mitchell v. Helms,* 530 U.S. 793 (2000), *rehearing denied,* 530 U.S. 1296 (2000), *on remand sub nom. Helms v. Picard,* 229 F.3d 467 (5th Cir. 2000); *Wolman v. Walter,* 433 U.S. 229 (1977).

Charles J. Russo

Z

Zelman v. Simmons-Harris

As part of a larger effort to address poor achievement in Cleveland's schools, the State of Ohio implemented the Pilot Project Scholarship Program to give educational choices to families in certain districts. The only district involved at the time of the filing of the case was the Cleveland City School District. In 1997 the district had failed to meet any of the state standards for minimal acceptable performance. Less than one-third of enrolled students graduated from high school and some who did graduate could not perform basic skills at levels demonstrated by students in other states. Eligible parents could participate in the program from kindergarten through eighth grade. Any tuition and fees not covered by the voucher program remained the responsibility of parents who chose to place their children in private schools. Private schools choosing to participate were required to agree not to discriminate. Both religious and nonreligious schools were eligible to participate, as well as public schools in adjacent school districts.

Tuition aid was granted according to parental financial need, with the parents having sole discretion as to the schools in which their children enrolled. During the school year 1999–2000, 82 percent of the private schools that participated were affiliated with a religion, no public schools in adjacent districts participated, and 96 percent of the students participating in the scholarship program attended schools with a religious affiliation. Sixty percent of participating students were from families at or below the poverty level. The amount of money available to qualified parents who chose religious schools was less than that available to those who chose public schools.

In 1996 a group of Ohio taxpayers sought to stop the program on both state and federal constitutional grounds. The Ohio Supreme Court ruled that the program violated some procedural requirements of the Ohio Constitution, but rejected the federal arguments. The Ohio legislature corrected the defective parts of the program. In 1999, respondents filed action in U.S. District Court to stop the implementation of the program on the grounds that it violated the Establishment Clause of the First Amendment, which states, "Congress shall make no law respecting an establishment of religion" made applicable to the individual states by the Fourteenth Amendment in the *Everson* (1947) decision. In 1999, the district court granted a preliminary injunction barring further program implementation; the U.S. Supreme Court stayed the injunction pending approval by a federal appellate court. In December 1999, the U.S. District Court granted respondents summary judgment. In December 2000, the Court of Appeals for the Sixth Circuit affirmed the lower court's judgment, holding that the program violated the Establishment Clause because it had a primary effect of promoting religion. On appeal, the U.S. Supreme Court granted certiorari.

The Solicitor General of the United States filed a brief of *amicus curiae* urging reversal of the lower court decision. Additional briefs of *amici curiae* urging reversal were filed by the State of Florida, by officials in eight states, as well as by the mayor of New York and a councilwoman, the American Education Reform Council, the American Civil Rights Union, the American Center for Law and Justice, the Association of Christian Schools International, the Becket Fund for Religious Liberty, the Black Alliance for Educational Options, the Catholic League for Religious and Civil Rights, the Center for Education Reform, and others. Briefs of *amici curiae* urging affirmation of the appellate decision were filed by the American Jewish Committee, the Anti-Defamation League, the Council on Religious Freedom, the NAACP Legal Defense and Educational Fund, and others.

Chief Justice William Rehnquist delivered the majority opinion of the deeply divided Court (5-4) in *Zelman v. Simmons-Harris* (2002), which held that Ohio's Pilot Project Program did not violate the Establishment Clause of the First Amendment. In answering the question whether Ohio's Pilot Scholarship Program in any way ran afoul of the Establishment Clause, the Court held: (1) the program has a secular purpose as it is available to all parents who may choose public or private schools to address the deficiencies in their children's education; (2) the primary effect of the program neither advances nor inhibits religion, the program is religiously neutral, the choice to use grant money for education in a religious school is that of those parents whose income level qualifies their children for the program, and the religious institutions have nothing to say in determining the granting of the aid or in the determination of where the aid money is spent; and (3) the program does not involve an excessive entanglement of government with religion. The state gives money to parents who make the choice where to use it. Other than ensuring compliance with nondiscrimination policies, the state has no relationship to the religious schools. Thus, the Court deemed the Ohio's Pilot Scholarship Program constitutional.

In his dissent, Justice David Souter, joined in part by Justice John Paul Stevens, argued that the fact that 96 percent of the scholarship recipients enrolled in religious schools demonstrated that parents lack choice and that the program favored religious schools. Justice Stephen Breyer, also dissenting, argued that the program fostered divisiveness and religious strife.

This case expands the theory of "accommodation of religion" as understood in Establishment Clause decisions. Thus it appears that so long as the primary effect of the accommodation is not the advancement or suppression of religion, the accommodation does not violate the Establishment Clause. *See also:* First Amendment Religion Clauses and the Supreme Court; Government Aid to Religious Schools; *Mitchell v. Helms; Mueller v. Allen;* Vouchers.

Further Reading: *Agostini v. Felton,* 521 U.S. 203 (1997); *Zelman v. Simmons Harris,* 122 S.Ct. 2460 (2002).

Mary Angela Shaughnessy

Zobrest v. Catalina Foothills School District

The U.S. Supreme Court's ruling in *Zobrest v. Catalina Foothills School District* (1993) signaled a dramatic shift in its Establishment Clause jurisprudence for students who attended religiously affiliated nonpublic schools. At issue in *Zobrest* was a school board's refusal to provide a sign-language interpreter, under the Individuals with Disabilities Education Act (IDEA), for a deaf student in Arizona whose parents sought to place him in a Roman Catholic high school. After the Ninth Circuit Court of Appeals affirmed that such an arrangement would have violated the Establishment Clause's prohibition against aid to religiously affiliated nonpublic schools by failing the tripartite *Lemon v. Kurtzman* (1971) test insofar as it had the primary effect of advancing religion, the Supreme Court agreed to hear an appeal.

On further review, a divided Supreme Court, in a 5-4 opinion authored by Chief Justice William Rehnquist, reversed in favor of the student. In finding that an interpreter provided neutral aid to the student without offering financial benefits to either his parents or the school, and there was no governmental participation in the instruction because the interpreter was only a conduit who effectuated his communications with school staff, Rehnquist cited two of the Court's earlier judgments, *Mueller v. Allen* (1983) and *Witters v. Washington Department of Services for the Blind* (1986), as a basis for his rationale. Relying on these cases, and other precedents from the Court, Rehnquist was of the view that governmental programs, including those such as fire and police protection, that provide aid generally to a broad class of citizens without regard to their religion backgrounds are not subject to Establishment Clause scrutiny. In *Mueller,* the Court upheld a state tax deduction for educational costs for all parents, regardless of where their children attended school. Further, in *Witters,* the Court sustained the constitutionality of extending a general vocational assistance program to a blind man who was studying to become a clergyman at a religious college. The Supreme Court of Washington, however, later ruled that the state constitution forbade such use of public funds (*Witters,* 1989a), and the Supreme Court refused to hear an appeal of the Washington court's decision (*Witters,* 1989b).

In eschewing the *Lemon* test in *Zobrest,* Chief Justice Rehnquist was satisfied that since the student, not his school, was the chief beneficiary of the aid provided by the sign-language interpreter, he was entitled to this form of assistance under the IDEA. In addition, he distinguished the duties of sign-language interpreters and teachers or guidance counselors. To this end, Rehnquist noted that a sign-language interpreter merely serves as a kind of conduit who is hired to pass on or translate information accurately in the manner in which it was intended. On the other hand, he observed that the role of teachers and guidance counselors is significantly different to the extent that they interact with students in a wide variety of ways. As such, in pointing out that the Court had not placed an absolute prohibition against allowing students such as the plaintiff to receive the assistance of a sign-language interpreter in the religiously affiliated nonpublic schools that their parents freely chose, Rehnquist concluded that this practice passed Establishment Clause muster. As author of the primary dissent, Justice Harry Blackmun voiced his concern that the Court turned its back on its long-standing principles by allowing aid that he thought violated the Establishment Clause. *See also:* First Amendment Religious Clauses and the Supreme Court; Government Aid to Religious Schools; *Mueller v. Allen.*

Further Reading: Individuals with Disabilities in Education Act, 20 U.S.C. §§ 1401 *et seq.* (1991); *Lemon v. Kurtzman,* 403 U.S. 602 (1971); *Mueller v. Allen,* 463 U.S. 388 (1983); *Witters* *v. State Commission for the Blind,* 771 P.2d 1119 (Wash.1989), *cert. denied,* 493 U.S. 850 (1989); *Witters v. Washington Department of Services for the Blind,* 474 U.S. 481 (1986); *Zobrest v. Catalina Foothills School District,* 509 U.S. 1 (1993).

Charles J. Russo

Zorach v. Clauson

Four years after striking down a program from Illinois that allowed religious leaders to enter public schools during the class day to provide religious instruction for students whose parents wished to have their children participate in the classes on the basis that it violated the Establishment Clause in *People of State of Illinois ex rel. McCollum v. Board of Education of School District No. 71, Champaign County* (1948), the U.S. Supreme Court revisited a similar dispute from New York City. At issue in *Zorach v. Clauson* (1952) was the New York City Board of Education's (NYCBOE) practice of allowing children to be dismissed early from their public schools, on the request of their parents, so that they could travel to religious schools to receive weekly instruction in their faiths.

Opponents of the plan unsuccessfully challenged the NYCBOE's practice of released time at all three levels of New York's state courts alleging that it violated the Establishment Clause. On further review, the U.S. Supreme Court affirmed that the program was constitutional.

Writing for the Court in its 6-3 judgment, Justice William Douglas, ordinarily a staunch separationist who opposed most incursions of religion in public education, began his analysis by observing that public officials have the authority to accommodate the religious wishes of parents by releasing their children in programs of this nature. To this end, Douglas explained that since no one was forced to attend religious instruction and that children attended the classes only after their parents voluntarily agreed that they should have been able to do so, there was no way that the controversy dealt with the issue of the free exercise of religion.

Turning from what he described as the nonissue of coercion, Justice Douglas rejected the plaintiffs' claim that the released-time program in *Zorach* implicated the establishment of religion. Distinguishing *Zorach* from the Court's earlier order in *McCollum,* he ruled that the released-time plan was constitutional because public school buildings were not used for religious instruction. Moreover, Douglas found that the program passed constitutional muster since it did not spend public funds in its implementation. In pointing out that this dispute, like so many other issues in constitutional interpretation, was one of the degrees of separation between church and state, he decided that the program was constitutional. Douglas specified that the program was acceptable insofar as it was similar to the approach that public school officials adopted in recognizing excused absences for children who were absent from school for other religious reasons such as the celebrations of specified holy days. In concluding that even though the released time program may have been "unwise and improvident from an educational or a community viewpoint," Douglas added that since the program did no more than accommodate parental wishes, the Justices could not impose their own personal standards or read hostility of religion into the Bill of Rights; therefore, he had no choice but to uphold its validity.

Justices Hugo Black, Felix Frankfurter, and Robert Jackson filed separate dissents. In sum, in refusing to acknowledge the differences between the programs in *McCollum* and *Zorach,* these justices were essentially of the opinion that the practice violated the Establishment Clause because it allowed religious institutions to use part of the public school day to provide students with "sectarian" instruction, even though it did not occur in public schools.

As evidence that controversy over released-time programs continues, more than 50 years after *Zorach,* the Second Circuit of Appeals upheld a similar program in New York in the face of litigation by a mother who objected to the practice. In upholding a grant of summary judgment in favor of the school board, the court reasoned that it passed constitutional muster because it did not use public funds or on-site religious instruction, it was totally voluntary, and officials in the public schools did not coerce or pressure students to participate (*Pierce ex rel. Pierce v. Sullivan West Central School District,* 2004). *See also: McCollum v. Board of Education ;* Released Time for Religious Instruction.

Further Reading: *People of State of Illinois ex rel. McCollum v. Board of Education of School District No. 71, Champaign County,* 333 U.S. 203 (1948); *Pierce ex rel. Pierce v. Sullivan West Central School District,* 379 F.3d 56 (2d Cir. 2004); *Zorach v. Clauson,* 343 U.S. 306 (1952).

Charles J. Russo

Appendix

United States Supreme Court Religious
Liberty Decisions

Supreme Court Cases on Religious Liberty

No.	Issue	Case	Citation	Year	Ratio	Author	Holding
1	Church Property	*Terrett v. Taylor*	13 U.S. (9 Cranch) 43	1815	7-0	Story, J.	State may not rescind the properly obtained charter of the Episcopal Church and expropriate the church's lands.
2	Charitable Bequest	*Vidal v. Girard's Executors*	43 U.S. (2 How.) 127	1844	7-0	Story, J.	Testamentary bequest for establishment of school for orphans is valid notwithstanding provisions derogatory of Christianity.
3	Federalism	*Permoli v. First Municipality of New Orleans*	44 U.S. (3 How.) 589	1844	8-0	Catron, J.	United States Constitution does not protect citizens' religious liberties in regards to the respective states.
4	Church Property	*Goesele v. Bimeler*	55 U.S. (14 How.) 589	1852	8-0	McLean, J.	Heirs of member of communitarian religious group cannot recover share of property from the religious society.
5	Church Property: Civil Court Relief	*Smith v. Swormstedt*	57 U.S. (16 How.) 288	1853	9-0	Nelson, J.	A Court may sit in equity and divide jointly held property to carry out a voluntarily reached agreement of the church.
6	Church Property	*Baker v. Nachtrieb*	60 U.S. (19 How) 126	1856	9-0	Campbell, J.	Defecting member of communitarian religious group may not recover share of property from the religious society.
7	Mandatory Oath	*Cummings v. Missouri*	71 U.S. (4 Wall.) 277; dissent attached to Ex parte Garland, 71 U.S. (4 Wall.) 397	1866	5-4	Field, J.	State may not deprive priest of the right to preach for failure to take a mandatory oath disavowing support/sympathy for the cause of the Confederate states.

#	Category	Case Name	Citation	Year	Vote	Justice	Holding
8	Church Property	Watson v. Jones	80 U.S. (13 Wall.) 679	1871	6-2	Miller, J.	Civil courts should defer to the judgment of the highest religious authority in determining which of two internal religious factions is entitled to disputed property.
9	Church Property: Internal Church Governance	Bouldin v. Alexander	82 U.S. (15 Wall.) 131	1872	9-0	Strong, J.	Courts have no power to question acts of internal church discipline or excommunication; the rule of the church's highest internal tribunal must govern property disputes dependent on doctrine.
10	Polygamy; First Application of Free Exercise Clause	Reynolds v. United States	98 U.S. 145	1879	9-0	Waite, C.J.	Upheld federal criminal law prohibiting polygamy and denied a Mormon's free exercise claim to the practice, stating that beliefs could not be regulated but actions could.
11	Polygamy	Murphy v. Ramsey	114 U.S. 15	1885	9-0	Matthews, J.	Upheld laws disenfranchising known and suspected bigamists.
12	Tax Exemptions	Gibbons v. District of Columbia	116 U.S. 404	1886	9-0	Gray, J.	Allowed property tax scheme that exempted "church buildings, and grounds actually occupied by such buildings" but not land owned by but not used for the church.
13	Church Property	Speidel v. Henrici	120 U.S. 377	1887	9-0	Gray, J.	Defecting member of communitarian religious group may not recover share of property from the religious group.
14	Polygamy	Davis v. Beason	133 U.S. 333	1890	9-0	Field, J.	Upheld a conviction for falsely taking a (mandatory) oath renouncing polygamy.

#	Topic	Case	Citation	Year	Vote	Justice	Holding
15	Polygamy	*The Late Corporation of the Church of Jesus Christ of Latter-day Saints v. United States*	136 U.S. 1	1890	6-3	Bradley, J.	Upheld government's dissolution of the Mormon Church's corporate charter and the confiscation of its property for continued advocacy of polygamy.
16	Church Staff Hiring	*Church of the Holy Trinity v. United States*	143 U.S. 457	1892	9-0	Brewer, J.	Refused to apply a new federal law forbidding contracts with foreign aliens to a church seeking to hire a foreign cleric.
17	Building Grants; First application of Disestablishment Clause	*Bradfield v. Roberts*	175 U.S. 291	1899	9-0	Peckham, J.	Upheld, against disestablishment clause challenge, the allocation and distribution of federal funds to build religious hospital.
18	Religious School Funding; Indian Trust Disbursement	*Quick Bear v. Leupp*	210 U.S. 50	1908	9-0	Fuller, C.J.	Upheld federal distribution of funds (under an Indian treaty) to Catholic schools that offered education to Native Americans.
19	Treaty; Church Property	*Ponce v. Roman Catholic Apostolic Church*	210 U.S. 296	1908	9-0	Fuller, C.J.	Confirmed church's title to property acquired from Spanish government before the U.S. annexation of Puerto Rico.
20	Church Property	*Order of St. Benedict v. Steinhauser*	234 U.S. 640	1914	9-0	Hughes, J.	Upheld communal ownership of property within monastic order and granted the Order title to the estate of deceased lifelong member.

#	Subject	Case	Citation	Year	Vote	Author	Holding
21	Conscientious Objection	Selective Draft Law Cases (*Arver v. United States*)	245 U.S. 366	1918	9-0	White, C.J.	Upheld as constitutional Congress's power to define conscientious objector status and Congress's restriction of the status to ordained ministers, theology students, and members of well-recognized pacifist sects.
22	Religious School Curriculum	*Meyer v. Nebraska*	262 U.S. 390; dissent attached to *Bartels v. Iowa*, 262 U.S. 412	1923	7-2	McReynolds, J.	State statute mandating English-only instruction in all grade schools held unconstitutional, as applied to private religious school.
23	Religious School Attendance	*Pierce v. Society of Sisters*	268 U.S. 510	1925	9-0	McReynolds, J.	Invalidated state law mandating attendance at public schools as violation of rights of private schools and of parents.
24	Religious School Regulation	*Farrington v. Tokushige*	273 U.S. 284	1927	9-0	McReynolds, J.	States may not impose unduly intrusive and stringent accreditation and regulatory requirements on religious and other private schools.
25	Naturalization Qualifications; Conscientious Objection	*United States v. Schwimmer*	279 U.S. 644	1929	6-3	Butler, J.	Permitted the denial of citizenship to pacifist who refused to swear an oath to take up arms in defense of the country.
26	Religious School Subsidization: Textbooks	*Cochran v. Louisiana Board of Education*	281 U.S. 370	1930	9-0	Hughes, C.J.	Upheld state policy of furnishing textbooks to public and religious school students over objection of taxpayer that this constituted a taking of his private property in violation of the Fourteenth Amendment due process clause.
27	Naturalization Qualifications	*United States v. Bland*	283 U.S. 636	1931	5-4	Sutherland, J.	Refusal to bear arms in defense of the United States is a valid reason to bar a person's naturalization as a U.S. citizen.

#	Topic	Case	Citation	Year	Vote	Author	Holding
28	Conscientious Objection	*Hamilton v. Regents of the University of California*	293 U.S. 245	1934	9-0	Butler, J.	Due Process Clause of Fourteenth Amendment, though to be construed broadly, confers no right to exemption for pacifists from mandatory R.O.T.C. training at state university.
29	Federal Jurisdiction; Distribution of Religious Literature	*Coleman v. City of Griffin*	302 U.S. 636, letting stand 189 S.E. 427 (Ga. Ct. App. 1936)	1937	9-0	Per curiam	No federal question presented in appeal of city ordinance prohibiting distribution of religious literature on religion grounds; same ordinance addressed substantively in *Lovell v. City of Griffin*, 303 U.S. 444 (1938).
30	Distribution of Religious Literature	*Lovell v. City of Griffin*	303 U.S. 444	1938	8-0	Hughes, C.J.	Invalidated city ordinance prohibiting distribution of religious literature for violating freedom of the press.
31	Distribution of Religious Literature	*Schneider v. State of New Jersey (Town of Irvington)*	308 U.S. 147	1939	7-1	Roberts, J.	Invalidated local ordinance prohibiting distribution of religious literature for violating freedom of speech and freedom of the press.
32	Licensing; Free Exercise Clause Incorporated	*Cantwell v. Connecticut*	310 U.S. 296	1940	9-0	Roberts, J.	Free Exercise Clause expressly applied to the states through the Fourteenth Amendment; city licensing law, requiring religious groups to procure a license in advance but giving discretion to local administrators to deny such licenses, held unconstitutional.
33	Flag Salute	*Minersville School Board v. Gobitis*	310 U.S. 586	1940	7/1-1	Frankfurter, J.	Providing no free exercise exemption from public school requirement of saluting and pledging allegiance to the American flag.

34	Licensing	*Cox v. New Hampshire*	312 U.S. 569	1941	9-0	Hughes, C.J.	City may require all groups to obtain a license/permit and pay a reasonable fee, consonant with the expense incurred by the city to administer the license and maintain public order during and after the parade/procession.
35	Fighting Words	*Chaplinsky v. New Hampshire*	315 U.S. 568	1942	9-0	Murphy, J.	Cursing a police officer is not the exercise of "religion" nor speech protected by the First Amendment.
36	Distribution of Religious Literature	*Jones v. Opelika (I)*	316 U.S. 584	1942	5-4	Reed, J.	Local ordinance requiring license fee on distribution of all literature, and reserving discretion of revocation, may constitutionally be applied to distributors of religious literature.
37	Distribution of Religious Literature	*Jamison v. Texas*	318 U.S. 413	1943	8-0	Black, J.	Local ordinance prohibiting distribution of religious pamphlets in the public square and door to door is unconstitutional.
38	Licensing	*Largent v. Texas*	318 U.S. 418	1943	8-0	Reed, J.	City ordinance that requires permit to solicit orders for books but reserves to city official discretion to deny permits is unconstitutional as applied to religious publications.

#	Topic	Case	Citation	Year	Vote	Author	Holding
39	Distribution of Religious Literature	Jones v. Opelika (II)	319 U.S. 103; dissents attached to Murdock v. Pennsylvania (City of Jeannette), 319 U.S. 117, and Douglas v. City of Jeannette, 319 U.S. 166	1943	5-4	Per curiam (relying on Justice Douglas's opinion in Murdock v. Pennsylvania, and Chief Justice Stone's dissent in Jones v. Opelika (I)	Explicitly overruled Jones v. Opelika (I), 316 U.S. 584 (1942); state may not prohibit distribution of religious literature; even if ordinance is "nondiscriminatory" on its face, the liberties guaranteed by the First Amendment are in a preferred position.
40	Distribution of Religious Literature; Flat License Tax	Murdock v. Pennsylvania (City of Jeannette)	319 U.S. 105; additional dissent attached to Douglas v. City of Jeannette, 319 U.S. 166 (1943)	1943	5-4	Douglas, J.	A flat tax on all persons soliciting or selling goods is a "prior restraint" on those exercising their constitutional right to exercise their religion through distributing tracts and is thus unconstitutional.
41	Distribution of Religious Literature	Martin v. Struthers	319 U.S. 141; additional dissent attached to Douglas v. City of Jeannette, 319 U.S. 166 (1943)	1943	5-4	Black, J.	Ordinance forbidding door-to-door distribution of religious pamphlets and circulars is unconstitutional because it violates free speech and press.
42	Federal Jurisdiction; Flat License Tax	Douglas v. City of Jeannette	319 U.S. 157	1943	7/2-0	Stone, C.J.	Case not properly in federal court; same ordinance addressed substantively in Murdock v. Pennsylvania (City of Jeannette), 319 U.S. 105 (1943).

43	Flag Salute	*West Virginia State Board of Education v. Barnette*	319 U.S. 624	1943	6-3	Jackson, J.	Overruled *Minersville School Board v. Gobitis*, 310 U.S. 586 (1940); First Amendment provides exemption from mandatory participation in rituals that parties conscientiously oppose—including saluting the flag in a public school classroom.
44	Parent/Guardian Rights	*Prince v. Massachusetts*	321 U.S. 158	1944	5-4	Rutledge, J.	State criminal law regulating child labor, applied to guardian of nine-year-old girl distributing religious tracts on the public streets in the evening, is not a denial or abridgment of free exercise rights.
45	Flat License Tax; Distribution of Religious Literature	*Follett v. Town of McCormick*	321 U.S. 573	1944	5/1-3	Douglas, J.	City may not impose flat license tax on minister distributing religious literature.
46	Religious Fraud	*United States v. Ballard*	322 U.S. 78	1944	5-4	Douglas, J.	Truth of religious belief is not subject to the scrutiny of a jury, but jury may be called upon to decide the sincerity of defendant's belief.
47	Conscientious Objection	*In re Summers*	325 U.S. 561	1945	5-4	Reed, J.	Refusal of bar admission to conscientious objector who refused to swear oath that he would serve in military not a free exercise violation.
48	Polygamy	*Chatwin v. United States*	326 U.S. 455	1946	7/1-0	Murphy, J.	Defendant who persuaded minor female to join him in "celestial" marriage not guilty of violating Federal Kidnapping Act.

49	Distribution of Religious Literature	*Marsh v. Alabama*	326 U.S. 501	1946	5-3	Black, J.	Statute imposing criminal penalties for distribution of religious literature in company owned town is unconstitutional, per Free Exercise and Speech Clauses.
50	Distribution of Religious Literature	*Tucker v. Texas*	326 U.S. 517	1946	5-3	Black, J.	Statute imposing criminal penalties for distribution of religious literature in company owned town is unconstitutional, per Free Exercise and Speech Clauses.
51	Naturalization Qualifications; First Application of Article VI Test Oath Clause	*Girouard v. United States*	328 U.S. 61	1946	5-3	Douglas, J.	Government may not require a party who is conscientiously opposed to swear a military test oath before receiving naturalized citizenship status, per Free Exercise Clause and Article VI ban on religious test oaths.
52	Polygamy	*Cleveland v. United States*	329 U.S. 14	1946	5/1-3	Douglas, J.	Upheld convictions of members of polygamous sect for transporting plural wives across state lines in violation of the Mann "White Slave" Act.
53	Conscientious Objection	*Eagles v. Samuels*	329 U.S. 304	1946	9-0	Douglas, J.	Civilian panel could properly determine that defendant failed to establish right to preministerial deferment under Selective Service Act.
54	School Transportation; Disestablishment Clause Incorporated	*Everson v. Board of Education*	330 U.S. 1	1947	5-4	Black, J.	Expressly applied disestablishment clause to the states through the Fourteenth Amendment; but it is not establishment of religion for states to provide school bus transportation to religious and public school children alike.

#	Category	Case	Citation	Year	Vote	Author	Holding
55	Polygamy	*Musser v. Utah*	333 U.S. 95	1948	5/1-3	Jackson, J.	Conviction for polygamy vacated and remanded for consideration of state law questions.
56	Public School On-Campus Release Time	*McCollum v. Board of Education*	333 U.S. 203	1948	6/1/1-1	Black, J.	Disallowed public school "release time" program, wherein students were released from regular classes once a week to be able to participate in religious classes, which were held on campus.
57	Religious Speech	*Saia v. New York*	334 U.S. 558	1948	5-4	Douglas, J.	City ordinance prohibiting sound amplification, reserving discretion to police chief but giving no criteria for exercising that discretion, violates free speech because it operates as a prior restraint.
58	Conscientious Objection	*Gara v. United States*	340 U.S. 857, affirming, by an equally divided Court, 178 F.2d 38 (6th Cir. 1949)	1950	4-4	Per curiam	Upheld conviction for counseling another person conscientiously to object to draft registration and for actively opposing Selective Service Act.
59	Licensing	*Niemotko v. State of Maryland*	340 U.S. 268	1951	7/1/1-0	Vinson, C.J.	City may not deny a permit to use a public park for religious purposes when the applicable statute lacks clear criteria for such denials.
60	Licensing	*Kunz v. New York*	340 U.S. 290; concurrence attached to *Niemotko v. Maryland*, 340 U.S. 273 (1991)	1951	6/1/1-1	Vinson, C.J.	City may not deny a license to a Baptist minister to preach in a public park because the licensing regulation improperly gave local officials discretion to deny licenses.

#	Topic	Case	Citation	Year	Vote	Justice	Holding
61	Standing	*Doremus v. Board of Education*	342 U.S. 429	1952	6-3	Jackson, J.	Party lacks standing to challenge Bible reading in public school when the student has already graduated.
62	Release Time from Public Schools	*Zorach v. Clauson*	343 U.S. 306	1952	6-3	Douglas, J.	Upheld the constitutionality of granting students release time from public schools to attend religious education or services.
63	Censorship	*Joseph Burstyn, Inc. v. Wilson*	343 U.S. 495	1952	6/2/1-0	Clark, J.	State law requiring permit for commercial showing of films but allowing censorship of films that are "Sacrilegious" is a prior restraint and thus an unconstitutional violation of freedoms of speech and press.
64	Church Property; Regulation of Churches: Internal Church Governance	*Kedroff v. Saint Nicholas Cathedral*	344 U.S. 94	1952	8-1	Reed, J.	State religious incorporation law may not prohibit foreign religious authority from selecting church leaders and shift control to local church authorities; internal church law must be allowed to decide who makes such a decision.
65	Public Forum	*Fowler v. Rhode Island*	345 U.S. 67	1953	7/1/1-0	Douglas, J.	Struck down ordinance that prohibited religious speech but allowed for religious services in a public park because it was religiously discriminatory.
66	Licensing	*Paulos v. New Hampshire*	345 U.S. 395	1953	6/1-2	Reed, J.	Ordinance that leaves officials no discretion in granting permits but nevertheless requires payment of a sliding-scale fee to pay for city expenses incurred because of the permitted activity is constitutional.

67	Conscientious Objection	*United States v. Nugent*	346 U.S. 1	1953	5-3	Vinson, C.J.	Conscientious objector refusing to submit to induction into armed services has not shown the statute to be unconstitutional; Selective Service not required to disclose full FBI file on claimants.
68	Conscientious Objection	*Sicurella v. United States*	348 U.S. 385	1955	7-2	Clark, J.	Willingness to fight in "theocratic" wars does not disqualify a Jehovahs Witness who would otherwise qualify for exemption as a conscientious objector.
69	Conscientious Objection	*Simmons v. United States*	348 U.S. 397	1955	5/2-2	Clark, J.	Reversed conviction of defendant who was denied fair conscientious objection hearing because of government's failure to supply him "fair resume" of materials from his FBI files.
70	Conscientious Objection	*Gonzales v. United States*	348 U.S. 407	1955	6-3	Clark, J.	Reversed conviction of defendant who was denied fair conscientious objection hearing because of government's failure to supply him "fair resume" of materials from his FBI files.
71	Loyalty Oath	*First Unitarian Church v. County of Los Angeles*	357 U.S. 545; concurrence and dissent attached to *Speiser v. Randall*, 357 U.S. 513, 538 (1958).	1958	7/1-1	Brennan, J.	Government may not require a party who is conscientiously opposed to swear a loyalty oath as a prerequisite to receiving a tax exemption.
72	Sunday Laws	*McGowan v. Maryland*	366 U.S. 420	1961	6/2-1	Warren, C.J.	Upheld state law proscribing certain business and commercial activity on Sunday against disestablishment clause challenge.

73	Sunday Laws	*Two Guys from Harrison Allentown, Inc. v. McGinley*	366 U.S. 582; concurrence and dissent attached to *McGowan v. Maryland*, 366 U.S. 459, 561 (1961)	1961	6/2-1	Warren, C.J.	Sunday closing law does not violate disestablishment clause.
74	Sunday Laws	*Braunfeld v. Brown*	366 U.S. 599; other opinions attached to *McGowan v. Maryland*, 366 U.S. 459, 561 (1961)	1961	Pluralities	Warren, C.J. (for the plurality)	Statute disallowing sales on Sunday does not violate free exercise rights of Jewish appellant, who is a strict Saturday sabbatarian.
75	Sunday Laws	*Gallagher v. Crown Kosher Super Market of Massachusetts*	366 U.S. 617; other opinions attached to *McGowan v. Maryland*, 366 U.S. 459, 561, and to *Braunfeld v. Brown*, 366 U.S. 610, 616	1961	Pluralities	Warren, C.J. (for the plurality)	Sunday closing law does not violate free exercise rights of owner of kosher supermarket, Orthodox Jewish customers, or rabbis with a duty to inspect kosher markets per Jewish dietary laws.
76	Mandatory Public Office Oath	*Torcaso v. Watkins*	367 U.S. 488	1961	7/2-0	Black, J.	Requirement of mandatory oath affirming belief in God as a prerequisite for holding public office is unconstitutional.
77	Prayer in Public School	*Engel v. Vitale*	370 U.S. 421	1962	6-1	Black, J.	Disallowed state program of daily (nondenominational) prayer in public school classrooms.

78	Federal Jurisdiction; Sunday Laws	*Arlan's Department Store v. Kentucky*	371 U.S. 218; letting stand 357 S.W.2d 708 (Ky. 1962)	1962	8-1	Per curiam	Dismissed for lack of federal question; state court decision allowed to stand, upholding regulation that provided exemption from Sunday closing law only for those whose religion required rest on another day.
79	Bible Reading in Public School	*Abington School District v. Schempp & Murray v. Curlett*	374 U.S. 203	1963	8-1	Clark, J.	Mandatory Bible reading and recitation of the Lord's Prayer in public school classrooms violates disestablishment clause.
80	Unemployment Compensation Benefits	*Sherbert v. Verner*	374 U.S. 398	1963	6/1-2	Brennan, J.	Free exercise clause forbids state to deny unemployment compensation to claimant discharged from a job that would require her to work on her Sabbath.
81	Bible Reading in Public School	*Chamberlin v. Public Instruction Board*	377 U.S. 402	1964	8-0	Per curiam	Reading of Bible and recitation of Lord's Prayer in public school is unconstitutional.
82	Prisoner's Rights	*Cooper v. Pate*	378 U.S. 546	1964	9-0	Per curiam	Muslim prisoner entitled to hear on the merits that he was denied access to religious publications.
83	Conscientious Objection	*United States v. Seeger*	380 U.S. 163	1965	9-0	Clark, J.	Section 6(j) of Selective Service Act should be construed broadly, such that claimants may qualify for conscientious objector status if their belief is "sincere and meaningful" and occupies in their life "a place parallel to that filled by the God of those admittedly qualifying for the exemption."

#	Category	Case	Citation	Year	Vote	Author	Holding
84	Medical Care; Parent/Guardian Rights	*Jehovah's Witnesses v. King County Hospital*	390 U.S. 598; affirming 278 F.Supp. 488 (W.D. Wash)	1968	7-2	Per curiam	Blood transfusions may be administered to children, even if the parents are religiously opposed.
85	Standing	*Flast v. Cohen*	392 U.S. 83	1968	8-1	Warren, C.J.	Federal taxpayer has standing to challenge appropriation of federal funds for religious schools under the disestablishment clause.
86	Religious School Subsidization: Textbooks	*Board of Education v. Allen*	392 U.S. 236	1968	6-3	White, J.	Upheld state law requiring textbooks of "secular subjects" be provided to all students in the state, whether attending public or private (religious or other) schools.
87	Teaching Evolution in Public Schools	*Epperson v. Arkansas*	393 U.S. 97	1968	8/1-0	Fortas, J.	State criminal law, which prohibited the teaching of evolution in a public school or state university violates the disestablishment clause.
88	Internal Church Governance; Church Property	*Presbyterian Church in the United States v. Mary Elizabeth Blue Hull Memorial Presbyterian Church*	393 U.S. 440	1969	9-0	Brennan, J.	Internal church disputes, including property disputes, should be governed by internal church law; civil courts may not use "departure from doctrine" standard, and should defer to the highest internal church authority.
89	Church Property	*Maryland and Virginia Churches v. Sharpsburg Church*	396 U.S. 367	1970	9-0	Per curiam	Civil courts may resolve church property disputes as long as they do not involve inquiry into church doctrine.

90	Tax Exemptions	*Walz v. Tax Commission*	397 U.S. 664	1970	8-1	Burger, C.J.	Upheld state property tax exemption for church property against disestablishment clause challenge.
91	Conscientious Objection	*Welsh v. United States*	398 U.S. 333	1970	4/1-3	Black, J. (for the plurality)	Section 6(j) must be construed broadly; persons whose consciences, "spurred by deeply held moral, ethical, or religious beliefs," do not allow them to be an "instrument of war" are entitled to conscientious objector status.
92	Conscientious Objection	*Gillette v. United States*	401 U.S. 437	1971	7/1-1	Marshall, J.	Congress may exempt persons opposed to participating in all wars, but not those objecting to participation in a particular war, from military service without violating the First Amendment.
93	Employment	*Dewey v. Reynolds Metals Co.*	402 U.S. 689; affirming, by an equally divided Court, 429 F.2d 324 (6th Cir. 1970)	1971	4-4	Per curiam	Rejected free exercise claim of a Sabbatarian who claimed he was wrongfully discharged on the basis of his religious beliefs.
94	Religious School Subsidization: Textbooks	*Lemon v. Kurtzman (I)*	403 U.S. 602	1971	6/1/1-0	Burger, C.J.	Disestablishment clause requires laws to have (1) a secular purpose; (2) primary effect that neither advances nor inhibits religion; and (3) no excessive entanglement of church and state; statute that reimbursed religious schools for costs of teaching secular subjects violates (3).

#	Topic	Case	Citation	Year	Pluralities	Author	Holding
95	Construction Grants	*Tilton v. Richardson*	403 U.S. 672; additional opinions attached to *Lemon v. Kurtzman (I)*, 403 U.S. 642, 661 (1971)	1971		Burger, C.J.	Upheld federal grants that supported construction of library, science, and arts buildings at religious colleges as well as secular colleges.
96	Prisoner's Rights	*Cruz v. Beto*	405 U.S. 319	1972	6/1/1-1	Per curiam	Buddhist prisoner must be given "reasonable" opportunities to free exercise of religion.
97	Compulsory Education	*Wisconsin v. Yoder*	406 U.S. 205	1972	6-1 (but dissenting opinion concured in part)	Burger, C.J.	Granted free exercise exemption to Amish, which exempted them from full compliance with compulsory school attendance law.
98	Religious School Subsidization	*Lemon v. Kurtzman (II)*	411 U.S. 192	1973	4/1-3	Burger, C.J. (for the plurality)	*Lemon v. Kurtzman (I)*, 403 U.S. 602 (1971), *should not be applied retroactively*.
99	Religious School Subsidization: Textbooks	*Norwood v. Harrison*	413 U.S. 455	1973	7/2-0	Burger, C.J.	State may loan textbooks on secular subjects to religious schools, but not if those schools discriminate on racial grounds.
100	Religious School Subsidization	*Levitt v. Committee for Public Education and Religious Liberty*	413 U.S. 472	1973	5/3-1	Burger, C.J.	States may not reimburse religious schools for most costs incurred to administer standardized tests and to prepare mandated state records.
101	Revenue Bonds	*Hunt v. McNair*	413 U.S. 734	1973	6-3	Powell, J.	Upheld issuance of revenue bonds for religious colleges.

				Pluralities		
102	Religious School Subsidization	*Committee for Public Education and Religious Liberty v. Nyquist*	413 U.S. 756	1973	Powell, J. (opinion of the Court)	Disallowed state reimbursement for low-income parents for part of religious school tuition; disallowed tax deduction for low-income parents whose children attended religious schools; disallowed direct grants to private schools; disallowed direct grants to private schools serving low-income students for maintenance and repair costs.
103	Religious School Subsidization	*Sloan v. Lemon*	413 U.S. 825; additional opinions attached to *Committee for Public Education and Religious Liberty v. Nyquist,* 413 U.S. 798, 813 (1973)	1973	6-3 Powell, J.	Disallowed state reimbursement to parents for portion of religious school tuition.
104	Education Benefits; Conscientious Objection	*Johnson v. Robinson*	415 U.S. 361	1974	8-1 Brennan, J.	Statute which grants education benefits to military draftees but not to craftees who perform civilian alternative service is not unconstitutional.
105	Education Benefits; Conscientious Objection	*Hernandez v. Veterans' Administration*	415 U.S. 391	1974	8/1-0 Brennan, J.	Vacated a Ninth Circuit dismissal, for lack of jurisdiction, of a former conscientious objector's challenge to the statute at issue in *Johnson v. Robinson,* 415 U.S. 361 (1974) and remanded for reconsideration in light of that case.

106	Title I; Religious School Subsidization	*Wheeler v. Barrela*	417 U.S. 402	1974	6/1/1-1	Blackmun, J.	State receiving Title I funds must provide "Comparable" but "not identical" services to disadvantaged students in both public and private schools, or forfeit Title I funds.
107	Conscientious Objection; Taxes	*United States v. American Friends Service Committee*	419 U.S. 7	1974	8-1	Per curiam	Upheld collection of taxes from those conscientiously opposed to having their taxes support the military.
108	Religious School Subsidization: Textbooks	*Meek v. Pittenger*	421 U.S. 349 overruled by *Mitchell v. Helms*, 530 U.S. 793 (2000)	1975	Pluralities	Stewart, J. (for the plurality)	State may loan textbooks, but not other various supplies and film, nor various counseling and other personnel, even if those were mandated by state policy.
109	Internal Church Governance	*Serbian Orthodox Diocese v. Milivojevich*	426 U.S. 696	1976	6/1-2	Brennan, J.	Internal church law must govern internal church matters, including removal from ecclesiastical posts; civil courts may not give marginal review to ecclesiastical decisions, even if they appear arbitrary, collusive, or fraudulent.
110	Construction Grants	*Roemer v. Maryland Public Works Board*	426 U.S. 736	1976	3/2-4	Blackmun, J. (for the plurality)	Upheld a state construction grant program that aided religious colleges alongside secular colleges.
111	Title VII; Employment	*Parker Seal Company v. Cummins*	429 U.S. 65, affirming, by an equally divided Court, 516 F.2d 544 (6th Cir. 1975)	1976	4-4	Per curiam	Employer did not make sufficient effort to accommodate Sabbatarian.

#	Topic	Case	Citation	Year	Vote	Opinion	Holding
112	State Motto	*Wooley v. Maynard*	430 U.S. 705	1977	Pluralities	Burger, C.J. (opinion of the Court)	State cannot require, upon pain of criminal sanctions, display of state motto upon vehicle license plates that violates owner's religious convictions
113	Title VII; Employment Accommodation	*Trans World Airlines, Inc. v. Hardison*	432 U.S. 63	1977	7-2	White, J.	Employer's attempted accommodation of employee's religious beliefs was reasonable; no obligation to violate union contracts or incur additional costs without express congressional intent.
114	Religious School Subsidization	*Wolman v. Walter*	433 U.S. 229, overruled by *Mitchell v. Helms*, 530 U.S. 793 (2000)	1977	Pluralities	Blackmun, J. (for the plurality)	State may provide various personnel, diagnostic services, and standardized testing but may not loan instructional materials to private schools or to parents or provide transportation for field trips by private schools.
115	Title VII; Employment Accommodation	*Parker Seal Company v. Cummins*	433 U.S. 903, vacating 429 U.S. 65 (1976)	1977	8-0	Vacated and remanded	Vacated and remanded for consideration in light of *Trans World Airlines, Inc. v. Hardison*, 432 U.S. 63 (1977).
116	Religious School Subsidization	*New York v. Cathedral Academy*	434 U.S. 125	1977	6-3	Stewart, J.	Disallowed reimbursement of religious schools for state-mandated record keeping.
117	Clergy Disqualified from Public Office	*McDaniel v. Paty*	435 U.S. 618	1978	4/2/1/1-0	Burger, J. (for the plurality)	State constitutional prohibition against clergy holding political office is unconstitutional.
118	Labor Law	*National Labor Relations Board v. Catholic Bishop of Chicago*	440 U.S. 490	1979	5-4	Burger, C.J.	Denied jurisdiction to the NLRB over a Catholic school's teachers, based on the rights of a religious group to function separately from the state.

119	Church Property; Internal Church Governance	*Jones v. Wolf*	443 U.S. 595	1979	5-4	Blackmun, J.	Courts may decide intrachurch property disputes using "neutral principles of law," and thus avoid deferring all decision making to internal church authorities.
120	Religious School Subsidization	*Committee for Public Education and Religious Liberty v. Regan*	444 U.S. 646	1980	5-4	White, J.	Upheld reimbursement of religious schools for "actual costs" of state-mandated tests and reporting.
121	Abortion and Religion	*Harris v. McRae*	448 U.S. 297	1980	5-4	Stewart, J.	Upheld congressional restrictions on Medicaid-funded abortions.
122	Ten Commandments in Public School	*Stone v. Graham*	449 U.S. 39	1980	5-4	Per curiam	Struck down state statute that required the posting of a plaque bearing the Ten Commandments on the wall of each public school classroom.
123	Unemployment Compensation Benefits	*Thomas v. Review Board, Indiana Employment Security Division*	450 U.S. 707	1981	7/1-1	Burger, C.J.	Government may not deny unemployment benefits to claimant who refused to accept employment, based on individual religious beliefs, at a job that produced parts that would be used in military armaments.
124	Religious Schools and Unemployment Compensation Taxes	*St. Martin Evangelical Lutheran Church v. South Dakota*	451 U.S. 772	1981	8/1-0	Blackmun, J.	The word "church" in the Federal Unemployment Tax Act exempting service performed in the employ of a church applies to schools that have no separate legal existence from a church.

#		Case	Citation	Year	Pluralities	Opinion	Description
125	Distribution of Religious Literature; Charitable Solicitation Law	*Heffron v. International Society for Krishna Consciousness*	452 U.S. 640	1981		White, J. (opinion of the Court)	Regulation requiring all persons and groups wishing to sell, exhibit, or distribute materials at a fair do so from a rented booth does not violate First Amendment rights of itinerant religious group.
126	Equal Access	*Widmar v. Vincent*	454 U.S. 263	1981	7/1-1	Powell, J.	When a state university creates a limited public forum open to voluntary student groups, religious groups must be given "equal access" to that forum.
127	Standing	*Valley Forge Christian College v. Americans United for Separation of Church and State*	454 U.S. 464	1982	5-4	Rehnquist, J.	Religious liberty litigant, as federal taxpayer, lacked standing to challenge federal donation of property to religious organizations.
128	Tax Exemption	*United States v. Lee*	455 U.S. 252	1982	8/1-0	Burger, C.J.	Denied free exercise exemption from social security taxes for Amish employer.
129	Prayer in Public School	*Treen v. Karen B.*	455 U.S. 913; affirming 653 F.2d 897 (5th Cir. 1981)	1982	9-0	Affirmed on appeal	Affirmed, without comment, a Fifth Circuit opinion that struck down a statute authorizing student volunteers to lead prayer in public school classrooms.
130	Charitable Solicitation Law	*Larson v. Valente*	456 U.S. 228	1982	5-4	Brennan, J.	Disallowed state law requiring only certain religious organizations to make revenue reports.

#	Topic	Case	Citation	Year	Vote	Author	Holding
131	Charitable Solicitation Law	*Rusk v. Espinoza*	456 U.S. 951; affirming 634 F.2d 477 (10th Cir. 1980)	1982	7-2	Affirmed on appeal	Affirmed, without comment, a Tenth Circuit opinion which struck, down ordinance that required officials to distinguish between "religious" and "secular" religious activities of religious bodies for licensing and regulation purposes.
132	Federal Jurisdiction; Unemployment Tax	*California v. Grace Brethren Church*	457 U.S. 393	1982	7-2	O'Connor, J.	Federal District Court did not have jurisdiction to hear case involving state tax.
133	Zoning; Delegation of Civil Power	*Larken v. Grendel's Den*	459 U.S. 116	1982	8-1	Burger, C.J.	States may not grant veto power to churches over whether a liquor license will be granted to a facility within 500 feet from the church property.
134	Tax Exempt Status	*Bob Jones University v. United States*	461 U.S. 574	1983	7/1-1	Burger, C.J.	Upheld IRS decision to remove federal tax exempt status from religious university that engaged in racial discrimination, on the basis of its religious convictions, in matriculation and employment decisions.
135	State Income Tax Deduction	*Mueller v. Allen*	463 U.S. 388	1983	5-4	Rehnquist, J.	Upheld state law that allowed parents of private school children to claim state income tax deductions for the costs of "tuition, transportation, and textbooks."
136	Legislative Prayer	Marsh v. Chambers	463 U.S. 783	1983	6-3	Burger, C.J.	Upheld, against disestablishment clause challenge, the state practice of appointing legislative chaplains to offer prayers at the General Assembly.

#	Topic	Case	Citation	Year	Vote	Opinion	Holding
137	Religious Display	*Lynch v. Donnelly*	465 U.S. 668	1984	5-4	Burger, C.J.	Upheld government practice of displaying nativity scene as part of holiday display in city park.
138	Conscientious Objection	*Wayte v. United States*	470 U.S. 598	1985	7-2	Powell, J.	"Passive enforcement policy" and "beg policy" of Selective Service System do not violate First (or Fifth) Amendment.
139	Religious Display	*Village of Scarsdale v. McCreary*	471 U.S. 83; affirming, by an equally divided Court, 739 F.2d 716 (2d Cir. 1984)	1985	4-4	Per curiam	Accommodation of displaying a nativity scene, at no expense to city, is not a violation of disestablishment clause.
140	Fair Labor Standards Act	*Tony and Susan Alamo Foundation v. Secretary of Labor*	471 U.S. 290	1985	9-0	White, J.	Application of Fair Labor Standards Act does not obstruct core religious functions of a foundation.
141	Moment of Silence in Public School	*Wallace v. Jaffree*	472 U.S. 38	1985	5/1-3	Stevens, J.	Struck down state law providing for moments of silence (for prayer or meditation) in public schools.
142	Driver's License Photograph	*Jensen v. Quaring*	472 U.S. 478, affirming, by an equally divided Court, 728 F.2d 1121 (8th Cir. 1984)	1985	4-4	Per curiam	Struck down requirement that applicant submit to having color photograph taken to affix on driver's license as an unconstitutional burden on applicant's free exercise of her sincerely held religious beliefs.
143	Sabbath Laws	*Estate of Thornton v. Caldor*	472 U.S. 703	1985	8-1	Burger, C.J.	Struck down state law that allowed private sector employees to pick their Sabbath, which employers must accommodate.

144	Religious School Subsidization: Shared Time Programs	*Grand Rapids School District v. Ball*	473 U.S. 373	1985	Pluralities	Brennan, J. (opinion of the Court)	States may not lend public school personnel to teach remedial and enrichment courses in religious schools.
145	Title I Remedial Services	*Aguilar v. Felton*	473 U.S. 402, overruled by *Agostini v. Felton*, 521 U.S. 203 (1997)	1985	5-4	Brennan, J.	States may not use public school teachers to hold remedial educational programs to indigent children in classrooms leased from religious schools.
146	State Aid for Vocational Education at Religious College	*Witters v. Washington Department of Services for the Blind*	474 U.S. 481	1986	8/1-0	Marshall, J.	Upheld state program furnishing aid to a visually impaired student attending a Christian college for vocational education.
147	Standing	*Bender v. Williamsport Area School District*	475 U.S. 534	1986	5-4	Stevens, J.	School board member has no standing, in his capacity as a parent, to appeal a board decision affecting the religious rights of his child in the school.
148	Military Regulations	*Goldman v. Weinberger*	475 U.S. 503	1986	5-4	Rehnquist, J.	Military officer does not have free exercise right to wear his yarmulke on duty.
149	Social Security Number Requirement	*Bowen v. Roy*	476 U.S. 693	1986	Pluralities	Burger C.J. (for the plurality)	Agency's use of social security number does not violate free exercise rights of Native American, who believes such use would impair his child's spirit.
150	Federal Jurisdiction	*Ohio Civil Rights Commission v. Dayton Christian Schools*	477 U.S. 619	1986	5/4-0	Rehnquist, J.	Federal District Courts should abstain from adjudicating pending state proceedings as long as federal plaintiff has opportunity to litigate his constitutional claim.

	Topic	Case	Citation	Year	Pluralities	Rehnquist, C.J. (opinion of the Court)	
151	Title VII; Employment Accommodation	*Ansonia Board of Education v. Philbrook*	479 U.S. 60	1986		Rehnquist, C.J. (opinion of the Court)	Employer not required to accept employee's preferred religious accommodation.
152	Unemployment Compensation Benefits	*Hobbie v. Unemployment Appeals Commission of Florida*	480 U.S. 136	1987	6/1/1-1	Brennan, J.	Government may not deny unemployment benefits to claimant, a new religious convert, who was discharged for refusal to work on her Sabbath.
153	Religious Discrimination	*Shaare Tefila Congregation v. Cobb*	481 U.S. 615	1987	9-0	White, J.	Jews may rely on racial clause of civil rights statute for cause of action against desecrators of synagogue.
154	Prisoner's Rights	*O'Lone v. Estate of Shabazz*	482 U.S. 342	1987	5-4	Rehnquest, C.J.	Denying free exercise accommodation for Muslim prisoner to engage in collective Friday worship.
155	Overbreadth Doctrine	*Airport Commissioners of Los Angeles v. Jesus for Jesus*	482 U.S. 569	1987	9-0	O'Connor, J.	Airport regulation banning all "first amendment activities" within a public (or nonpublic) forum is a violation of the free speech clause.
156	Creationism in Public School	*Edwards v. Aguillard*	482 U.S. 578	1987	6/1-2	Brennan, J.	Struck down state statute that required, in public schools, teaching of both creation and evolution, if a theory of origins was taught at all.
157	Employment Discrimination	*Corporation of the Presiding Bishop of the Church of Jesus Christ of Latter-day Saints v. Amos*	483 U.S. 327	1987	5/2/1/1-0	White, J.	Upheld exemption of religious school from Civil Rights prohibition against religious discrimination; religious employer not required to retain employee who has lapsed from its faith.

158	Standing	*Karcher v. May*	484 U.S. 72	1987	8/1-0	O'Connor, J.	State legislators cannot appeal a disestablishment case involving a moment of silence law for which they voted, but which the legislature has chosen not to appeal.
159	Native American Rights	*Lyng v. Northwest Indian Cemetery Protective Association*	485 U.S. 439	1988	5-3	O'Connor, J.	Construction of road through section of national forest regarded as sacred ground by three tribes does not violate Free Exercise Clause; American Indian Religious Freedom Act provides no cause of action.
160	Unemployment Compensation Benefits	*Employment Division, Oregon v. Smith (I)*	485 U.S. 660	1988	5-3	Stevens, J.	State must determine whether religious use of peyote is legal under state law.
161	Standing	*United States Catholic Conference v. Abortion Rights Mobilization*	487 U.S. 72	1988	8-1	Kennedy, J.	A nonparty witness held in contempt had standing to challenge federal court's jurisdiction over case.
162	Religious Social Agency Subsidization	*Bowen v. Kendrick*	487 U.S. 589	1988	5-4	Rehnquist, C.J.	Upheld federal funding of Catholic counseling centers for pregnant teenagers, in implementation of the Adolescent Family Life Act.
163	Tax Exemption	*Texas Monthly v. Bullock*	489 U.S. 1	1989	3/2/1-3	Brennan, J. (for the plurality)	State sales tax exemption exclusively for religious periodicals violates disestablishment clause.

#	Category	Case	Citation	Year	Vote	Opinion	Holding
164	Unemployment Compensation Benefits	*Frazee v. Illinois Department of Employment Security*	489 U.S. 829	1989	9-0	White, J.	State may not deny unemployment benefits to claimant who refused to take a job that might require him to work on Sunday.
165	Tax Deductions	*Hernandez v. Commissioner of Internal Revenue*	490 U.S. 680	1989	5-2	Marshall, J.	Upheld denial of charitable deduction for contributions to the Church of Scientology, given in return for religious services.
166	Religious Display	*County of Allegheny v. ACLU*	492 U.S. 573	1989	Pluralities	Blackmun, J. (for the plurality)	Disallowed county's practice of allowing a privately funded nativity scene in front of its courthouse but upheld the display of a menorah on courthouse grounds.
167	Tax Exemption	*Jimmy Swaggart Ministries v. Board of Equalization of California*	493 U.S. 378	1990	9-0	O'Connor, J.	Levy of state sales and use taxes on religious articles is not a prior restraint.
168	Unemployment Compensation Benefits	*Employment Division, Oregon v. Smith (II)*	494 U.S. 872	1990	5/1-3	Scalia, J.	Denial of unemployment compensation benefits to Native American who was discharged for sacramental use of peyote, a proscribed narcotic, does not violate Free Exercise Clause.
169	Public Safety Exemption	*Minnesota v. Hershberger*	495 U.S. 901	1990	7-2	Vacating and remanding on appeal	Vacated a state supreme court holding that Amish were entitled to free exercise exemption from a law requiring them to place reflective triangles on their buggies for public safety reasons and remanded for reconsideration in light of *Employment Division v. Smith (II)*, 494 U.S. 872 (1990).

170	Tax Deductions	*Davis v. United States*	495 U.S. 472	1990	9-0	O'Connor, J.	Upheld denial of charitable deduction for contribution in return for religious services.
171	Equal Access	*Board of Education of the Westside Community Schools v. Mergens*	496 U.S. 226	1990	4/2/2-1	O'Connor, J. (for the plurality)	Equal Access Act, which applies *Widmar v. Vincent*, 454 U.S. 263 (1981) rule to public high schools, does not violate disestablishment clause.
172	Title VII; Employment Discrimination	*EEOC v. Arabian American Oil Co.*	499 U.S. 244	1991	5/1-3	Rehnquist, C.J.	Nondiscrimination in employment rules of Title VII do not apply outside United States to U.S. employers who employ U.S. citizens abroad.
173	Graduation Prayers in Public School	*Lee v. Weisman*	505 U.S. 577	1992	5-4	Kennedy, J.	Ecumenical prayer by Jewish rabbi at a public middle school graduation ceremony violates disestablishment clause.
174	Forum Analysis; Religious Solicitation	*International Society for Krishna Consciousness v. Lee*	505 U.S. 672	1992	Pluralities	Rehnquist, C.J. (opinion of the Court)	An airport terminal operated by a public authority is a nonpublic forum, and therefore a ban on distribution of religious literature and solicitation need only satisfy a reasonableness standard; the ban on solicitation here is reasonable.
175	Distribution of Religious Literature	*Lee v. International Society for Krishna Consciousness*	505 U.S. 830	1992	5-4	Per curiam	Ban on distribution of religious materials in airport terminals is invalid under First Amendment, as it does not satisfy a reasonableness standard.
176	Mootness, IRS Summons	*Church of Scientology of California v. United States*	506 U.S. 9	1992	9-0	Stevens, J.	Compliance with an enforcement order to surrender taped conversations does not render moot an appeal concerning the lawfulness of the search claim.

177	Equal Access	*Lamb's Chapel v. Center Moriches Union Free School District*	508 U.S. 384	1993	6/2/1-0	White, J.	Public school that opens its school facilities, during nonschool time, to various voluntary community groups may not exclude only those with religious viewpoint; equal access must be given.
178	Ritual Sacrifice of Animals	*Church of the Lukumi Babalu Aye, Inc. v. City of Hialeah*	508 U.S. 520	1993	9-0, but concurring opinions	Kennedy, J. (opinion of the Court, except as to Part II.A.2)	Local ordinance discriminating against ritual sacrifice of animals violates the free exercise clause.
179	Religious School Subsidy: Interpreter	*Zobrest v. Catalina Foothills School District*	509 U.S. 1	1993	5-4	Rehnquist, C.J.	State's provision of an interpreter to disabled student at religious high school does not violate disestablishment clause.
180	Delegation of Civil Power	*Board of Education of Kiryas Joel Village School District v. Grumet*	512 U.S. 687	1994	4/1/1-3	Souter, J. (for the plurality)	State's creation of a single public school district within an exclusively Satmar Hasidic community violates disestablishment clause.
181	Religious Display	*Capitol Square Review and Advisory Board v. Pinette*	515 U.S. 753	1995	4/3-2	Scalia, J. (for the plurality)	City may not ban private display of KKK cross in an otherwise open public forum.
182	Equal Access	*Rosenberger v. University of Virginia*	515 U.S. 819	1997	5-4	Kennedy, J.	State university must grant equal access to funding for voluntary religious student groups as for voluntary nonreligious student group.

183	Title I Remedial Services	*Agostini v. Felton*	521 U.S. 203	1997	5-4	O'Connor, J.	Overturned *Aguilar v. Felton* (1985); the mere presence of a state employee in a religious institution is not per se unconstitutional, and thus the state may provide Title I remedial services to students at religious schools.
184	Free Exercise Standard of Review	*City of Boerne v. Flores*	521 U.S. 507	1997	5/1-3	Kennedy, J.	Religious Freedom Restoration Act (1993), which required use of the compelling state interest test for free exercise cases, declared unconstitutional, as applied to the state.
185	Religious School Subsidy: Interpreter	*Mitchell v. Helms*	530 U.S. 793	2000	4/2/3	Thomas, J.	Federally funded state policy to lend educational materials directly to public and private schools does not violate the disestablishment clause simply because many of the private schools receiving aid are religiously affiliated; *Meek v. Pittinger* (1975) and *Wolman v. Walter* (1977) overruled.
186	Student Prayer at Public School Football Games	*Santa Fe Independent School District v. Doe*	530 U.S. 290	2000	6-3	Stevens, J.	School policy instituting student-led, student-initiated "invocations" prior to public high school football games violates the disestablishment clause.
187	Equal Access	*Good News Club v. Milford Central School*	533 U.S. 98	2001	4/1/1/1/2	Thomas, J.	Public middle school's exclusion of Christian children's club from meeting on school property after hours was unconstitutional viewpoint discrimination, and was not required to avoid establishment of religion.

188	Licensing	*Watchtower Bible and Tract Society v. Village of Stratton*	536 U.S. 150	2002	6-2/1	Stevens, J.	Ordinance requiring door-to-door solicitors and canvassers to obtain a permit containing one's name violates constitutional free speech and free exercise rights because of its breadth and unprecedented nature, and is not narrowly enough tailored to the stated interest of preventing fraud, crime, and privacy intrusion.
189	Religious School Subsidy: Voucher	*Zelman v. Simmons-Harris*	536 U.S. 639	2002	5-4	Rehnquist, C.J.	School voucher program, enacted for valid secular purpose of providing educational assistance to poor children in demonstrably failing public school system, does not violate the disestablishment clause, because program was neutral toward religion and government aid to religious schools was the result of parents' "true private choices."
190	State Scholarship Program	*Locke v. Davey*	540 U.S. 712	2004	7-2	Rehnquist, C.J.	State scholarship program established to assist payment of academically gifted students' postsecondary education expenses for all students, except those pursuing a theology degree, does not violate the free exercise clause
191	Pledge of Allegiance/ Standing	*Elk Grove Unified School District v. Newdow*	542 U.S. 1	2004	5/1/1/1-0	Stevens, J.	Noncustodial father lacked standing to bring disestablishment case on behalf of his minor daughter challenging school district's policy that required teacher-led recitation of the Pledge of Allegiance, with phrase "One Nation Under God."

#	Category	Case	Citation	Year	Vote	Justice	Holding
192	Prisoner's Rights	*Cutter v. Wilkinson*	544 U.S. 709	2005	9-0	Ginsburg, J.	RLUIPA is upheld
193	Religious Display	*Van Orden v. Perry*	545 U.S. 677	2005	5-4	Rehnquist, C.J.	A display of the Ten Commandments outside the Texas State Capitol in the context of other memorials is found to be constitutional.
194	Religious Display	*McCreary County v. ACLU*	545 U.S. 844	2005	5-4	Souter, J.	County display of the Ten Commandments in the courthouse is held unconstitutional because of the circumstances of the display; the Court looks at the resolution that is passed and the speech surrounding the unveiling of the Commandments and determines that the reasons for the display are religious.
195	Sacramental Tea	*Gonzales v. O'Centro*	546 U.S. 418	2006	8-0	Roberts, C.J.	Use of hoasca, which contains a prohibited drug, is permitted under the Religious Freedom Restoration Act of 1993, since the government failed to demonstrate a compelling interest in regulating the use of the drug for religious purposes.
196	Standing	*Hein v. Freedom from Religion Foundation*	127 S.Ct. 2553	2007	5-4	Alito, J.	Taxpayers do not have standing to challenge on no establishment grounds actions of the Executive Branch funded by general appropriations for administrative costs (in this case the cost of conferences to promote faith-based initiatives).

Index

Mann, Horace, 294–96; appointment to
Massachusetts state board of education, 93,
160; on the Bible, 9, 93–94, 252, 294–95;
common school movement, 5–8, 50, 93–
94, 159–61, 294–96, 328, 352; elected to
Congress, 7; final report on common
schools, 7; as Unitarian, 4, 6, 7, 94, 294–
96, 352

Mapplethorpe, Robert, 130

Maritain, Jacques, 123

Marsh, Christopher, 269

Marshall, Ian, 431

Marshall, Thurgood: *Committee for Public
Education v. Nyquist,* 314; *Edwards v.
Aguillard,* 183–84; *Meek v. Pittenger,* 299;
*Witters v. Washington Department of Services
for the Blind,* 219

Marsh v. Alabama, 486

Marsh v. Chambers, 500

Martin Luther College, 288

Martin v. Struthers, 484

Marty, Bishop Martin, 145, 176, 369

Marx and Marxists, 408, 410, 412

*Mary Elizabeth Blue Hull Memorial
Presbyterian Church, Presbyterian Church in
the United States v.,* 492

Maryland, 3

Maryland, McGowan v., 489

*Maryland and Virginia Churches v. Sharpsburg
Church,* 492

Maryland Board of Public Works, Roemer v.,
216, 496

Mason, George, 291

Masons, 276, 342

Massachusetts: creation of state board of
education, 160, 161, 294, 296; first
education laws in the New World, 1;
*Largess v. Supreme Judicial Court for
Massachusetts,* 285; Lowell Plan, 8, 199,
286–87, 349; Mann and the Common
School in Massachusetts, 5–8; "Old
Deluder Law," 1

Massachusetts, Prince v., 485

Massen, John B., 437

May, Karcher v., 504

May, Samuel J., 296

Mayer, Rabbi Isaac, 97

Maynard, Wooley v., 497

McClellan, B. Edward, 12

McCloskey, Archbishop John, 349

McCollum v. Board of Education, 296–97;
described, 98, 208–9, 296–97, 362;
enrollment in released-time programs at
time of decision, 20, 98; reaction to decision, 24, 25; separation of church and state
rhetoric, 208–9, 297, 362, 420; Southern
Baptist Convention (SBC) support for,
429; Supreme Court case facts, 487; *Zorach*
compared to, 363, 474–75

McCreary, Village of Scarsdale v., 501

McCreary County v. ACLU, 335, 510

McDaniel v. Paty, 497

*McGinley, Two Guys from Harrison Allentown,
Inc. v.,* 490

McGowan v. Maryland, 489

McGuffey, William Holmes, 12, 95

McGuffey Readers, 11–13, 50, 95, 142, 297–
98, 352

McLean v. Board of Education, 167

McNair, Hunt v., 216, 494

McRae, Harris v., 498

McReynolds, James C.: *Meyer v. Nebraska,*
301, 302; *Pierce v. Society of Sisters,* 275,
343

McSweeney, Reverend Patrick F., 349

Mead, Edwin, 14

Mead, Sidney, 145

Meals, Muslim, 445

Meals, prayer in the public school prior to,
147, 355, 357

Media, 415

Medicaid, 150

Medical Care; Parent, 492

Meek v. Pittenger, 54–55, 221, 298–99, 304,
468–69, 496

Meese, Ed, 445

Meixner, Linda L., 463

"Memorial and Remonstrance against
Religious Assessments" (Madison), 292

Mencken, H. L., 405, 406

Mendlowitz, Rabbi Shraga Feivel, 443

Mennonite Church USA, 74–75. *See also*
Amish/Mennonite Schools

Mensa Research Journal, 243

Mercer, Charles, 390

Mergens, Board of Education of the Westside

Protestant Christian establishment and schools: academic achievement of students, 364–65, 366–67; Catholic-Protestant conflict (*see* Anti-Catholicism in education); colleges to train clergy, 50; colonial era, 2, 133; common schools (*see* Common school movement); control of public education until late nineteenth century, 49–50; King James Version of the Bible, 9–10, 96–97, 122, 181, 273–74, 336, 439; the Reformation, 115–16, 407, 414; statistics, 397; Ten Commandments version, 439. *See also* Christian day schools; Lutherans and Lutheran schools

The Protestant Crusade (Billington), 336

Protestants and Other Americans United (POAU) for the Separation of Church and State, 78–79. *See also* Americans United for the Separation of Church and State (AU)

The Protestant Tutor (Harris), 2

Prussia, 295

PTA (National Parent Teacher Association), 156, 224, 331–33

Public Education Religion Studies Center (PERSC), 369, 463

Public education studies of the Bible. *See* Academic study of the Bible

Public forum, 488

Public Funds for Public Schools v. Byrne, 447

Public Health Service Act, 426

Public magnet schools, 397–98

Public safety exemption, 505

Public's Attitudes toward the Public Schools (Gallup Poll), 309

"Public Schools and Religious Communities: A First Amendment Guide" (First Amendment Center), 157, 202, 450

"Public Schools and Sexual Orientation: A First Amendment Framework for Finding Common Ground," 141, 158, 202, 204

Public School Society, 5, 9, 244–45, 336

"Punishing Disturbers of Religious Worship and Sabbath Breakers" (Jefferson), 262

Purcell, Archbishop John, 97

Puritans, 2, 91, 101, 206, 350

Quakers: Bible taught to slaves by, 101; colonial era, 2, 350; Friends Council on

Education, 164, 226; Friends (Quaker) schools, 225–26; influence on foundation of American schooling, 9, 350; mid-1960s, 28; post–Civil War, 18; post–World War I, 22; Public School Society, 5, 9, 244–45, 336

Quaring, Jensen v., 501

Quayle, Dan, 132

Quick Bear v. Leupp, 215, 480

Radio, 405

Raikes, Robert, 92

Railsbach, Gary, 81

Raleigh District of North Carolina Conference of United Methodist Church, Smith v., 434–35

Ramsey, Murphy v., 479

Ray, Brian, 28, 241–42

Reagan, Ronald: on American as "city upon the hill," 145; Equal Access Act (EAA), 190, 355, 427; Moral Majority support for, 312–13; school prayer amendment, 100, 313, 316, 355

Reconstruction, 274–75

Rector and Visitors of the University of Virginia, Rosenberger v., 55–56, 213, 229, 507

Red Scare (1919), 275

Reed, Ralph, 130–31, 132, 313, 445

Reed, Stanley F., 297, 420

Reed v. Van Hoven, 355

The Reformation, 115–16, 407, 414

Reform Jews, 33, 86, 264, 265, 443, 444

Regan, Committee for Public Education and Religious Liberty v., 152–54, 321, 498

Regent Law School, 63, 140

Regents of the University of California, Hamilton v., 482

Regulation of religious schools, 89–90, 433–35, 447–48, 458–59, 467–68

Rehnquist, William: *Aguilar v. Felton*, 55, 220; *Committee for Public Education and Religious Liberty v. Nyquist*, 152; *Edwards v. Aguillard*, 183–84; *Locke v. Davey*, 222–23; *Meek v. Pittenger*, 299; *Mitchell v. Helms*, 34, 303–4; *Mueller v. Allen*, 218–19, 313–14; *Santa Fe Independent School District v. Doe*, 34; *Wallace v. Jaffree*, 218, 420, 462; *Zelman v. Simmons-Harris*, 34, 221–22,

About the Editors and Contributors

The Editors

James C. Carper is Professor of Social Foundations of Education at the University of South Carolina, where he has been a faculty member since 1989. His research interests include the history of American education, education and religion, and private schools. He has published in numerous journals, including *Journal of Church and State, Kansas History, History of Education Quarterly, Educational Leadership, Register of the Kentucky Historical Society, Kappa Delta Pi Record, Educational Forum,* and *Educational Policy. The Dissenting Tradition in American Education* (with Thomas C. Hunt) is his most recent book. He received his B.A. from Ohio Wesleyan University and his Ph.D. from Kansas State University.

Thomas C. Hunt received his Ph.D. from the University of Wisconsin–Madison in 1971. He joined the faculty at Virginia Tech that year where he served in numerous leadership positions and received awards for teaching, research, and service, most notably, perhaps, the most prestigious teaching award given by Virginia Tech. In 1996 he joined the faculty of the University of Dayton. In 2002 the University of Dayton bestowed on him its Alumni Scholarship Award. He has authored or edited 16 books in the past 23 years, all but one on religion and education. He has served as co-editor of *Catholic Education: A Journal of Inquiry and Practice,* the only refereed journal on Catholic schools in the nation, and is a past-president of the Associates for Research on Private Education (ARPE), a special interest group of the American Educational Research Association (AERA).

The Contributors

M. David Alexander is Chairman of the Department of Educational Leadership and Policy Studies, School of Education, Virginia Tech. He is co-author of five books, one of which, *American Public School Law,* currently in the sixth edition, co-authored with Kern Alexander, is widely used in graduate courses. *The Law of Schools, Students and Teachers in a Nutshell,* co-authored with Kern Alexander, is a popular book for practitioners. He has also written numerous research reports and articles.

Francis J. Beckwith is Professor of Philosophy and Church-State Studies, Baylor University, where he is also a Fellow and Faculty Associate in the Institute for the Studies of Religion. He has published scores of articles that have appeared in a wide variety of academic periodicals in the fields of philosophy, law, theology, medicine, and ethics. Among his over one dozen books are *Defending Life: A Moral and Legal Case Against Abortion Choice* (2007) and *Law, Darwinism, and Public Education: The Establishment Clause and the Challenge of Intelligent Design* (2003).

Mark A. Chancey is Associate Professor and Chair of the Department of Religious Studies at Southern Methodist University in Dallas. He received his doctorate in New Testament and Christian Origins from Duke University. A member of the Society of Biblical Literature's Working Group on the Bible and Public Education and the American Academy of Religion's Religion in the Schools Task Force, he is the author of several studies on academic, political, and legal aspects of public school Bible courses. His other research interests include ancient Judaism and the archaeology of Palestine in the Roman period.

Bruce S. Cooper is Professor of School Leadership at Fordham University's Graduate School of Education. He has written extensively on private education, politics of education, school finance, and education policy. His recent books are *Home Schooling in Full View* and *Better Policies, Better Schools*. He currently edits the *Private School Monitor.*

Derek H. Davis is Dean of the College of Humanities and Dean of the Graduate School at University of Mary Hardin-Baylor and Director of the UMHB Center for Religious Liberty. He was formerly Director of the J. M. Dawson Institute of Church-State Studies at Baylor University and Editor of *Journal of Church and State*. In addition to publishing numerous articles, he has authored or edited 16 books, including *Original Intent: Chief Justice Rehnquist & the Course of American Church-State Relations* and *Religion and the Continental Congress, 1774–1789: Contributions to Original Intent.*

Mark DeForrest is Assistant Professor of Legal Research and Writing at Gonzaga University School of Law in Spokane, Washington. He holds a B.A. degree in history from Western Washington University and a J.D. from Gonzaga, where he was a Thomas More Scholar and an associate editor of the *Gonzaga Law Review*. He has published articles on First Amendment topics in the *University of Utah Law Review, Harvard Journal of Law and Public Policy, Tulsa Law Review,* and *Regent University Law Review.*

Joan DelFattore is Professor of English and Legal Studies at the University of Delaware, where she teaches courses on intellectual freedom, free speech, and religious liberty. She has published on topics related to religion, law, and education in numerous journals including *University of Pennsylvania Journal of Constitutional Law* and *Rutgers Journal on Law and Religion*. Her *The Fourth R: Conflicts Over Religion in America's Public Schools* was published by Yale University Press in 2004.

Daniel L. Dreisbach is Professor of Justice, Law and Society in the School of Public Affairs at American University. He has authored or edited seven books, including *Thomas Jefferson and the Wall of Separation between Church and State* and *The Founders on God and Government*. He has published over 50 book chapters, reviews, and articles in scholarly journals, including *American Journal of Legal History, Constitutional Commentary, Emory Law Journal, Journal of Church and State, North Carolina Law Review,* and *William and Mary Quarterly.*

James W. Fraser is an historian of American education and a professor at the Steinhardt School of Culture, Education, and Human Development at New York University. He is the author of numerous books and articles including *Between Church and State: Religion and Public Education in a Multicultural America* and most recently *Preparing America's Teachers: A History.* He is an ordained minister in the United Church of Christ and pastor emeritus of Grace Church, Federated in East Boston, and Union Congregational Church in Winthrop, Massachusetts.

Lyndon G. Furst recently retired from the deanship of the School of Graduate Studies at Andrews University, a Seventh-day Adventist institution in Berrien Springs, Michigan. Previous to that position he served as Professor of Educational Administration. He also worked in the Seventh-day Adventist school system for 21 years as elementary teacher and principal, high school principal, and educational superintendent for a two-state region. He holds an Ed.D. in Educational Administration from the University of the Pacific.

Mary Ellen Giess is a master's degree candidate at Harvard Divinity School where she is focusing on religion and American government. She received a B.A. in Religious Studies at the University of North Carolina at Chapel Hill.

Charles L. Glenn, Jr. is Professor of Education Policy at Boston University, where he teaches history and comparative policy. From 1970 to 1991 he was Director of Urban Education and Equity for the Massachusetts Department of Education. His books include *The Myth of the Common School, Educational Freedom in Eastern Europe, Educating Immigrant Children: Schools and Language Minorities in Twelve Nations, The Ambiguous Embrace: Government and Faith-based Schools and Social Agencies,* and *Balancing Freedom, Autonomy, and Accountability in Education* (with Jan De Groof), a study of 40 countries. He is completing a two-volume history of educational policy since Antiquity.

Bruce Grelle is Professor of Religion in the Department of Religious Studies and Director of the Religion and Public Education Resource Center at California State University, Chico. He has served on the American Academy of Religion's Task Force on "Religion in the Schools" and on the steering committee for the California 3 Rs Project (Rights, Responsibilities, Respect): A Program for Finding Common Ground on Issues of Religion and Values in Public Schools. He is co-editor of *Explorations in Global Ethics* and serves on the editorial board of *Religion & Education* and the international advisory board of the *British Journal of Religious Education*.

Hans J. Hacker has taught at the University of Maryland, The College of William and Mary, Johns Hopkins University, and Stephen F. Austin State University. Currently, he is an assistant professor in the Department of Political Science at Arkansas State University where he serves as Co-Director of the Pre-Law Center, pre-law advisor, and coach of the department's Moot Court Team. He is the author of *The Culture of Conservative Christian Litigation* and of articles in the areas of constitutional law and history, law and society, and public administration theory.

Charles C. Haynes is Senior Scholar at the Freedom Forum's First Amendment Center in Washington, D.C. Over the past two decades, he has helped communities across the nation find common ground on conflicts involving religion in schools. He is a principal organizer and drafter of consensus guidelines on religious liberty in schools endorsed by a broad range of religious and educational organizations. He is author or co-author of seven books, including *Finding Common Ground: A First Amendment Guide to Religion and Public Schools.* Haynes holds a master's degree from Harvard Divinity School and a doctorate from Emory University.

William Jeynes is Professor of Education at California State University in Long Beach and a Non-resident Scholar at Baylor University. He has written numerous books and articles on religious education and educational history. His most recent book is *American Educational History: School, Society, and the Common Good.* His articles have appeared in *Teacher's College Record, Elementary School Journal, Cambridge Journal of Education, Journal of Negro Education,* and many other academic journals. He has worked with the Harvard Family Research Project and is a member of the International Network of Scholars based at Johns Hopkins University.

Karen E. Keyworth has worked for over 20 years as a faculty member and administrator at the university and K–12 levels with a wide range of responsibilities: ESL, developmental writing/reading, language arts (lower elementary), consulting, teacher training, curriculum, and governance. In 1996, she was the founding Principal of the Greater Lansing Islamic School. Two years later she co-founded and currently serves as the Director of Education for the Islamic Schools League of America, a virtual organization dedicated to facilitating quality education in K–12 Islamic schools.

Charles R. Kniker retired from the Board of Regents, State of Iowa, in 2002, where he served as Associate Director of Academic Affairs since 1998. Most of his professional life work was as a professor of education at Iowa State University. While there, he founded the journal, *Religion & Public Education* (now *Religion & Education*). He became president of Eden Theological Seminary in Webster Groves, Missouri, in 1993. In 1996, he became pastor of Faith United Church of Christ, Bryan, Texas. Earlier, his ministries included a year in Honduras and at churches in Missouri, California, and New Jersey. His research areas include religion and education, values education, and teacher education.

Rebecca P. Lewis is a doctoral candidate at Boston College in Curriculum and Instruction, researching the current curriculum controversy over the teaching of evolution. She has worked as a curriculum developer and researcher at Education Development Center, Inc. (EDC) in Massachusetts since 2000. Prior to joining EDC, she was a middle- and high-school classroom teacher in math and science in Boston.

Casey Luskin is an attorney working in Public Policy and Legal Affairs with the Discovery Institute in Seattle, Washington. He holds a B.S. and M.S. in Earth Sciences from the University of California, San Diego and earned his J.D. at the University of San Diego. He is co-founder of the Intelligent Design and Evolution Awareness (IDEA) Center, a nonprofit based in southern California helping students worldwide to investigate evolution by starting "IDEA Clubs" on college and high school campuses across the country. His work has been published in both law and science journals, including *Journal of Church and State; Montana Law Review; Geochemistry, Geophysics, and Geosystems;* and *Progress in Complexity, Information, and Design.* He is co-author of *Traipsing Into Evolution: Intelligent Design and the* Kitzmiller v. Dover *Decision.*

William Martin is the Harry and Hazel Chavanne Professor Emeritus of Religion and Public Policy in the Department of Sociology at Rice University and Chavanne Senior Fellow at the James A. Baker III Institute for Public Policy at Rice. He holds a B.A. and M.A. from Abilene Christian University and a B.D. and Ph.D. from Harvard. His books include *A Prophet with Honor: The Billy Graham Story* and *With God on Our Side: The Rise of the Religious Right in America,* companion volume to the PBS series of the same title.

Ralph D. Mawdsley is Professor of Educational Administration, Cleveland State University, where he teaches school law, special education law, and sports law. In 2007 he was appointed the Sir Alan Sewell Visiting Professor of Education and Law, Griffith University, Brisbane, Australia, and in 2005, was a Fulbright Scholar at the University of Pretoria, South Africa, where he was Visiting Professor of Law and Education. He is the author of over 450 publications in the area of education law, and served as the president of Education Law Association (ELA) in 2001 and received ELA's Marion McGhehey Award for outstanding contributions to the field of education law in 2004.

Joseph McTighe has been Executive Director of the Council for American Private Education (CAPE) since 1996. Prior to his service at CAPE, he worked for 15 years as Associate Director at the New York State Catholic Conference, where he served as Executive Secretary to the NYS Council of Catholic School Superintendents and the NYS Council of Diocesan Directors of Religious Education. Before that, he worked in the Catholic schools office for the Diocese of Albany, New York, served as principal of a Catholic elementary school in Albany, and taught at an inner-city Catholic school in Manhattan. He received a B.A. in philosophy from Manhattan College and an M.A. in philosophy from the New School for Social Research.

Diane L. Moore is Professor of the Practice in Religious Studies and Education, and Director of the Program on Religious and Secondary Education at the Harvard Divinity School. She is the author of *Overcoming Religious Illiteracy: A Cultural Approach to Teaching About Religion in Secondary Education* as well as numerous articles relating to religion, democracy, and education.

Monalisa M. Mullins holds a doctorate in educational leadership from the University of Dayton, where she currently teaches both undergraduate and graduate courses in the philosophy of education. Mullins has co-authored, with Thomas C. Hunt, *Moral Education in America's Schools: The Continuing Challenge.*

Warren A. Nord was Director of the interdisciplinary Program in the Humanities and Human Values at the University of North Carolina at Chapel Hill from 1979 to 2004. He continues to teach the philosophy of religion and the philosophy of education at UNC. He is the author of more than 30 articles and book chapters, and two books: *Religion and American Education: Rethinking a National Dilemma,* a comprehensive study of religion in both secondary and higher education; and, with Charles C. Haynes, *Taking Religion Seriously Across the Curriculum,* a guidebook for educators on "taking religion seriously" across the K–12 curriculum.

Ronald J. Nuzzi, a priest of the Diocese of Youngstown, Ohio, is Director of the ACE Leadership Program at The University of Notre Dame. A nationally known speaker and scholar, he has led dozens of staff development days, in-services, and retreats for Catholic school teachers and administrators in the United States, Canada, Mexico, and Italy. He serves as co-editor of the journal, *Catholic Education: A Journal of Inquiry & Practice,* and has edited and contributed to major research publications in Catholic education including: *Catholic Schools Still Make a Difference, A Handbook of Research on Catholic Education, A Handbook of Research on Catholic Higher Education,* and *Catholic School Leadership.* He holds a Ph.D. in Educational Administration from the University of Dayton.

Staci L. H. Ramsey earned a B.A. in History at the University of Virginia, where she was inducted as a member of Phi Alpha Theta History Honor Society. She also holds a master's degree in higher education from Virginia Tech. She currently serves as an adjunct faculty member at Franklin University, Kaplan University, and Rasmussen College, where she teaches first-term college students and assists with writing courses.

Brendan Randall is a Master of Theological Studies candidate in the Program for Religion and Secondary Education at Harvard Divinity School. He is a former lawyer who became an instructor at an independent high school where he taught various classes, including applied ethics and world religions. He is a graduate of Harvard College, the University of Minnesota Law School, and the Harvard Graduate School of Education where he recently graduated with a Master of Education degree. His current interests include moral and spiritual development.

Brian D. Ray is internationally known for his research on homeschooling (home-based education) and is president of the National Home Education Research Institute in Salem, Oregon. He has been a professor at the undergraduate and graduate levels, a classroom teacher in public and private schools, and an expert witness before many courts and legislatures. His most recent book is *Worldwide Guide to Homeschooling*. He holds an M.S. in zoology from Ohio University and a Ph.D. from Oregon State University.

William G. Ross is Professor of Law at the Cumberland School of Law at Samford University in Birmingham, Alabama, where he has taught since 1988. His courses include legal history, constitutional law, ethics, and civil procedure. A graduate of Stanford and Harvard Law School, he is the author of three books about American constitutional history and two books about the ethics of legal fees. He also has published widely on various subjects, including separation of powers and judicial ethics.

Charles J. Russo is the Joseph Panzer Chair in Education in the School of Education and Allied Professions and Adjunct Professor in the School of Law at the University of Dayton. The author or co-author of more than 600 articles and 28 books, he has spoken extensively on a wide array of topics in education law on all six inhabited continents and in 20 nations.

Shipley Robertson Salewski received her Master of Theological Studies degree from Harvard Divinity School in 2007, where she also completed the Program in Religion and Secondary Education (PRSE). She has taught Religious Studies and English at Stuart Hall High School in San Francisco, and currently teaches English Language Arts at KIPP Summit Academy, a public charter school in San Lorenzo, California.

Mary Angela Shaughnessy, SCN, is Executive Director of the Education Law Institute at St. Catharine College in Springfield, Kentucky. She is Professor of Education Emerita at Spalding University in Louisville, Kentucky. A former high school principal, she has held administrative posts in higher education and has served as adjunct and visiting professor in many colleges and universities. She is the author of over 30 texts and hundreds of articles on the topic of law and education. A practicing attorney, she specializes in school law.

David Sikkink is Associate Professor of Sociology at the University of Notre Dame, and a fellow in the Center for the Study of Religion and Society and the Center for Research on Educational Opportunity. He has published numerous articles in *Social Forces, Social Problems,* and the *Journal for the Scientific Study of Religion.* He is currently working on a book on religious schools, and an analysis of the relationship between religion and academic achievement in early childhood.

David Streight spent three decades as an educator and school psychologist in public, Catholic, and private independent schools. He is a past president of the Oregon School Psychologists Association and past secretary for the United States to the Association Internationale pour la Défense des Langues et Cultures Ménacées. Fluent in four languages, he has translated a number of books on philosophy and religion, primarily Islam, for academic presses. He is the translator/author of *Théodore Aubanel: Sensual Poetry and the Provençal Church,* editor of *Parenting for Character: Five Experts, Five Practices,* and host to the PBS/WNET Web site for Religion and Ethics Newsweekly. He is currently Executive Director of the Council for Spiritual and Ethical Education.

Julie Underwood, a nationally recognized authority on school law, is the eighth Dean of the University of Wisconsin (UW) Madison School of Education. She received her doctorate in Educational Leadership from the University of Florida as well as a law degree from Indiana University. She taught at UW–Madison from 1986 to 1995 on the faculty of the Department of Educational Administration. She returned to Madison after serving as dean of Miami University's School of Education and Allied Professions and as associate executive director and general counsel for the National School Boards Association (NSBA) in Washington, D.C. At the NSBA, she led a legal advocacy program on behalf of the nation's public school boards, including producing friend-of-the-court briefs and legal strategies before the U.S. Supreme Court and lower courts.

Steven C. Vryhof, a former Director of Teacher Education, is an independent researcher and the founder of Daystar School and Education Centre in Chicago. He is the author or co-author of five books, including *Between Memory and Vision: The Case for Faith-based Schooling*. His focus is on functional community in faith-based schools and how these schools contribute to the common good.

Timothy Walch is the Director of the Herbert Hoover Presidential Library and Associate Editor of the *U.S. Catholic Historian*. Educated at the University of Notre Dame and Northwestern University, he is the author or editor of 16 books, including *Parish School: American Catholic Parochial Education from Colonial Times to the Present*, which Father Andrew M. Greeley has heralded as "the best summary review of the history of Catholic education in the last half century."

John Witte, Jr. is the Jonas Robitscher Professor of Law and Director of the Center for the Study of Law and Religion at Emory University in Atlanta. A specialist in legal history, religious liberty, and marriage and family law, he has published 120 articles, 9 journal symposia, and 21 books, including *Religion and the American Constitutional Experiment; Modern Christian Teachings on Law, Politics, and Human Nature; God's Joust, God's Justice: Law and Religion in the Western Tradition;* and *The Reformation of Rights: Law, Religion, and Human Rights in Early Modern Calvinism*.